Origami Symphony No. 12

Where are the Gnomes?

Books by John Montroll
www.johnmontroll.com
Instagram: @montrollorigami

Origami Symphonies

Origami Symphony No. 1: The Elephant's Trumpet Call
Origami Symphony No. 2: Trio of Sharks & Playful Prehistoric Mammals
Origami Symphony No. 3: Duet of Majestic Dragons & Dinosaurs
Origami Symphony No. 4: Capturing Vibrant Coral Reef Fish
Origami Symphony No. 5: Woodwinds, Horns, and a Moose
Origami Symphony No. 6: Striped Snakes Changing Scales
Origami Symphony No. 7: Musical Monkeys
Origami Symphony No. 8: An Octet of Cats
Origami Symphony No. 9: Ode to Australia
Origami Symphony No. 10: Lucky & Dangerous Sides of Origami
Origami Symphony No. 11: Folding on Land, Air and Sea
Origami Symphony No. 12: Where are the Gnomes?

Animal Origami

Jungle Origami
Arctic Animals in Origami
Origami Aquarium
Dogs in Origami
Perfect Pets Origami
Dragons and Other Fantastic Creatures in Origami
Bugs in Origami
Horses in Origami: Second Edition
Origami Birds: Second Edition
Origami Gone Wild
Dinosaur Origami
Origami Dinosaurs for Beginners
Prehistoric Origami: Dinosaurs and other Creatures: Third Edition
Mythological Creatures and the Chinese Zodiac Origami
Origami Sea Life: Third Edition
Bringing Origami to Life: Second Edition
Origami Sculptures: Fourth Edition
African Animals in Origami: Third Edition
North American Animals in Origami: Third Edition
Origami for the Enthusiast: Second Edition
Animal Origami for the Enthusiast: Second Edition

Geometric Origami

The Magic of Origami Polyhedra
Origami Stars: Second Edition
Galaxy of Origami Stars: Second Edition
Origami and Math: Simple to Complex: Second Edition
Origami & Geometry
3D Origami Platonic Solids & More: Second Edition
3D Origami Diamonds
3D Origami Antidiamonds
3D Origami Pyramids
A Plethora of Polyhedra in Origami: Third Edition
Classic Polyhedra Origami
A Constellation of Origami Polyhedra
Origami Polyhedra Design

General Origami

Magical Origami Gnomes: 38 Gnomes. Infinite Fun.
Origami Fold-by-Fold
DC Super Heroes Origami
Origami Worldwide
Teach Yourself Origami: Third Edition
Christmas Origami: Second Edition
Storytime Origami
Origami Inside-Out: Third Edition

Dollar Bill Origami

Dollar Origami Treasures: Second Edition
Dollar Bill Animals in Origami: Second Revised Edition
Dollar Bill Origami
Easy Dollar Bill Origami

Simple Origami

Fun and Simple Origami: 101 Easy-to-Fold Projects: Second Edition
Origami Twelve Days of Christmas: And Santa, Too!
Super Simple Origami
Easy Dollar Bill Origami
Easy Origami
Easy Origami 2
Easy Origami 3
Easy Origami Coloring Book
Easy Origami Animals
Easy Origami Polar Animals
Easy Origami Ocean Animals
Easy Origami Woodland Animals
Easy Origami Jungle Animals
Meditative Origami

To Bonnie and Rocky

Origami Symphony No. 12: *Where are the Gnomes?*

Copyright © 2025 by John Montroll. All rights reserved.
No part of this publication may be copied or reproduced by any means without the express written permission of the author.

ISBN-10: 1-877656-73-9
ISBN-13: 978-1-877656-73-6

Antroll Publishing Company

Introduction

Welcome to the world premier of the Twelfth Origami Symphony! Modeled after the structure of a musical symphony, this collection is crafted in four movements, each bringing its own magic and adventure. Nighttime animals, woodland creatures that share the forest with gnomes, mysterious flying saucers, sparkling gems, and finally, the playful gnomes themselves—all appear through origami.

Nighttime animals include a bat, sloth, raccoon with a striped tail, and striped skunk. Some of the forest animals that live with the gnomes are a dragonlfy, frog, turtle, and squirrel. A spotted mushroom shows the clever side of origami. Flying saucers and gems with varying number of sides show the geometric side of origami. Detailed gnomes bring origami to life. Together, the 39 models in this Origami Symphony represent not just clever techniques, but also imagination woven into paper.

As I continue to develop origami design, I take great care to make my work as approachable as possible, given their complexity. The rabbit is diagrammed in 19 steps, the squirrel in 20 steps, and the spotted mushroom in 21 steps. The final gnome—the most intricate of the set—requires 33 steps, standing as the most elaborate design in the symphony. The balance of simplicity within complexity gives the models their life-force. It allows folders to enjoy the process while still arriving at a design that is rich and complete.

The diagrams are drawn in the internationally approved Randlett-Yoshizawa style. You can use any kind of square paper for these models, but the best results will be achieved with standard origami paper, which is colored on one side and white on the other (in the diagrams in this book, the shading represents the colored side). Large sheets, such as nine inches squared, are easier to use than small ones.

Origami supplies can be found in arts and craft shops, or at Dover Publications online: www.doverpublications.com. You can also visit OrigamiUSA at www.origamiusa.org for origami supplies and other related information including an extensive list of local, national, and international origami groups.

Please follow me on Instagram @montrollorigami to see posts of my origami.

I thank the folders who have encouraged me to develop the presentation of origami through an origami symphony.

Origami Symphony No. 12 is a celebration of both creativity and craft: part story, part geometry, and part magic. Enjoy the folds, and watch the gnomes spring to life.

John Montroll
www.johnmontroll.com

Contents

Symbols 9
The Four Phases of Learning a New Skill 9
Origami Symphony No. 12 10
    First Movement 11
    Second Movement 41
    Third Movement 70
    Fourth Movement 96

★ Simple
★★ Intermediate
★★★ Complex
★★★★ Very Complex

First Movement
Allegro: Songs of the Nighttime Animals

11 Bat ★★
14 Sloth ★★
16 Snail ★★
19 Owl ★★
21 Nightingale ★★
25 Anteater ★★
29 Raccoon ★★
33 Skunk ★★
37 Opossum ★★★

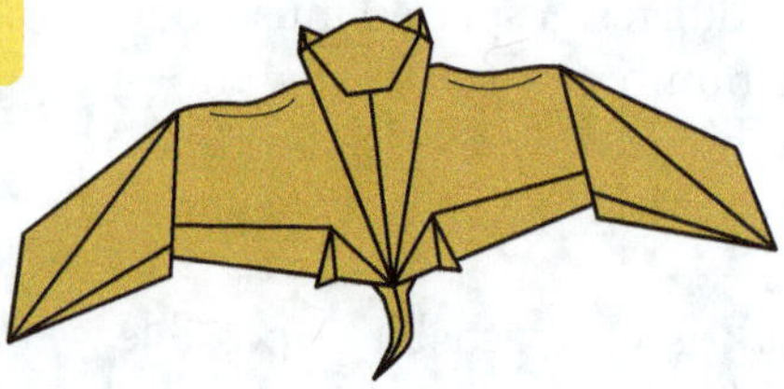

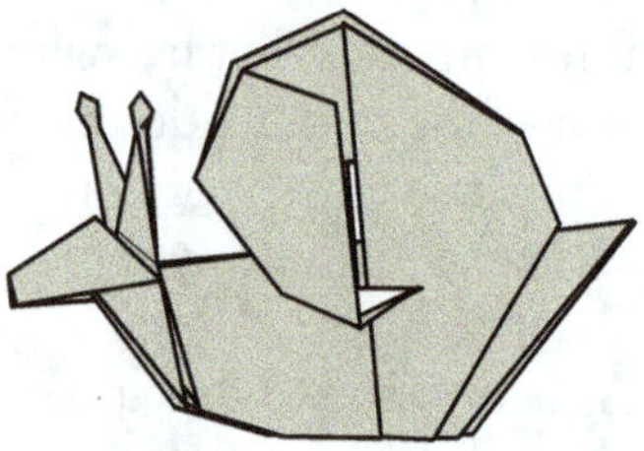

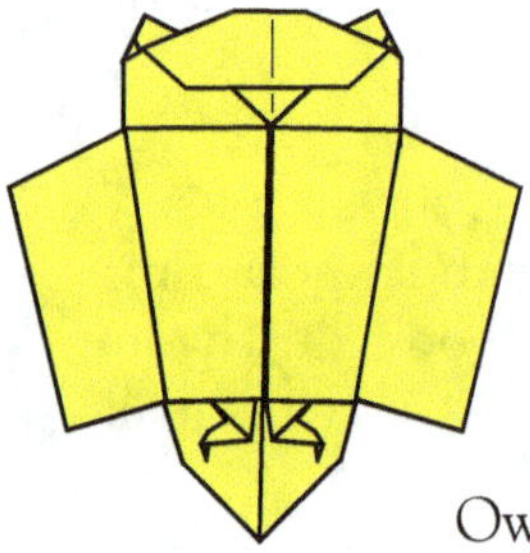

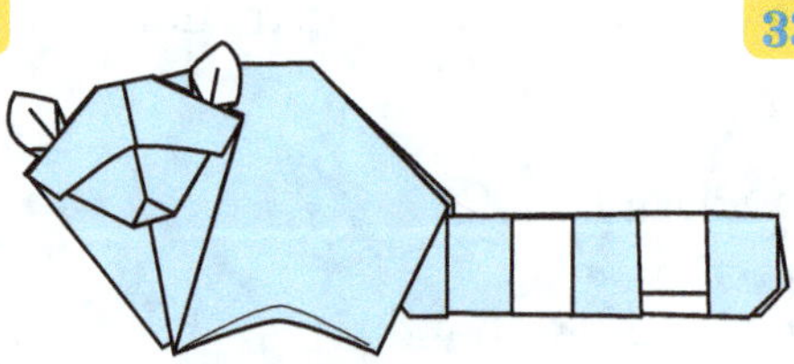

Second Movement
Andante: Nature for the Hidden Gnomes

41 Butterfly ★
43 Dragonfly ★★
46 Frog ★★

6 *Origami Symphony No. 12*

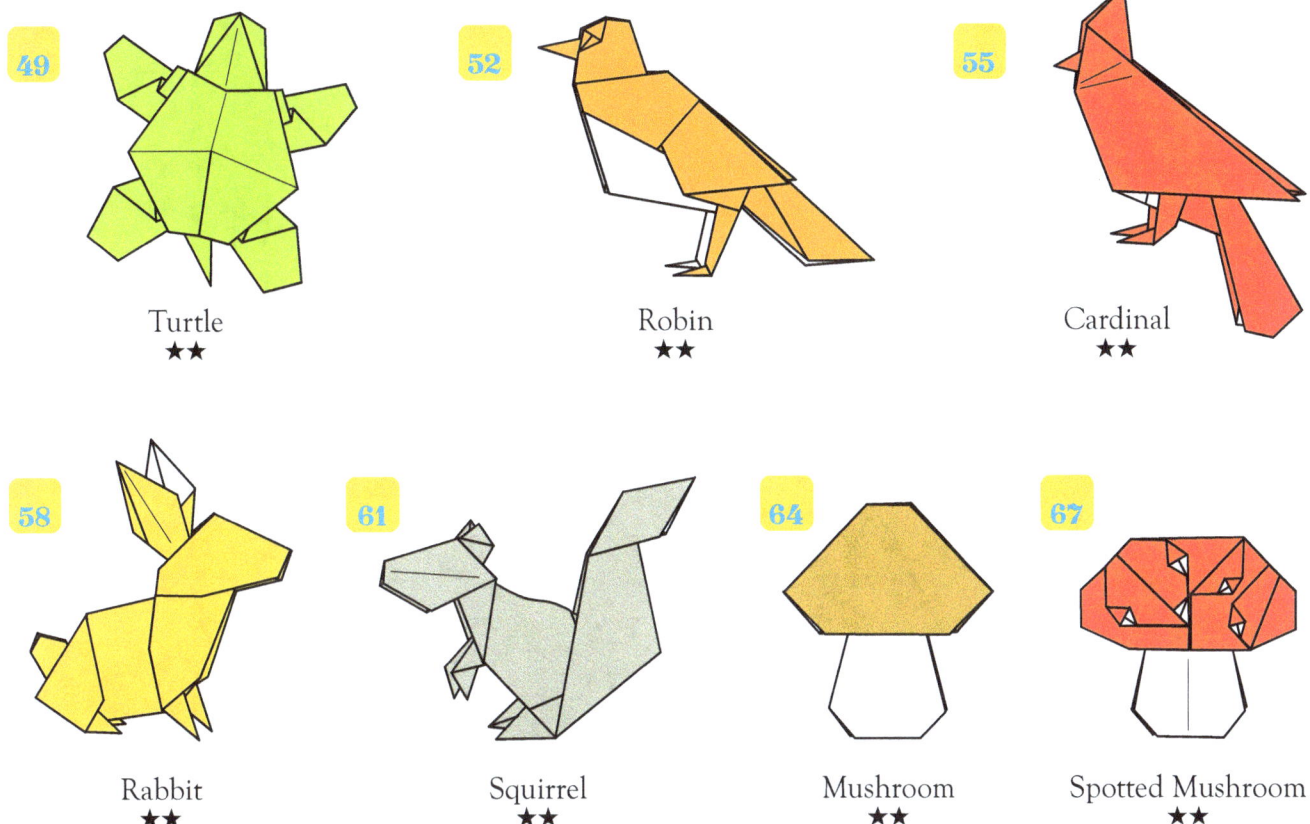

| 49 Turtle ★★ | 52 Robin ★★ | 55 Cardinal ★★ |

| 58 Rabbit ★★ | 61 Squirrel ★★ | 64 Mushroom ★★ | 67 Spotted Mushroom ★★ |

Third Movement
Minuet of Flying Saucers with a Trio of Gems

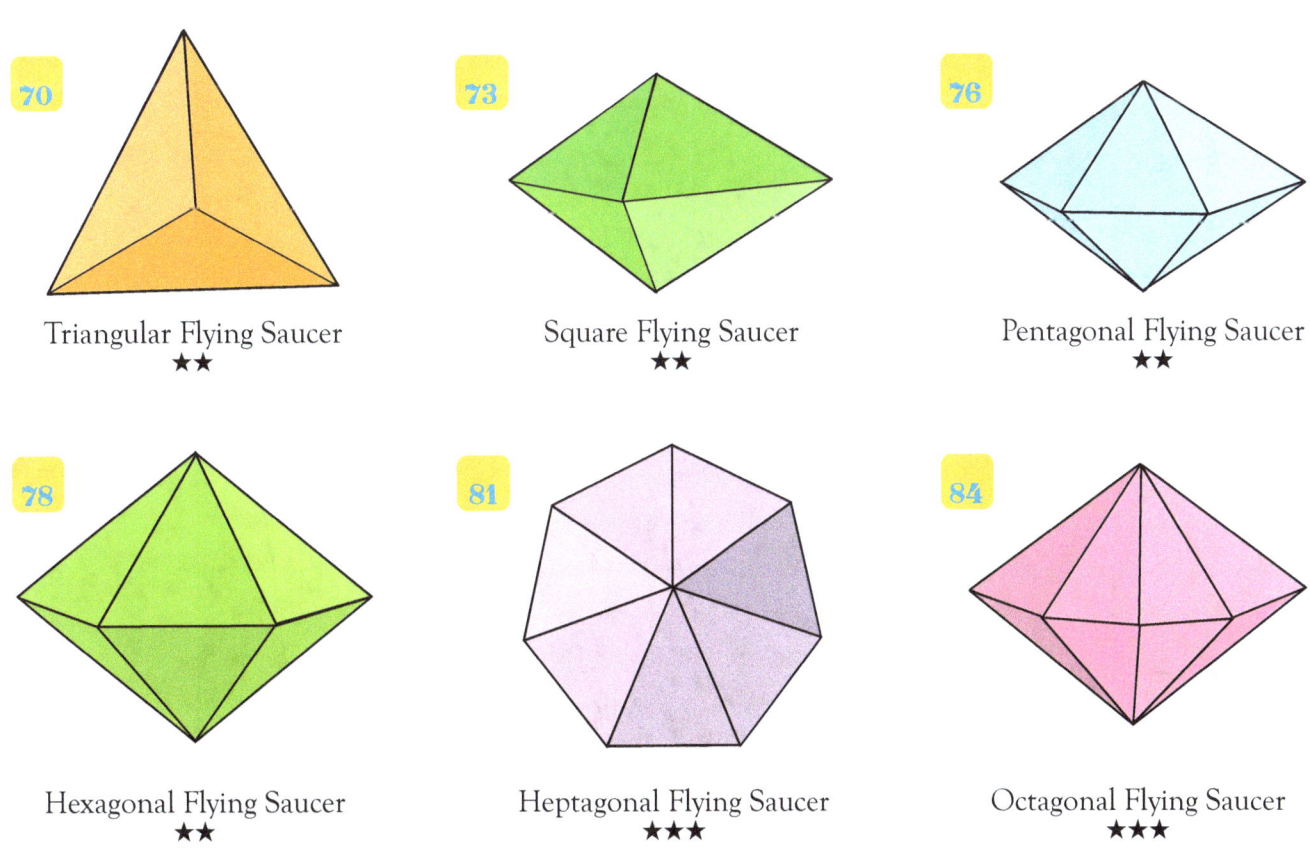

| 70 Triangular Flying Saucer ★★ | 73 Square Flying Saucer ★★ | 76 Pentagonal Flying Saucer ★★ |

| 78 Hexagonal Flying Saucer ★★ | 81 Heptagonal Flying Saucer ★★★ | 84 Octagonal Flying Saucer ★★★ |

Contents

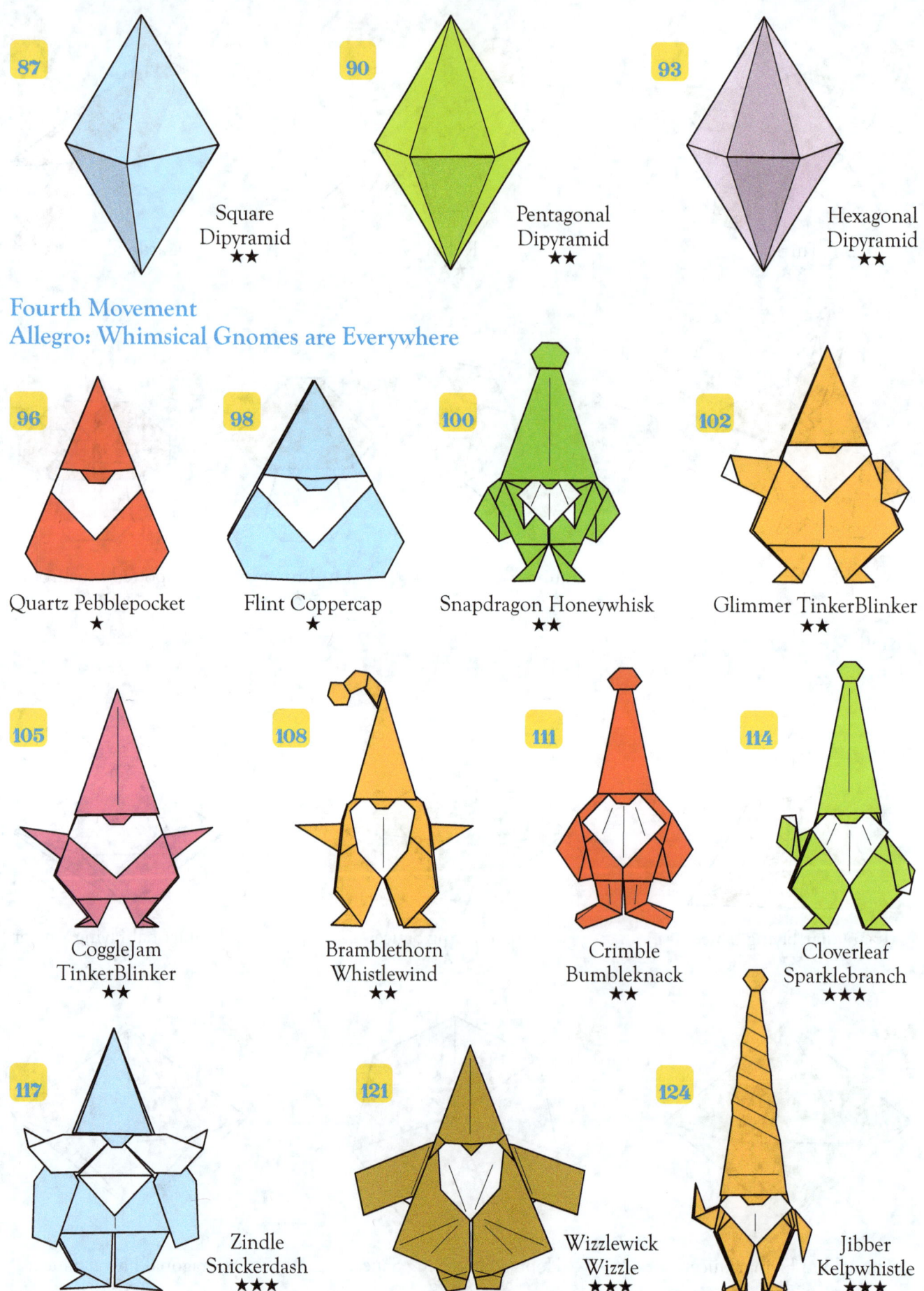

87 Square Dipyramid ★★

90 Pentagonal Dipyramid ★★

93 Hexagonal Dipyramid ★★

Fourth Movement
Allegro: Whimsical Gnomes are Everywhere

96 Quartz Pebblepocket ★

98 Flint Coppercap ★

100 Snapdragon Honeywhisk ★★

102 Glimmer TinkerBlinker ★★

105 CoggleJam TinkerBlinker ★★

108 Bramblethorn Whistlewind ★★

111 Crimble Bumbleknack ★★

114 Cloverleaf Sparklebranch ★★★

117 Zindle Snickerdash ★★★

121 Wizzlewick Wizzle ★★★

124 Jibber Kelpwhistle ★★★

8 *Origami Symphony No. 12*

Symbols

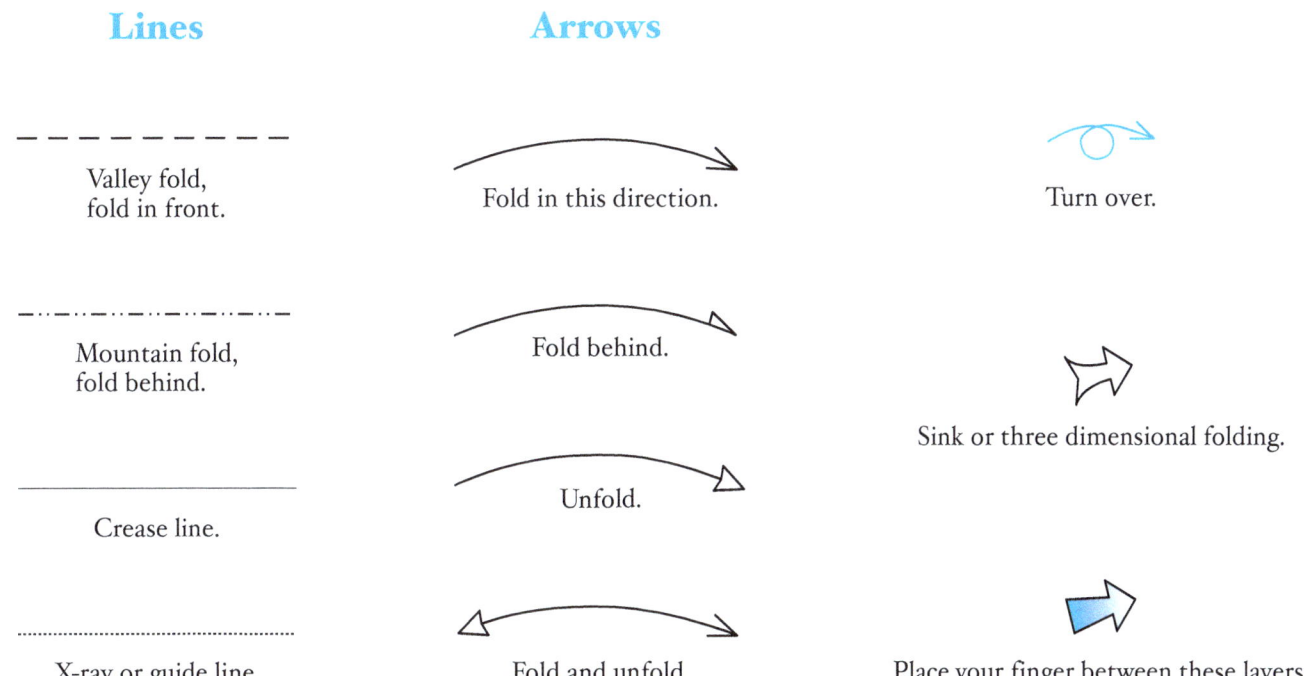

The Four Phases of Learning a New Skill

Learning a new skill is exciting, frustrating, and deeply rewarding all at once. Whether it's origami, playing piano, driving a car, or cooking a decent meal, the path to mastery follows a familiar journey.

Phase 1: Unconscious Incompetence

At the beginning, you don't know what you don't know.

At origami meetings, children sometimes ask me to teach them the intricate dragon with scales and claws displayed in the exhibit room. I ask, "Have you folded the cup or the traditional crane?" They shake their head. "No, I want to learn the dragon." At that stage, there isn't much I can do—unless I fold the dragon for them.

It's the same with driving: the new driver eagerly turns the key, only to bump into the nearest trash can. Enthusiasm is high, but awareness is low.

Phase 2: Conscious Incompetence

Here, reality sets in: this is harder than it looks.

Now you fold slowly and carefully, struggling through the steps. On the piano, you place your fingers deliberately on each note, trying to coordinate hands and rhythm. It's clumsy and difficult, yet you feel the spark of progress.

This is frustrating, but it's also inspiring—because every mistake means you are learning.

Phase 3: Conscious Competence

With practice, things start to click.

You're driving smoothly, but still paying close attention to every detail. Cooking a recipe works out better, though you follow each instruction carefully. On the piano, you're actually making music, but concentration is still required.

The skill is within reach—just not second nature yet.

Phase 4: Unconscious Competence

Finally, the magic happens: the skill becomes effortless.

You can drive while chatting with passengers. You can cook while holding a conversation in the kitchen. You can play the piano beautifully while your mind drifts to other thoughts.

In origami, your hands fold while you enjoy the background music or the company around you. The process has become second nature.

The Fun Twist

The real joy comes when you're in Phase 4 and meet someone in Phase 1. You watch them struggle with what feels as natural to you as breathing. It's a reminder of how far you've gone—and that every expert was once a beginner staring wide-eyed at the impossible dragon.

Origami Symphony No. 12

Many adventures unfold when origami comes to life. Somewhere, there are gnomes—though, as gnomes tend to do, they keep themselves invisible. And so this origami symphony begins at night, when all is quiet. By morning, we find ourselves in a forest filled with small animals and mushrooms, whispering to gnomes we cannot see. Flying saucers carry us to other worlds—perhaps crafted by gnomes, perhaps even piloted by them. Gems sparkle with perfection, surely the handiwork of gnomes. And finally, in the fourth movement, the gnomes step out of hiding, playful and wise, ready to teach us what life is all about.

The first movement, Allegro: Songs of the Nighttime begins in the dark with a Bat flying around. A patient Sloth and Snail encourage us to take our time to fold them well, with care. Night music surrounds us with an Owl and Nightingale. Voices of an Anteater, Raccoon, Skunk, and Opossum lead us deeper into adventure.

The tempo softens in the second movement: Andante: Nature for the Hidden Gnomes as we enter a woodland dream. Butterflies and Dragonflies shimmer through the air. By the water's edge, a Frog and Turtle play their part. A hopping Robin, a perched Cardinal, a Rabbit, and a Squirrel each reveal their charm. Mushrooms rise from the earth—plain and spotted alike—whispering that the gnomes are near, even if they remain unseen.

The third movement: Minuet of Flying Saucers with a Trio of Gems, shows the geometric side of origami. The flying saucers and gems were all crafted by the gnomes. Flying saucers range from a triangular base to an octagonal base. Beautiful gems sparkle, as origami was used to craft these otherwise sculpted stones.

The arrival of the fourth movement, Allegro: Whimsical Gnomes are Everywhere, fills the forest, mountains, and gardens with their quiet magic and mischievous fun. The endless possibilities of creating gnomes through origami design confirms that the universe is magical.

Combining all these models shows a fun, playful, yet deep side of origami. May these gnomes carry you on their saucers through the forest and into the stars.

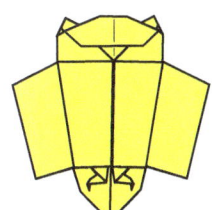

First Movement

Allegro: Songs of the Nighttime Animals

When most of us are fast asleep, some amazing animals are just waking up! The forest, fields, and even your backyard are full of creatures that can't wait for nighttime. Sloths slowly climb though the trees, anteaters tiptoe quietly on the hunt for tasty ants and termites. Skunks shuffle through the grass. Even snails come out of hiding, sliding across leaves and soil on tiny trails in the cool night air. The nighttime is full of secret adventures, quiet explorers, and tiny surprises.

Bat

These amazing flying mammals zoom through the night sky like tiny superheroes. They use echolocation to find and catch tasty bugs like mosquitoes and moths. Some bats prefer sweet nectar from flower, helping plants grow by spreading pollen.

During the day they snuggle upside-down in caves or trees, but at night they flap, swoop, and dive with super-fast wings. A single bat can gobble hundreds of insects in an hour.

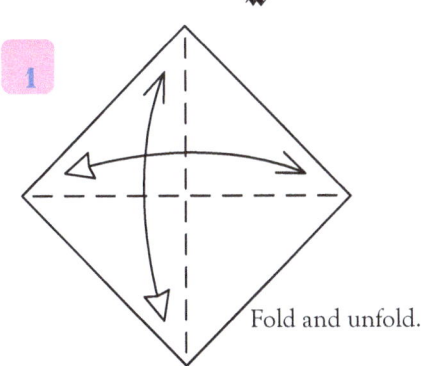

1. Fold and unfold.

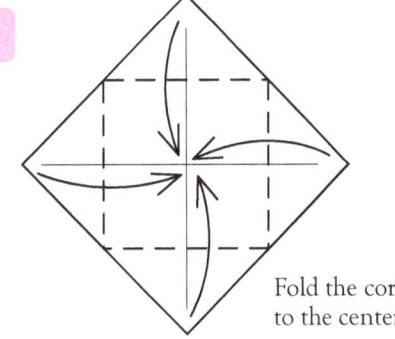

2. Fold the corners to the center.

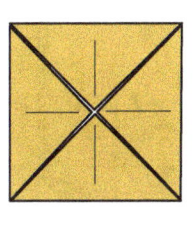

3. Rotate.

Bat 11

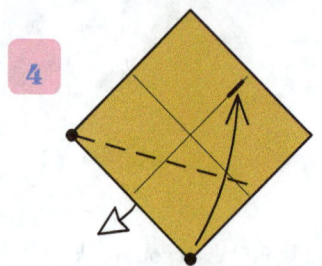

Bring the lower dot to the bold line. Swing out from behind.

Squash-fold and swing out from behind.

Squash-fold.

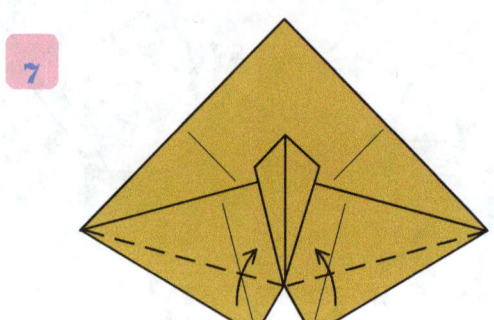

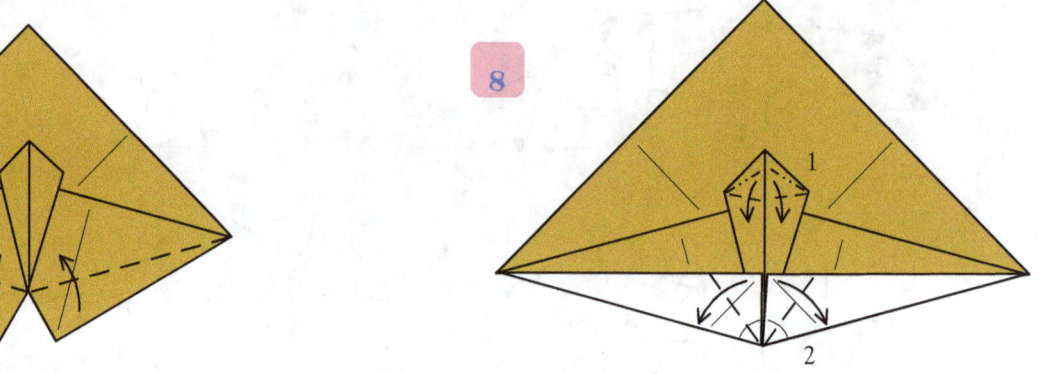

1. Spread while folding down.
2. Bisect the angles.

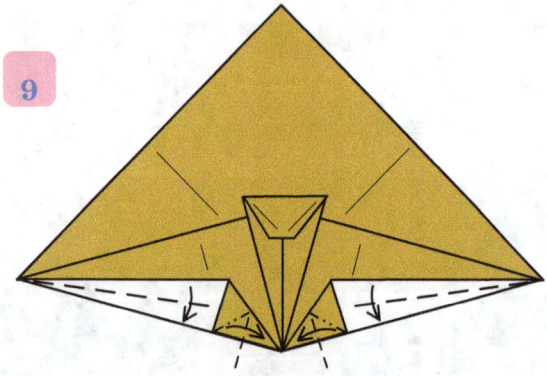

Make squash folds.

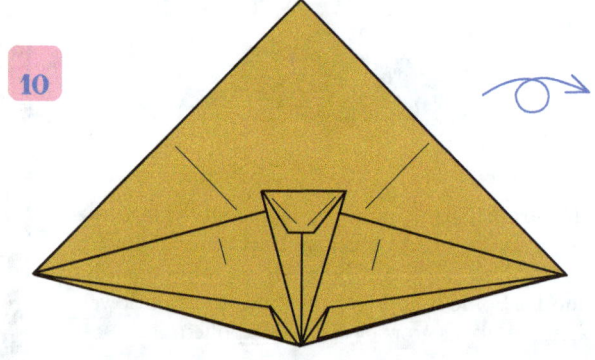

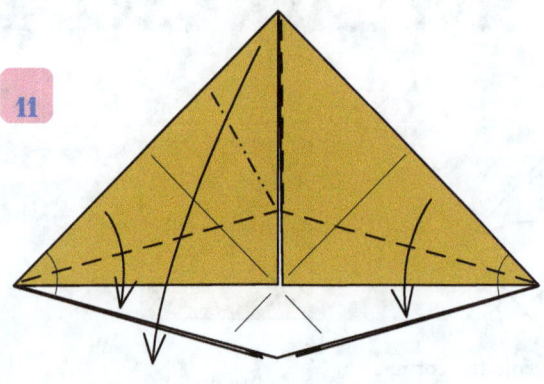

Rabbit-ear.

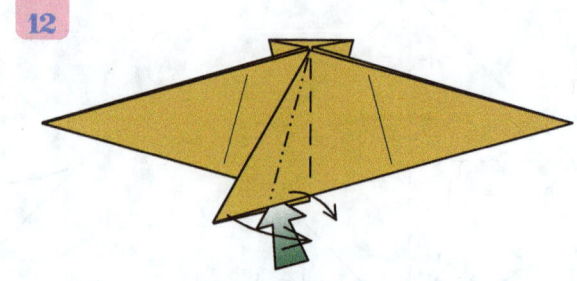

Squash-fold.

12 *Origami Symphony No. 12*

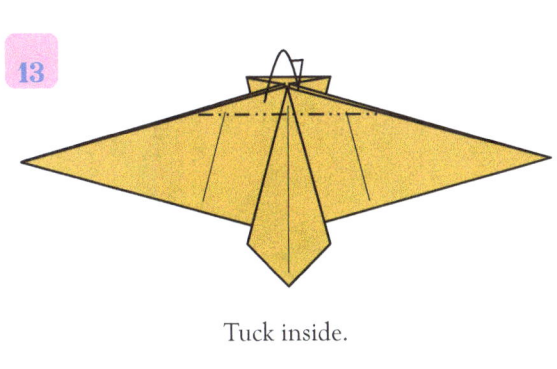

Tuck inside.

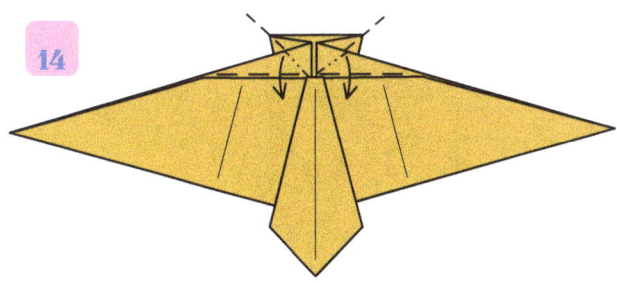

Make squash folds.

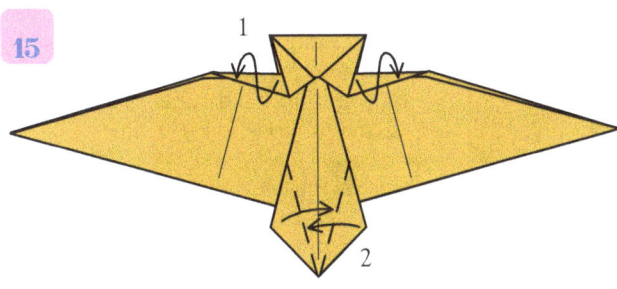

1. Tuck inside.
2. Divide in thirds.

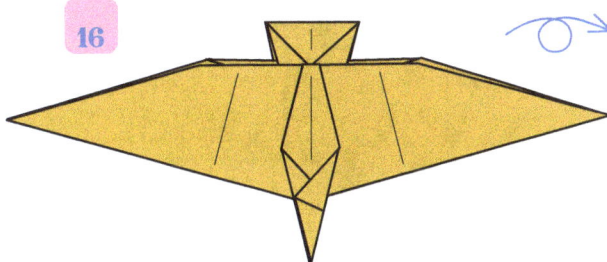

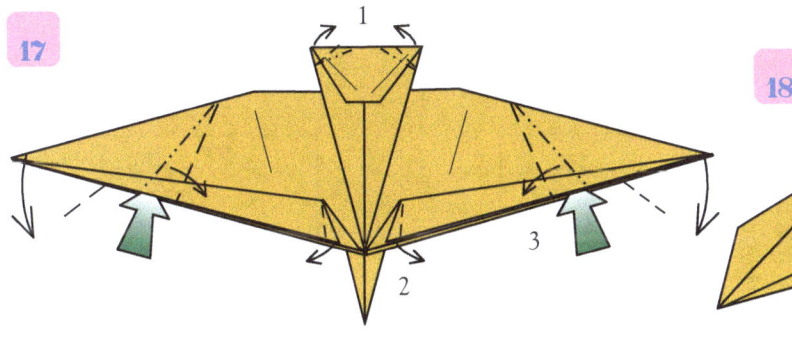

1. Make pleat folds.
2. Make valley folds.
3. Make squash folds.

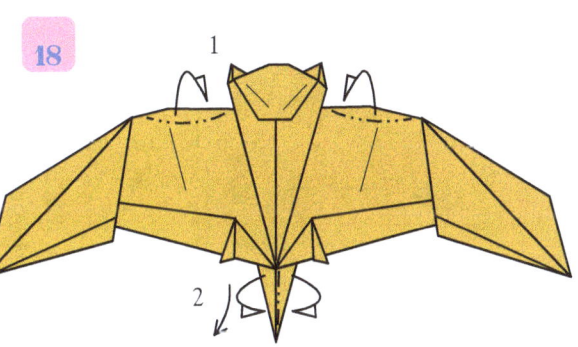

1. Shape the wings.
2. Thin and curl the tail.

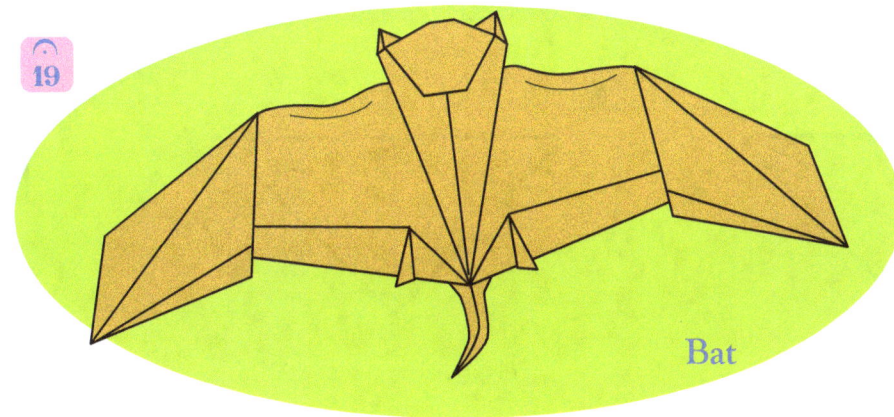

Bat

Sloth

Sloths spend most of their lives hanging upside-down in tress, munching leaves and taking very long naps. But here's the secret: while many sloths are famous for snoozing all day, most of them are actually busiest at night.

When the forest gets dark, sloths quietly climb from branch to branch looking for fresh leaves and tasty buds. Their slow moves help them stay hidden from night-time predators. They have great grip, strong claws, and super-quiet movements—perfect for a midnight snack run. After a little nighttime exploring, they curl back up in their leafy spots for more rest.

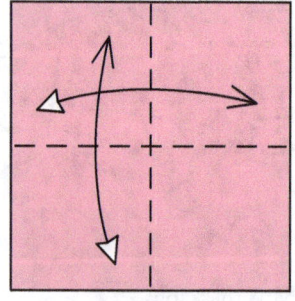

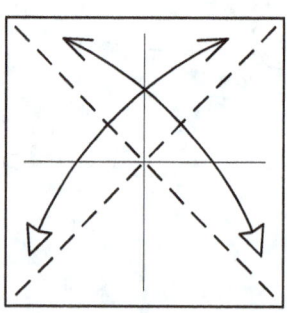

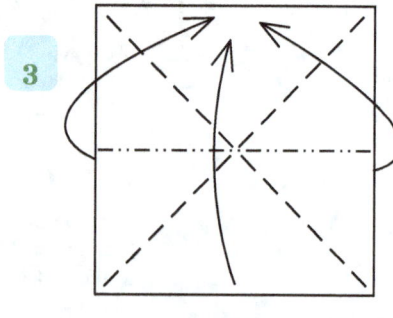

Fold and unfold.

Fold and unfold.

Collapse along the creases.

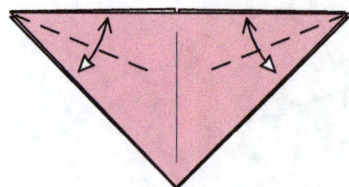

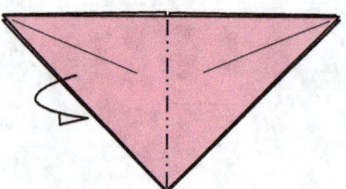

This is the Waterbomb Base. Fold and unfold all the layers.

Fold in half and rotate 90°.

Rabbit-ear and repeat behind.

14 *Origami Symphony No. 12*

7

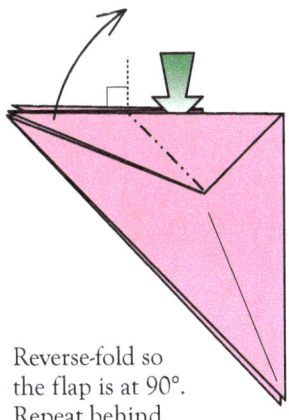

Reverse-fold so the flap is at 90°. Repeat behind.

8

Repeat behind.

9

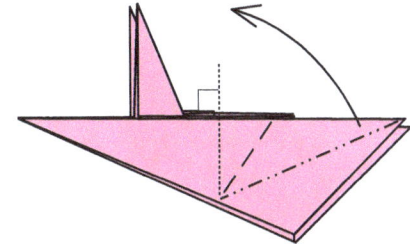

Squash-fold so the flap is at 90°. Repeat behind.

10

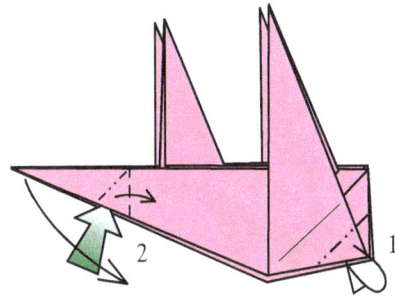

1. Fold inside, repeat behind.
2. Squash-fold.

11

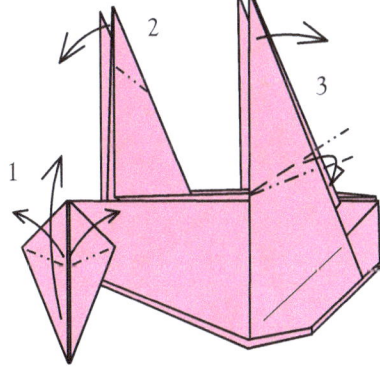

1. Open while folding up.
2. Reverse-fold, repeat behind.
3. Crimp-fold, repeat behind.

12

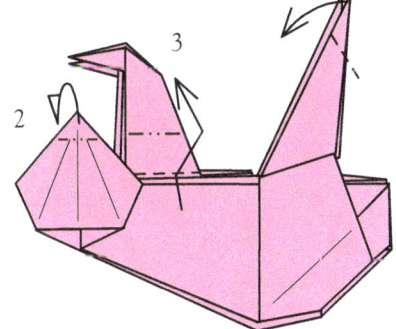

1. Outside-reverse-fold, repeat behind.
2. Fold behind.
3. Bend the legs, repeat behind.

13

Sloth

Sloth 15

Snail

Snails are tiny nighttime explorers! During the day they hide in cool, damp places so they don't dry out. When the sun goes down, they slide out of their hiding spots and glide slowly across leaves, soil, and sidewalks looking for yummy plants to nibble. Their shiny slime trail helps them move smoothly and keeps their bodies from getting hurt.

1. Fold and unfold.

2. Fold and unfold.

3. Bisect the angles.

4. Fold and unfold.

5.

6. Tuck inside.

16 *Origami Symphony No. 12*

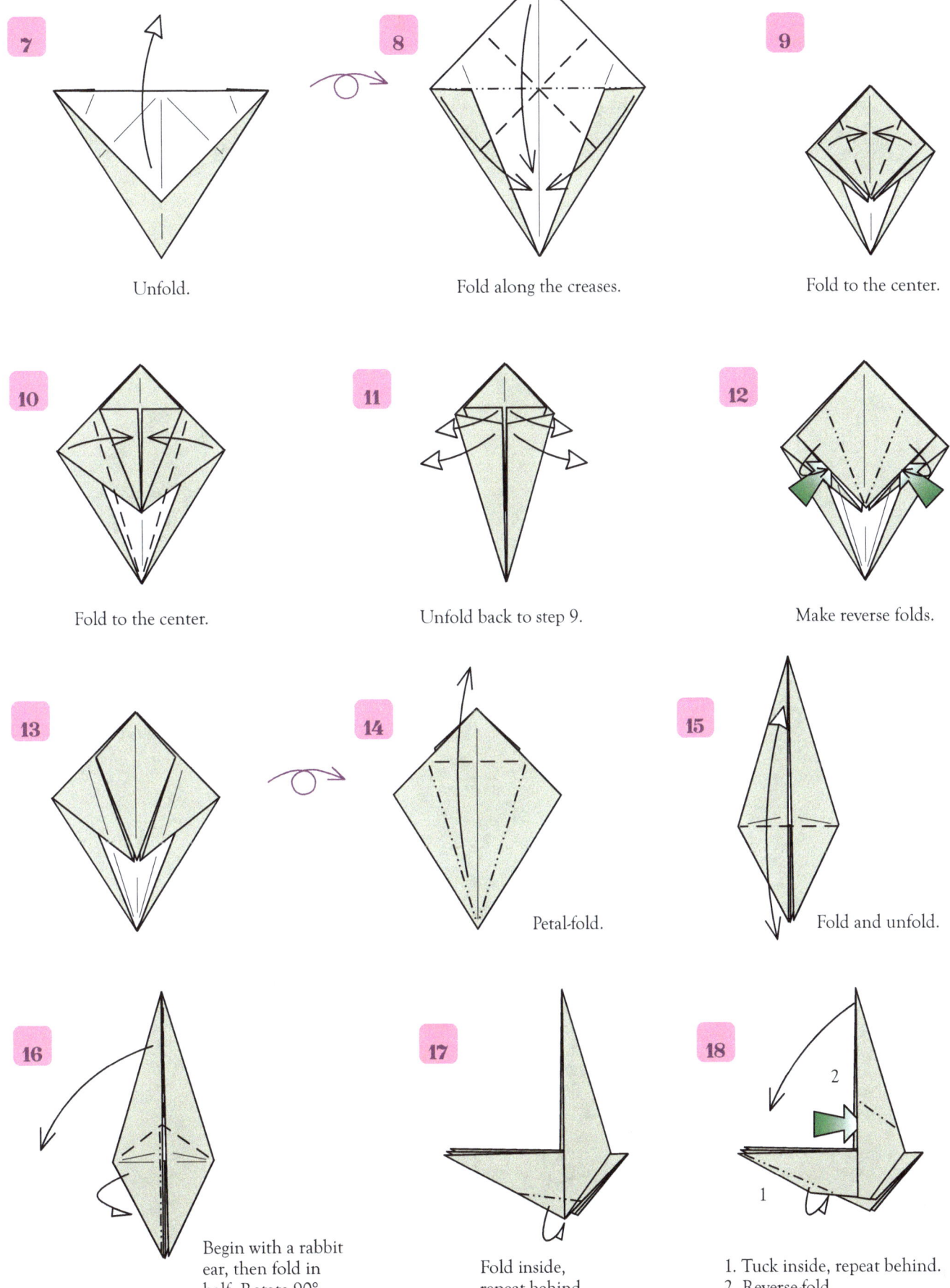

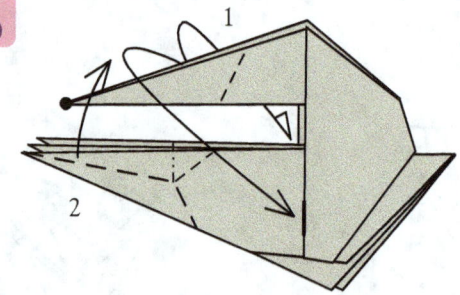

1. Outside-reverse-fold so the dot meets the bold line.
2. Rabbit-ear, repeat behind.

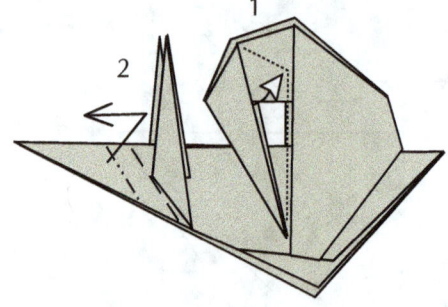

1. Pull out, repeat on the other side.
2. Make outside reverse folds.

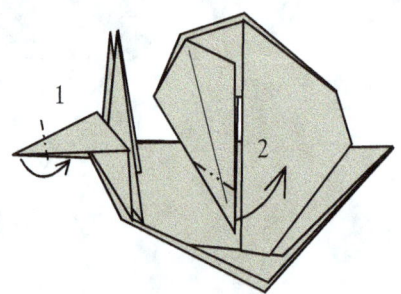

1. Reverse-fold.
2. Reverse-fold.

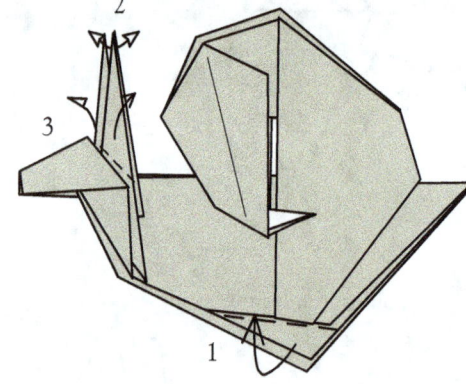

1. Tuck inside.
2. Spread to make a knob at the top.
3. Spread the antennae.
Repeat behind.

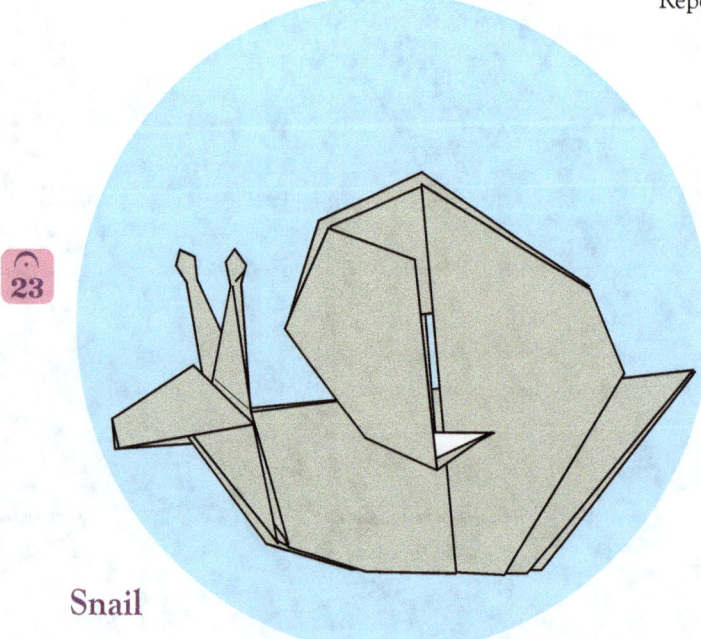

Snail

18 Origami Symphony No. 12

Owl

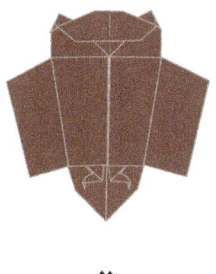

Owls are the super-silent flyers of the dark. All day long the sit very still in trees, looking like part of the bark, but when the sun goes down, they open their huge round eyes and swoop in the dark.

Owls have incredible hearing and excellent night vision, so they can spot mice, insects, and frogs even in almost total darkness. Their soft, special features let them fly without making a sound. An owl's "hoo-hoo" call is its way of talking to other owls in the dark.

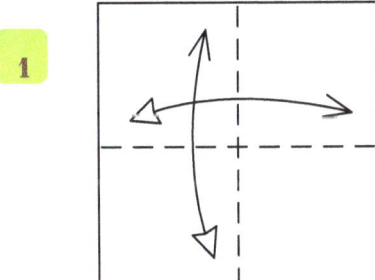

1

Fold and unfold.

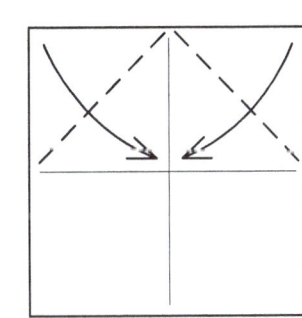

2

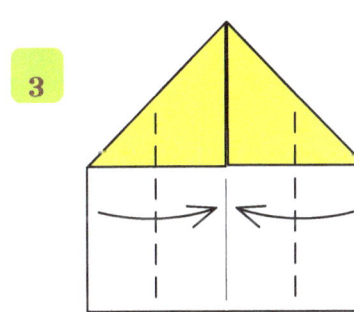

3

Fold to the center.

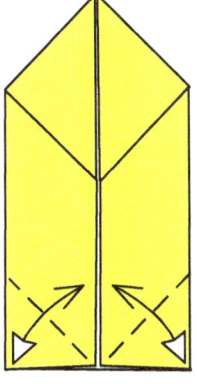

4

Fold and unfold.

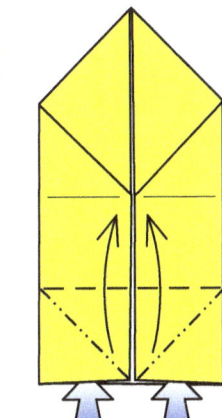

5

Make squash folds.

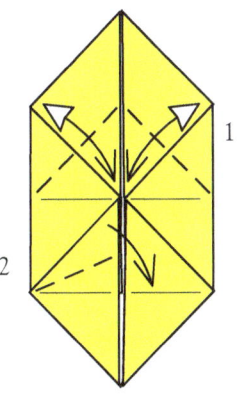

6

1. Fold and unfold.
2. Fold on the left.

Owl **19**

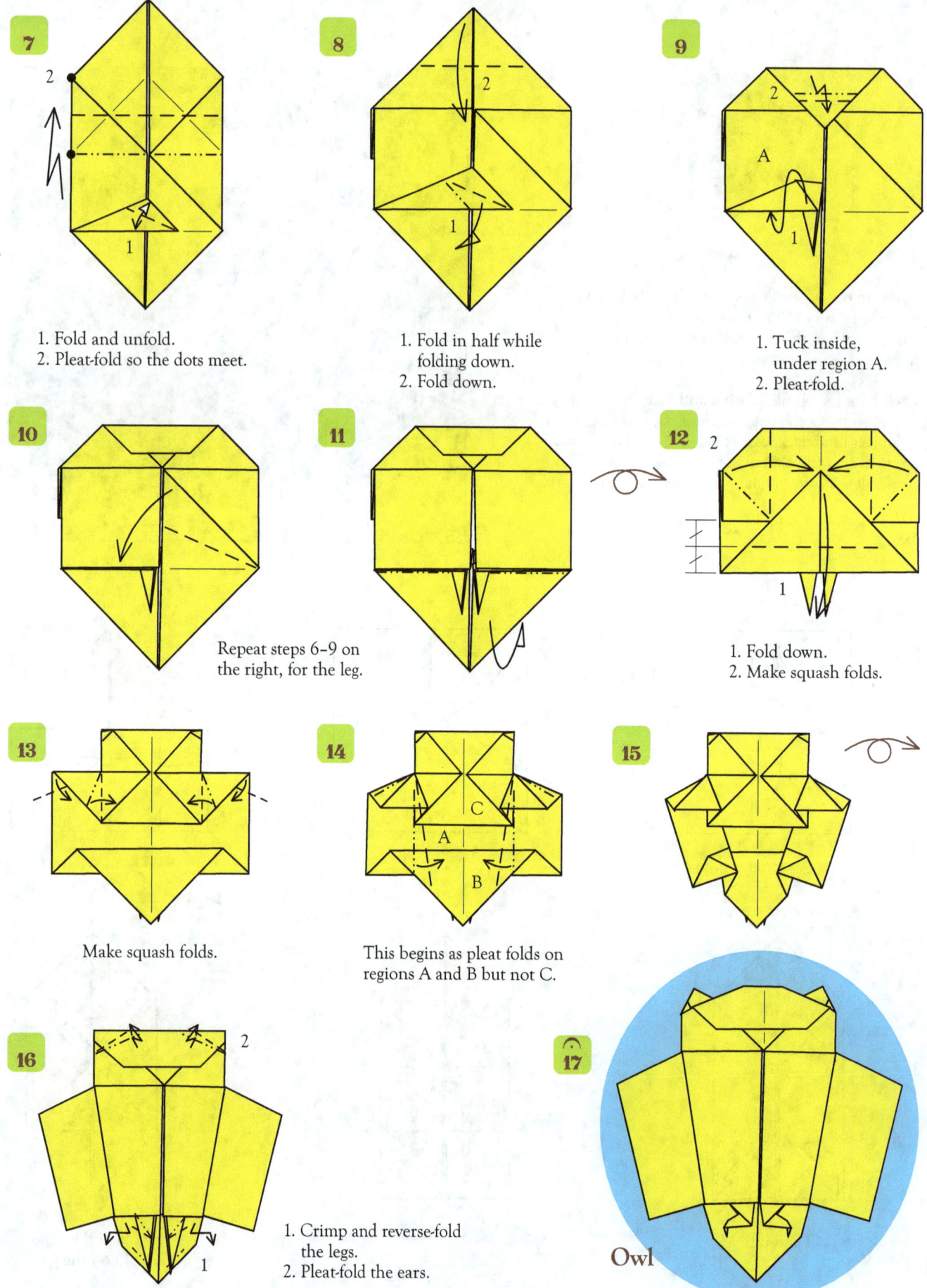

Nightingale

Nightingales are tiny brown birds with giant voices. They're famous for singing after sunset when most other birds are quiet. Their nighttime songs are full of whistles, chirps, and trills that can carry far across the forest, telling other nightingales "This is my place!" or "Meet me here!"

1

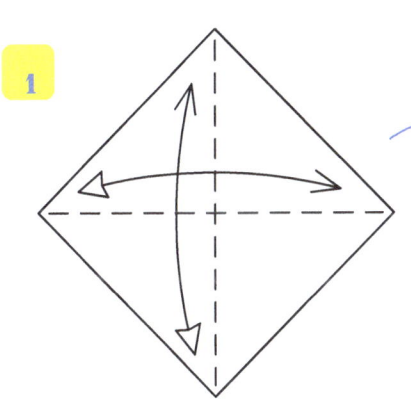

Fold and unfold.

2

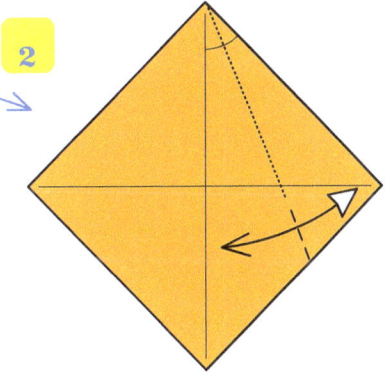

Fold and unfold on the edge.

3

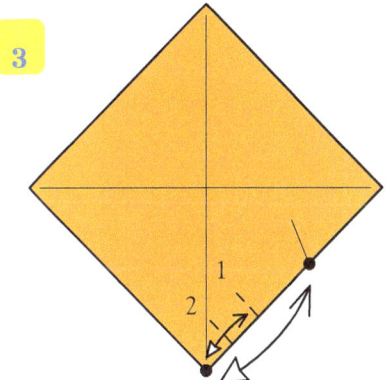

Fold and unfold on the edge at 1 and 2.

4

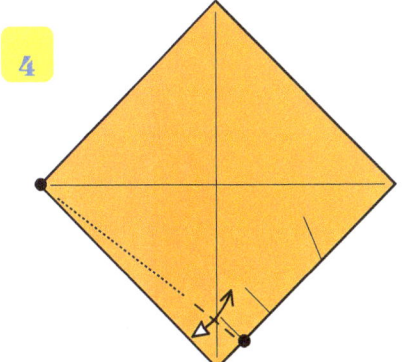

Fold and unfold.

5

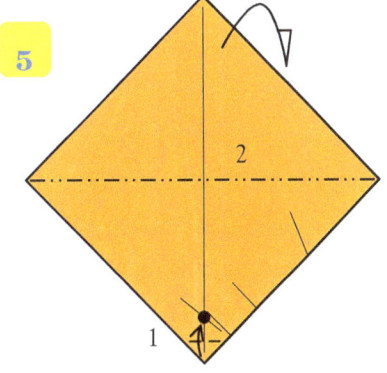

1. Fold up.
2. Fold behind.

6

Fold and unfold.

Nightingale **21**

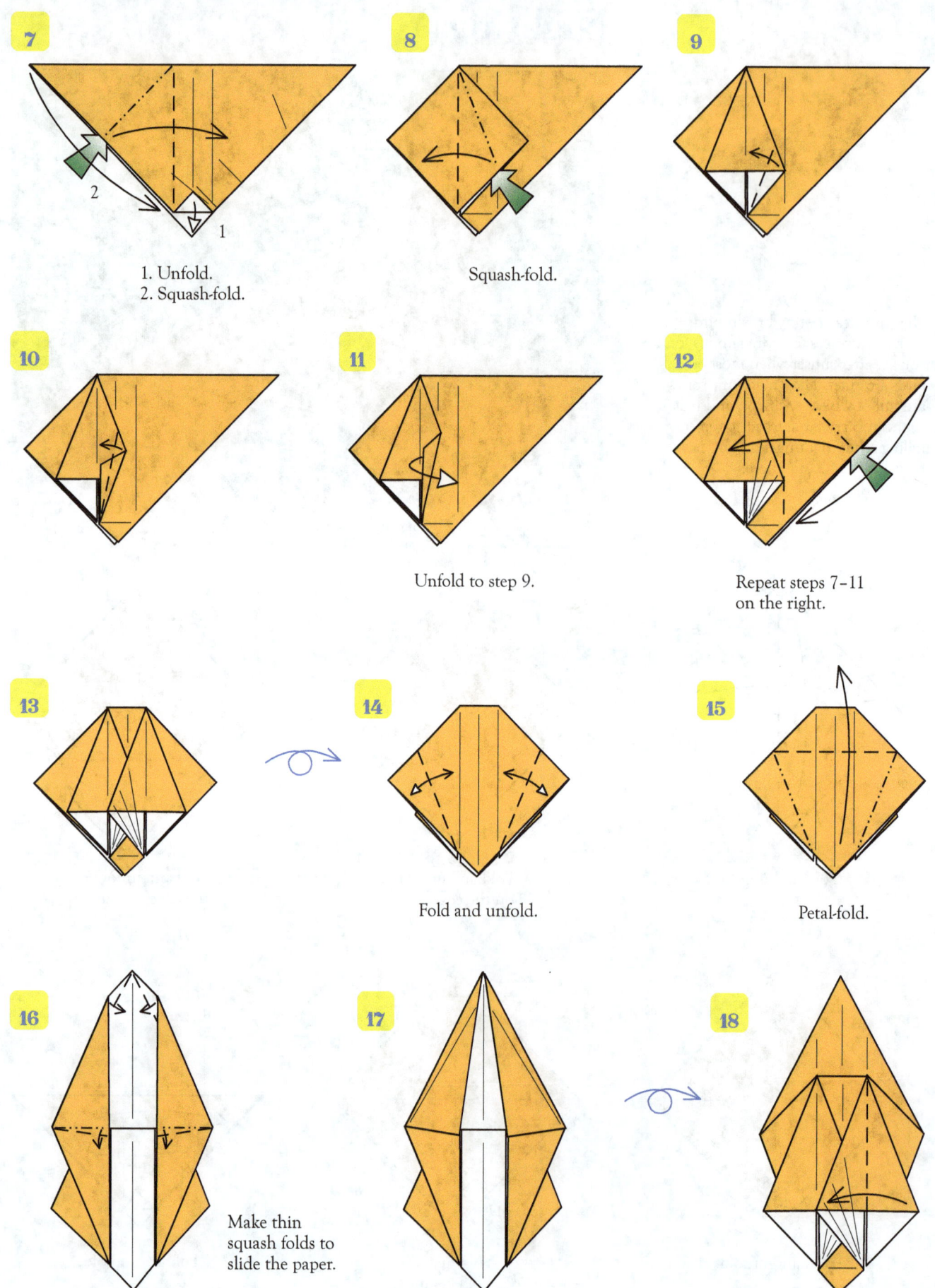

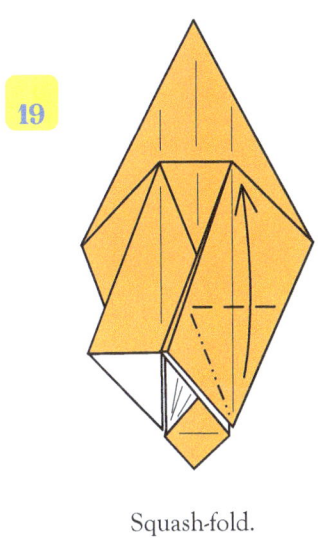

Squash-fold.

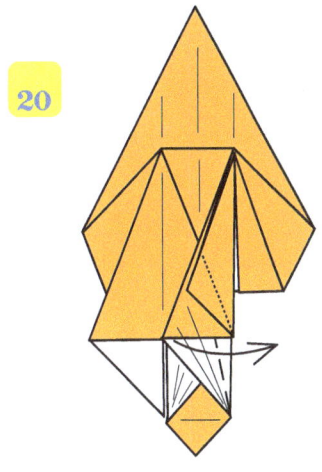

Valley-fold along the crease for this reverse fold.

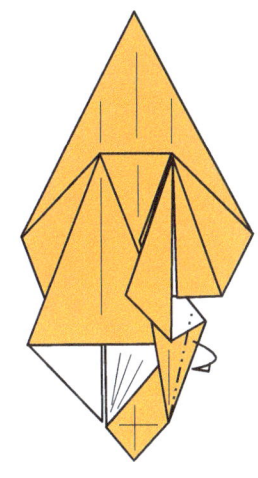

Fold behind along the crease.

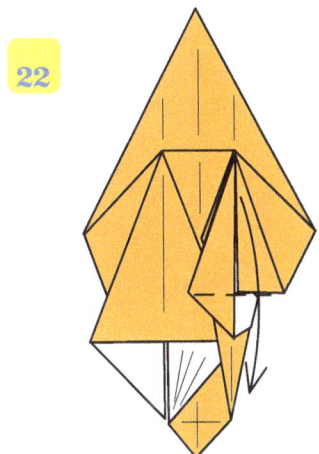

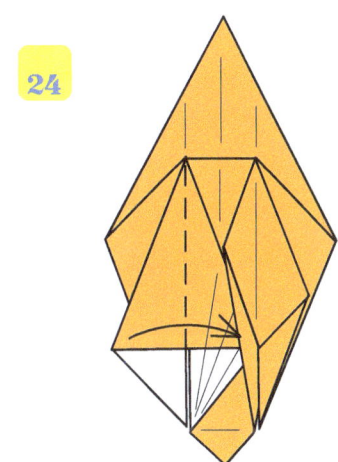

Repeat steps 18–23 on the left.

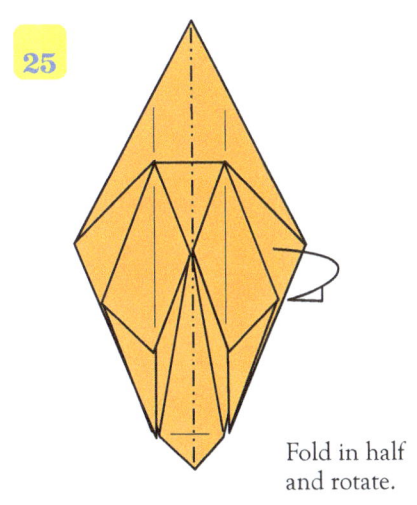

Fold in half and rotate.

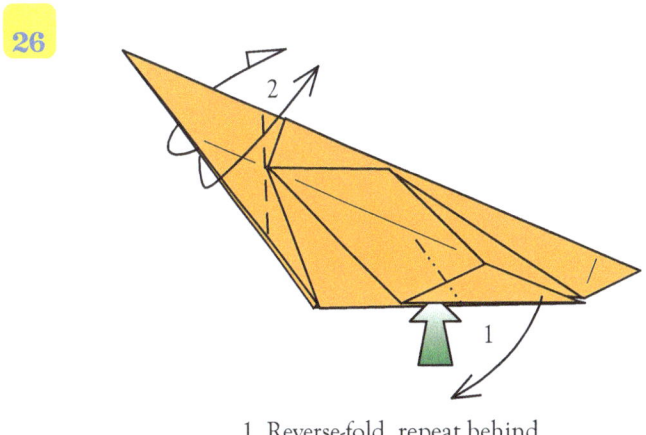

1. Reverse-fold, repeat behind.
2. Outside-reverse-fold.

Nightingale **23**

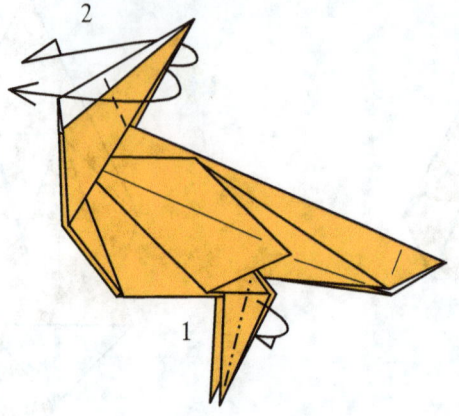

1. Fold inside on the front and back, repeat behind.
2. Outside-reverse-fold.

1. Make crimp folds, repeat behind.
2. Crimp-fold.
3. Fold inside, repeat behind.

Nightingale

Anteater

Anteaters are the bug-eating superheroes of the animal world! They don't have teeth, but they do have super-long, sticky tongues that can slurp up thousands of ants and termites in a single night. Many anteaters spend the hot daytime curled up in the shade or in a tree. When evening arrives, they wake up and quietly pad though the forest or grasslands with their big claws and bushy tails.

Moving slowly and gently in the dark keeps them cool and safe from predators while they search for tasty insects. So even though they look sleepy during the day, anteaters turn into silent, nighttime snack hunters once the sun goes down.

1 Fold and unfold.

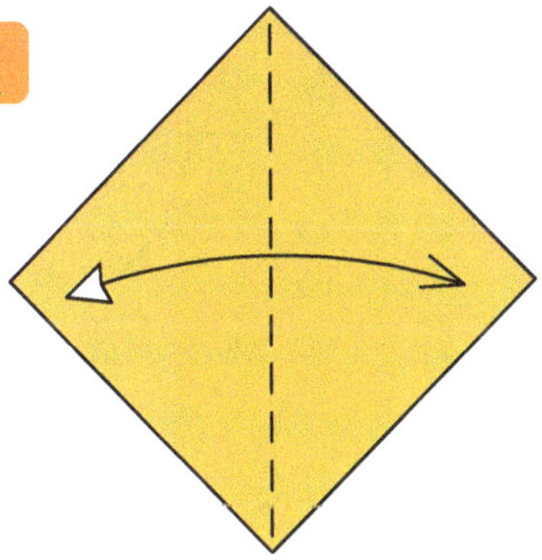

2 Fold and unfold on the edge.

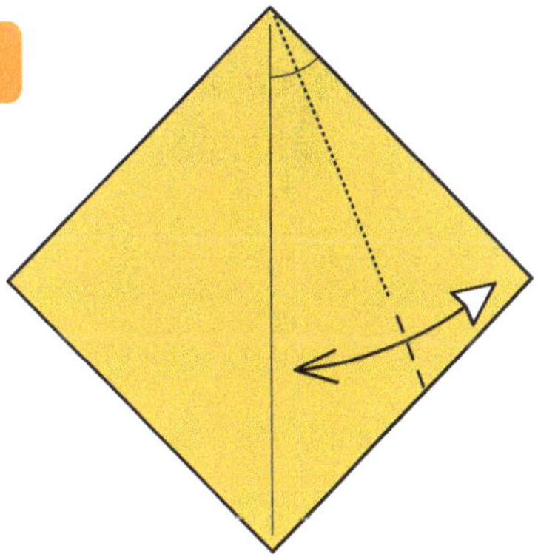

3 Fold and unfold on the edge.

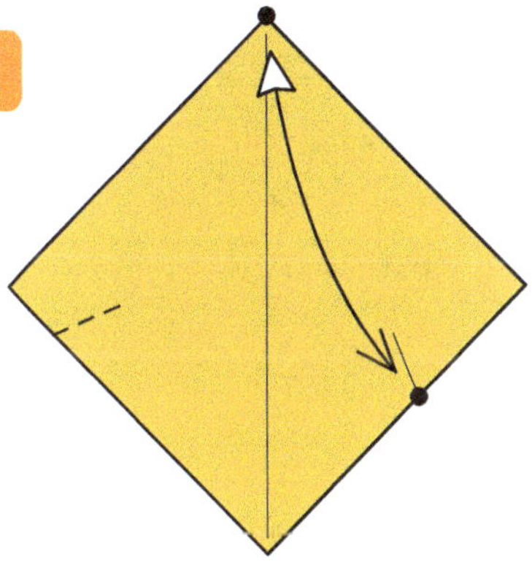

4 Fold and unfold on the diagonal.

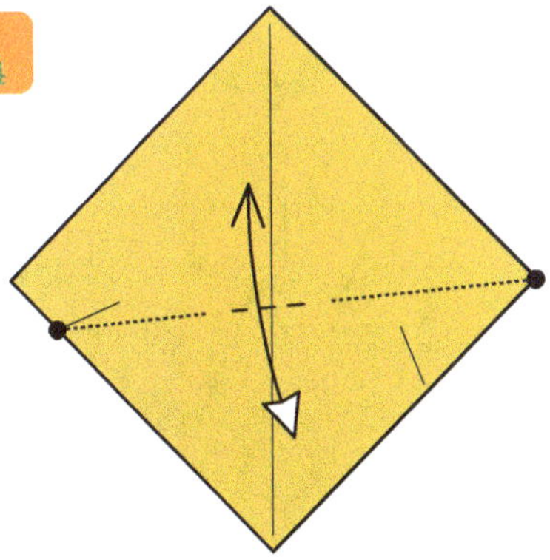

5 Fold and unfold. Rotate 180°.

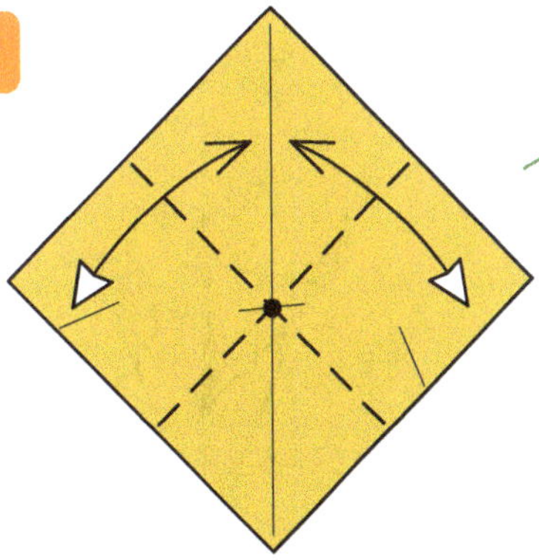

6 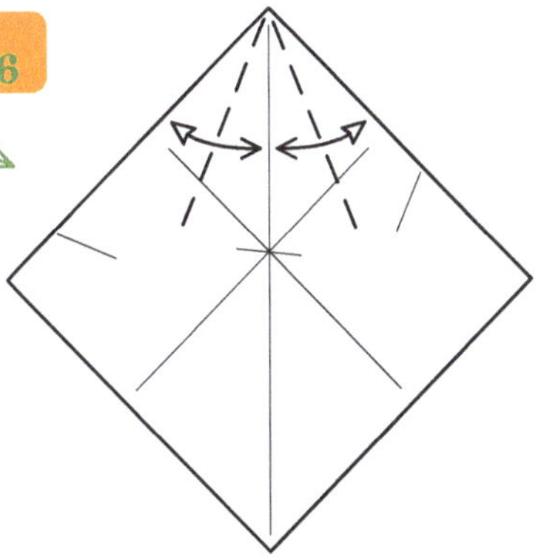 Fold to the center and unfold.

Anteater **25**

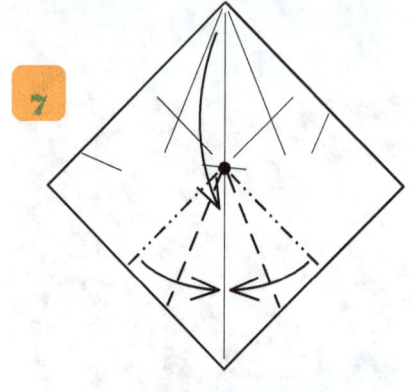

Push in at the dot. Mountain-fold along the creases.

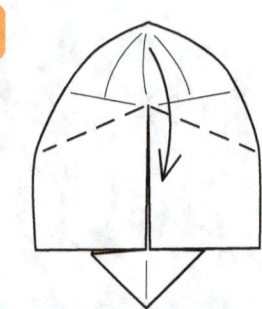

This is 3D. Flatten.

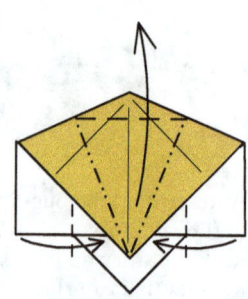

Petal-fold.

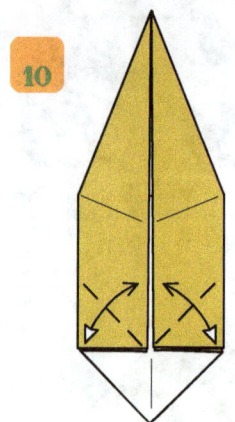

Fold and unfold.

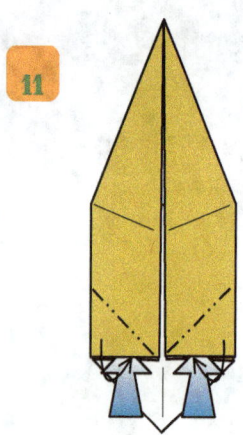

Make reverse folds.

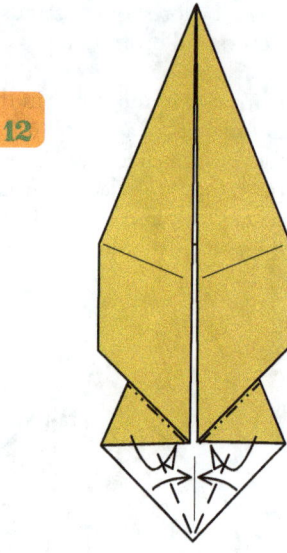

Make reverse folds.

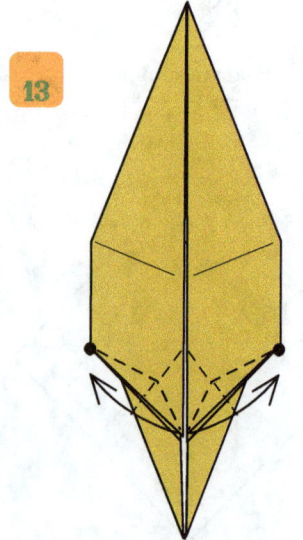

Make rabbit ears so the points end slightly below the dots.

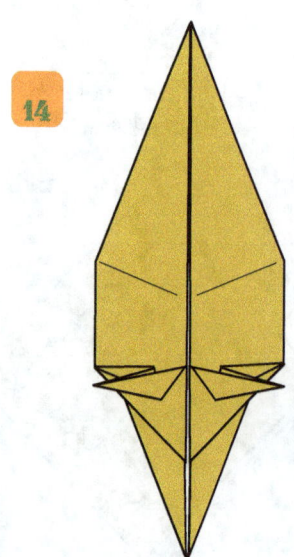

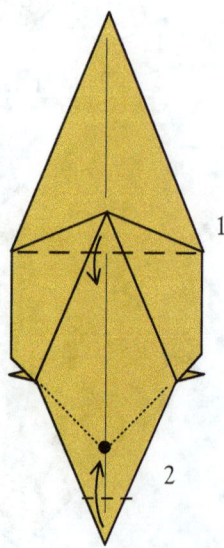

1. Fold down.
2. Fold up.

26 *Origami Symphony No. 12*

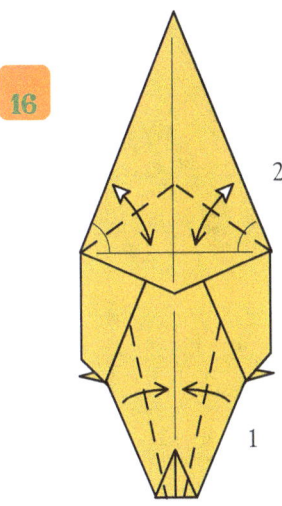
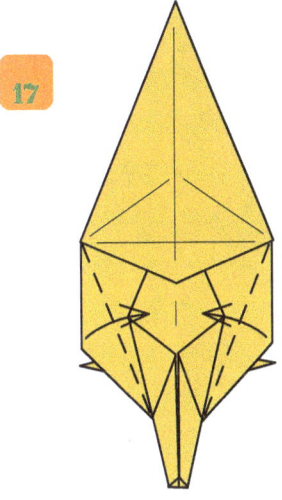
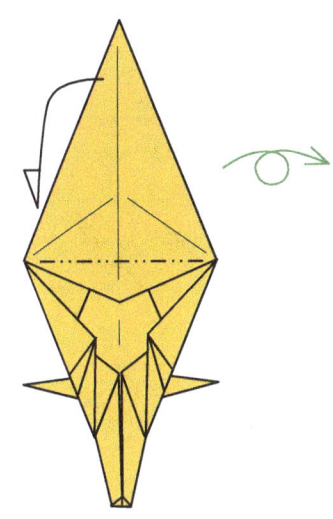

1. Fold to the center.
2. Fold and unfold.

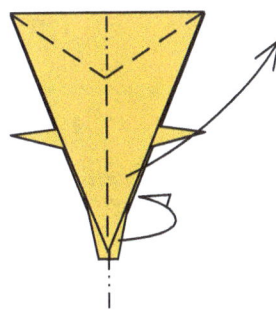
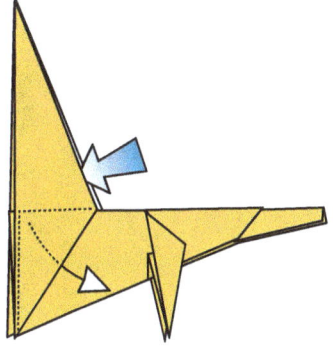

Lift the tail up while folding the body in half. Rotate 90°.

Unlock and pull out some paper. Repeat behind.

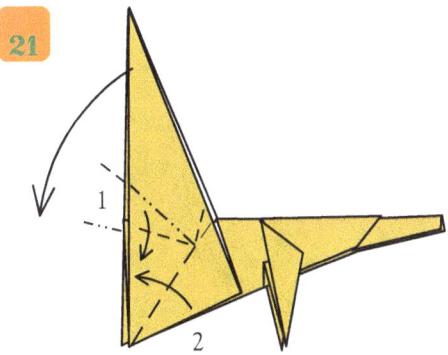
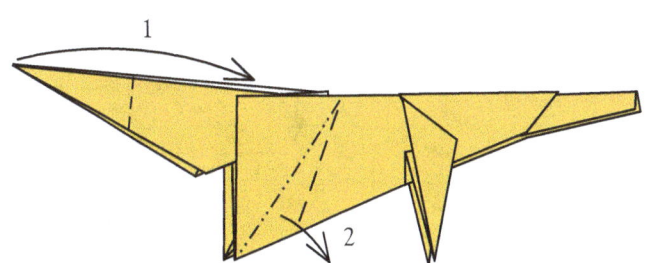

This is a combination of folds.
1. Begin a crimp fold while
2. folding the flap up, repeat behind.

1. Outside-reverse-fold.
2. Crimp-fold.

Anteater **27**

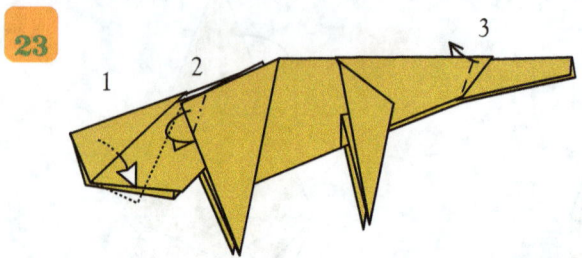

1. Pull out.
2. Fold behind.
3. Fold up.
Repeat behind.

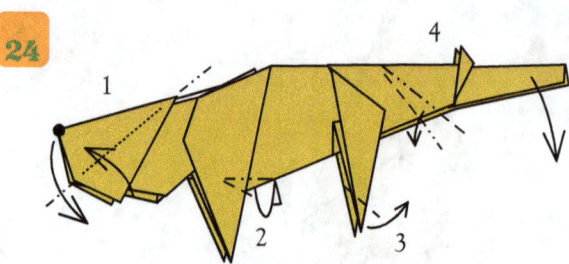

1. Push in at the dot and fold up on the front and back.
2. Shape the body with a small hidden squash fold, repeat behind.
3. Outside-reverse-fold, repeat behind.
4. Crimp-fold.

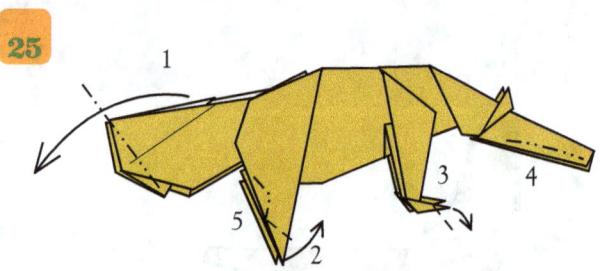

1. Reverse-fold.
2. Outside-reverse-fold.
3. Outside-reverse-fold.
4. Shape the head.
5. Shape the legs.
Repeat behind.

Anteater

Raccoon

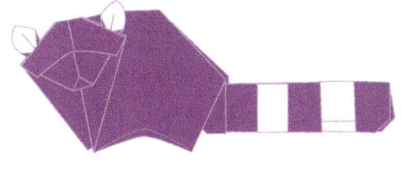

Raccoons are the little "masked bandits" of the night! Those dark rings around their eyes aren't just cute—they help cut down glare so raccoons can see better in the dark, While they spend the day curled up in trees, dens, or attics, they become busy explorers once the sun goes down.

At night raccoons pad quietly through yards, forests, and streams using their nimble hands to flip rocks, open shells, and even lift lids to find food. They'll munch berries, insects, fish, or leftovers—almost anything they can find. Their glowing eyes and striped tails make them look like tiny superheroes on a nighttime treasure hunt.

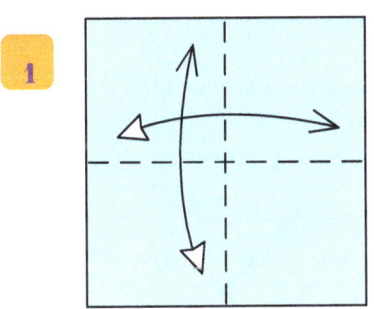

1

Fold and unfold.

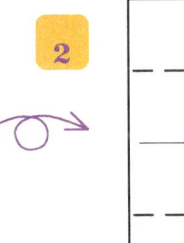

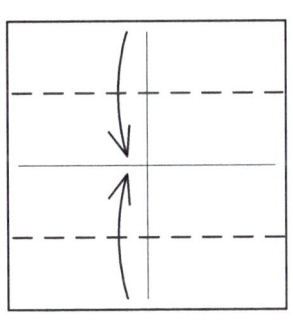

2

Fold to the center.

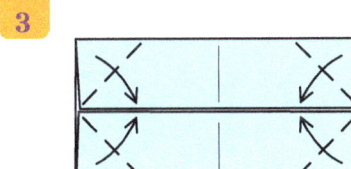

3

Fold to the center.

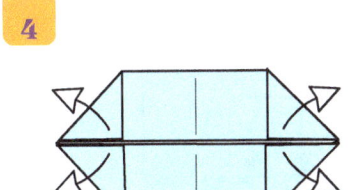

4

Unfold.

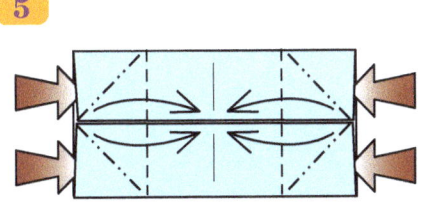

5

Make squash folds.

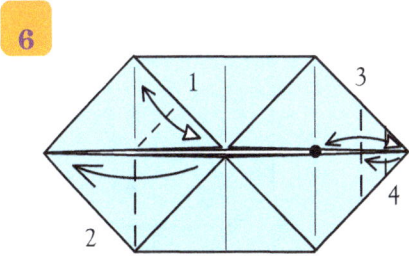

6

1. Fold and unfold.
2. Fold to the left.
3. Fold and unfold.
4. Fold to the left.

Raccoon **29**

7

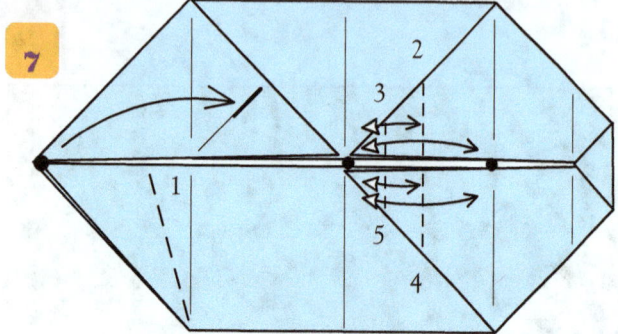

1. Bring the dot to the line.
2–5. Fold and unfold.

8

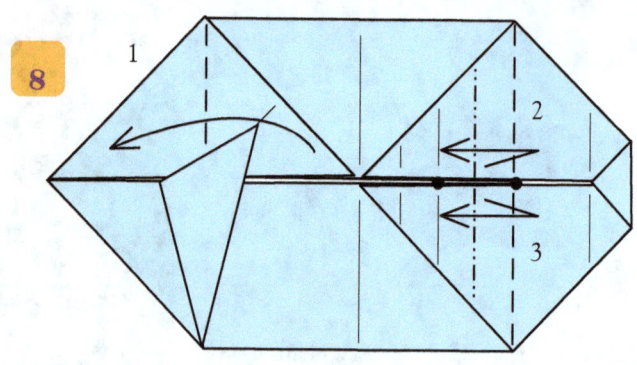

1. Fold to the left.
2–3. Pleat-fold so the dots meet.

9

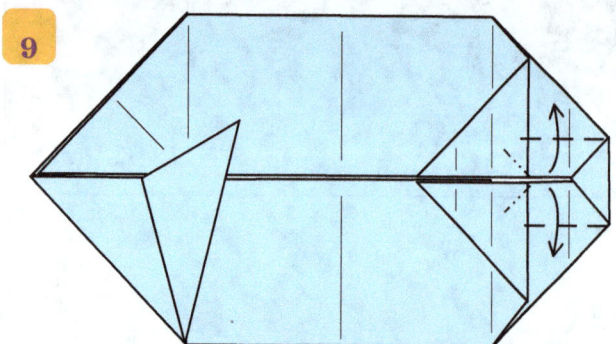

Fold the top layer. This is similar to making petal folds.

10

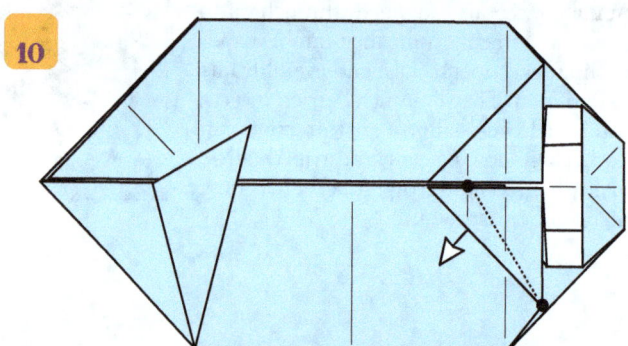

Pull out some paper. Fold a hidden layer along the dotted line. Rotate 90°.

11

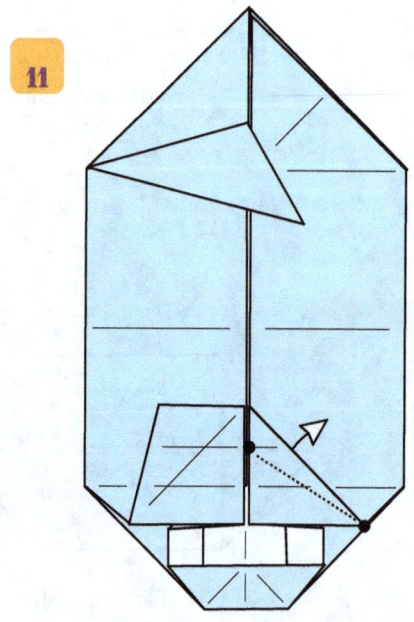

Repeat step 10 on the right.

12

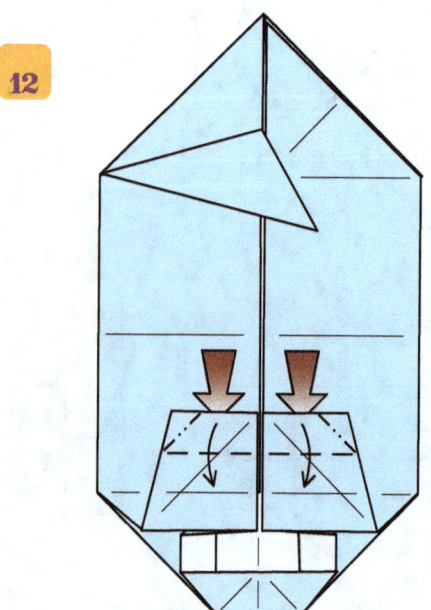

Make squash folds.

30   Origami Symphony No. 12

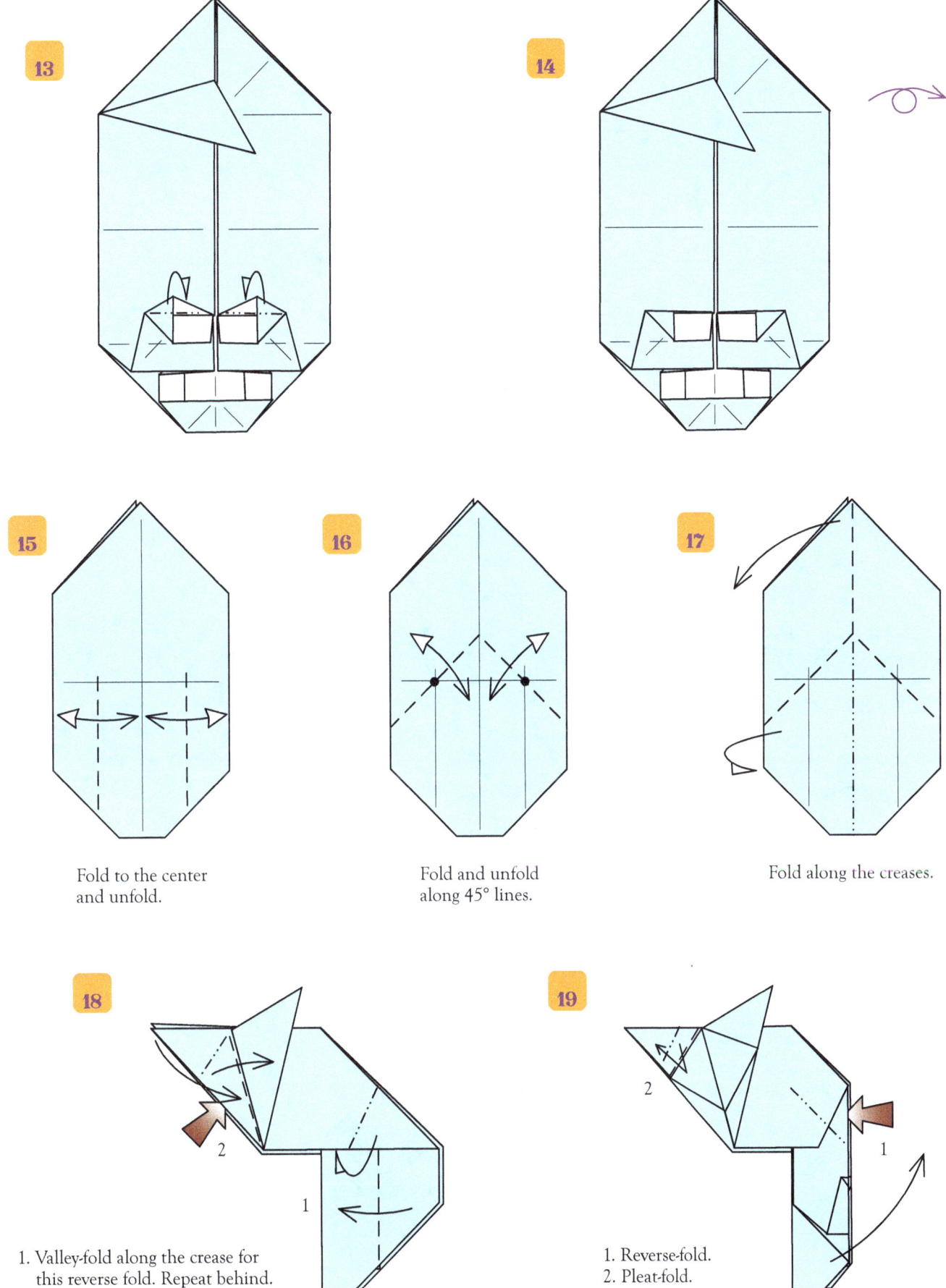

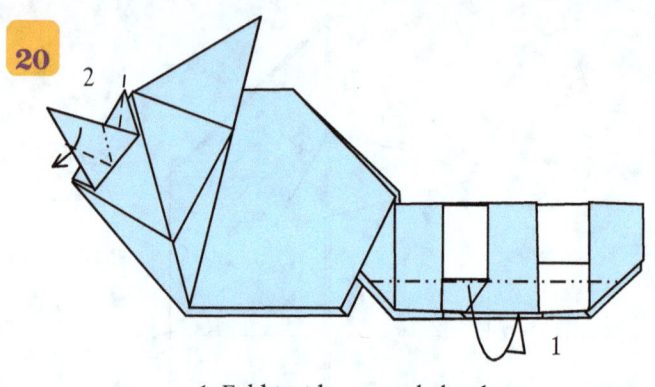

1. Fold inside, repeat behind.
2. Squash-fold.

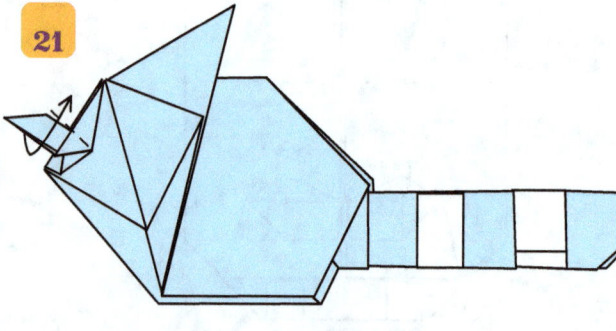

Open.

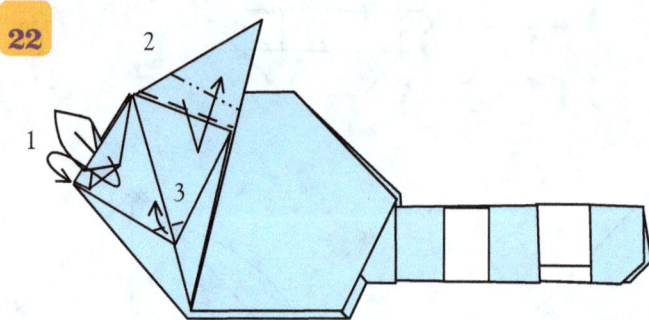

1. Tuck inside.
2. Repeat steps 19–22 on the right.
3. Fold up.

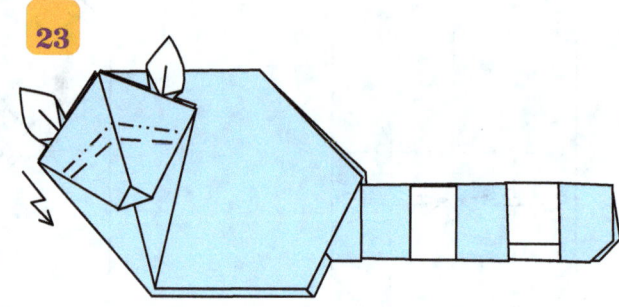

Shape the face with pleat folds. The head will be 3D.

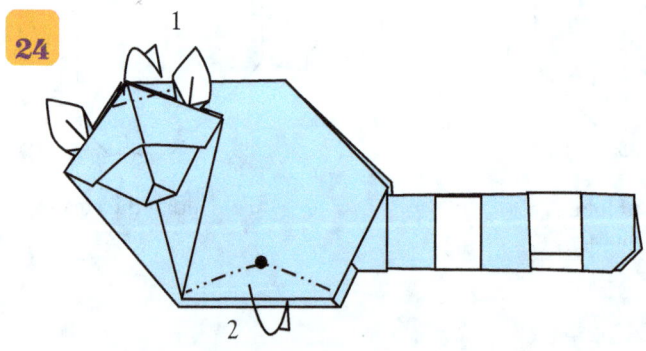

1. Fold behind.
2. Shape the legs and puff out at the dot. The body will be 3D. Repeat behind.

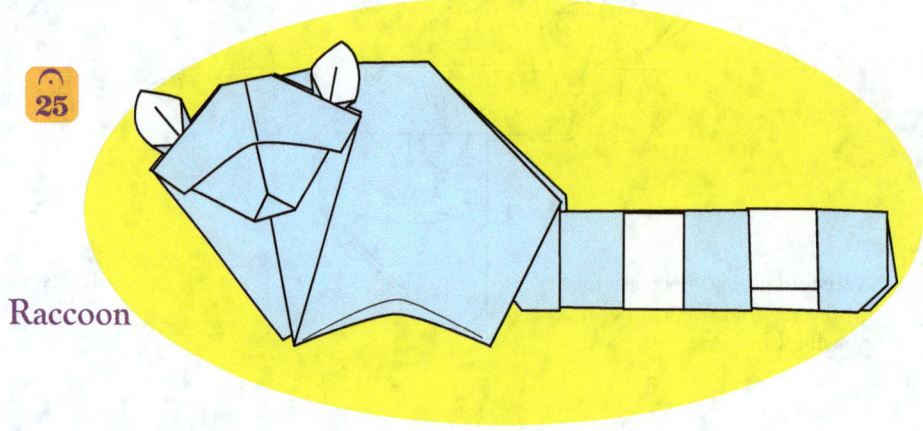

Raccoon

Skunk

Skunks are the shy, gentle wanderers with a very famous secret weapon—their stinky spray! During the day they hide in burrows, hollow logs, or under porches to stay safe and cool. When the sun sets, they shuffle out on little black-and-white paws to explore fields, forests, and backyards.

At night skunks look for tasty treats like insects, worms, berries, and fallen fruit. If something scares them, they stamp their feet and lift their fluffy tails as a warning before letting off their super-smelly mist. Most of the time, these striped night explores are quietly sniffing around, helping keep insect numbers down while glowing like little shadows under the moonlight.

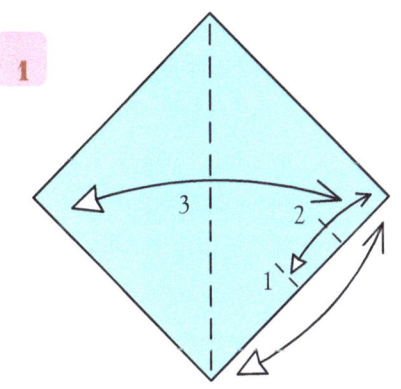

Fold and unfold at 1, 2, and 3.

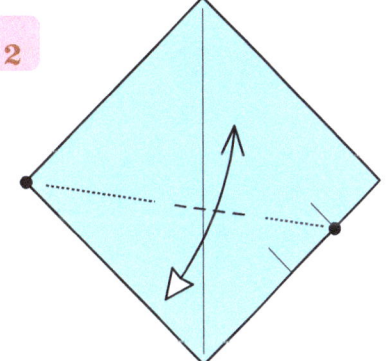

Fold and unfold on the diagonal.

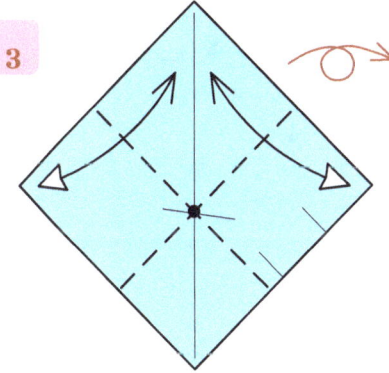

Fold and unfold. Rotate 180°.

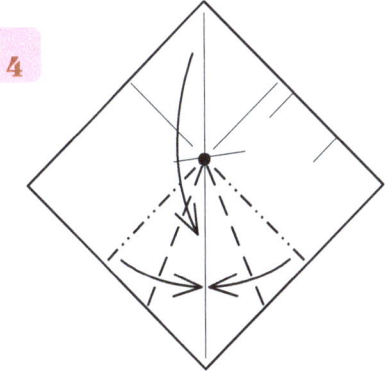

Push in at the dot. Mountain-fold along the creases.

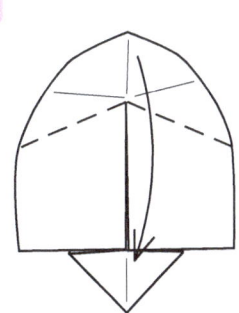

This is 3D. Flatten.

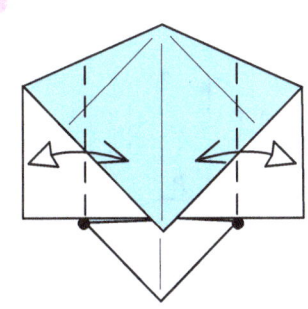

Fold and unfold.

Skunk 33

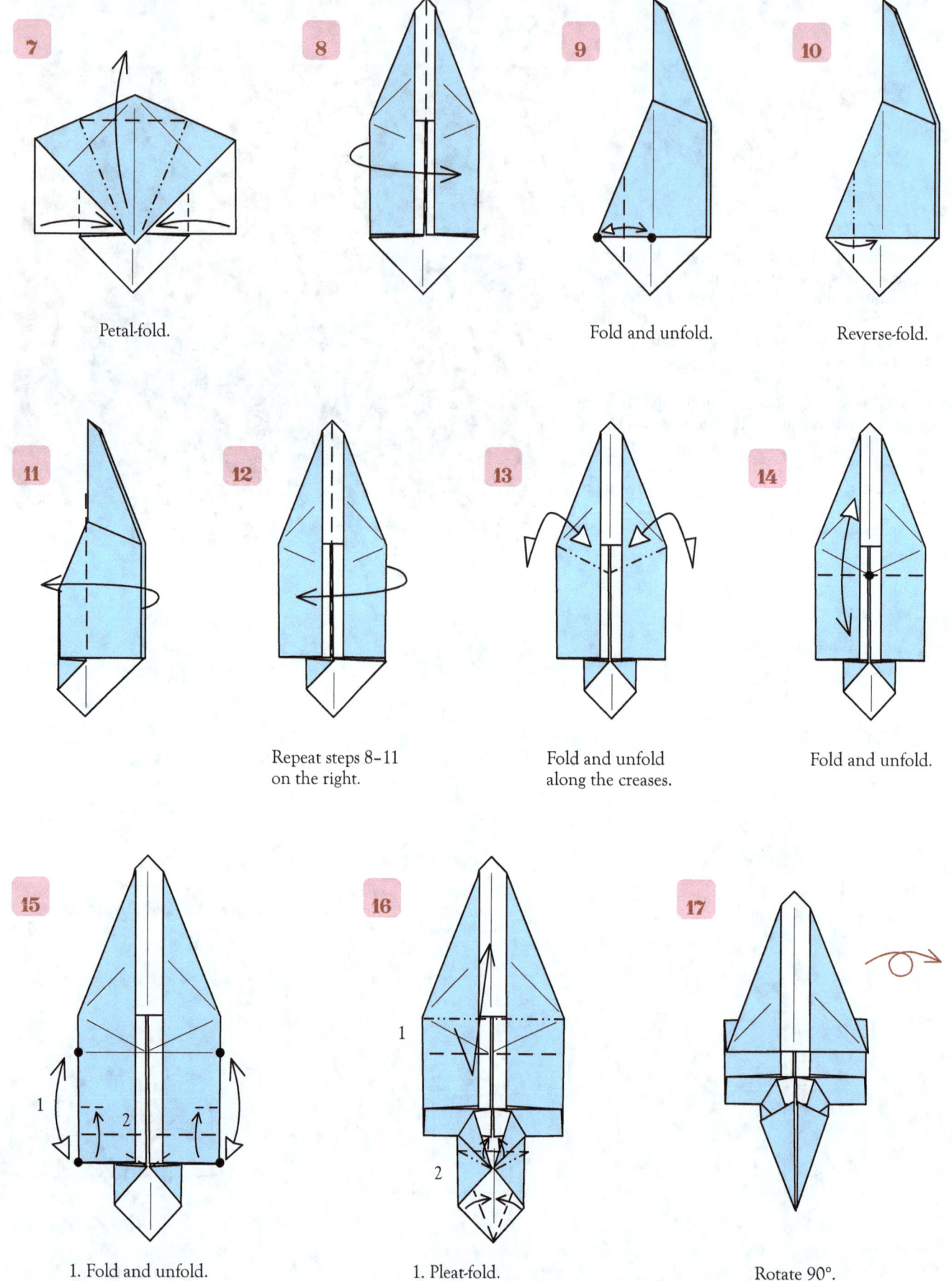

34 Origami Symphony No. 12

18

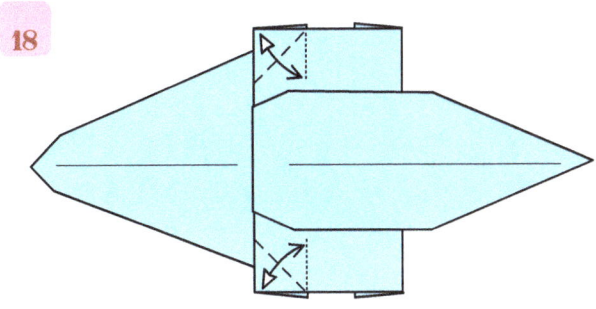

Fold and unfold.

19

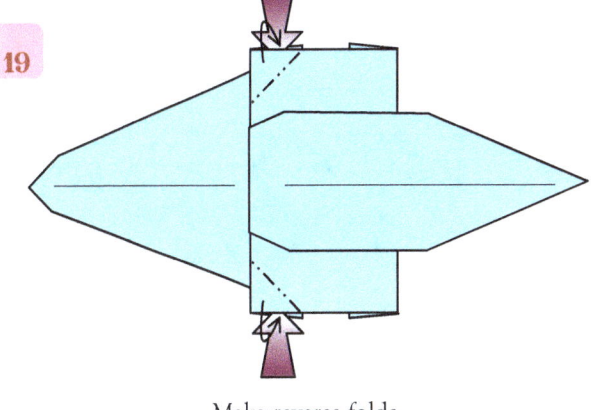

Make reverse folds.

20

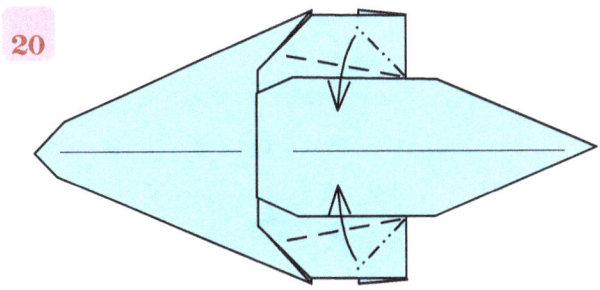

Make squash folds.

21

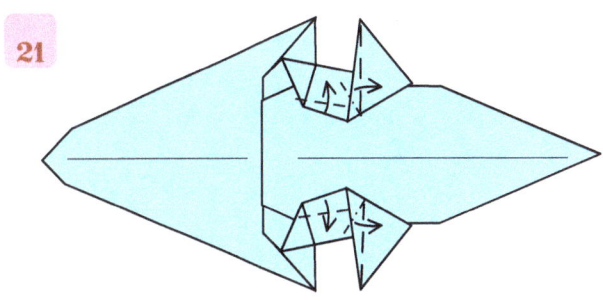

Make squash folds.

22

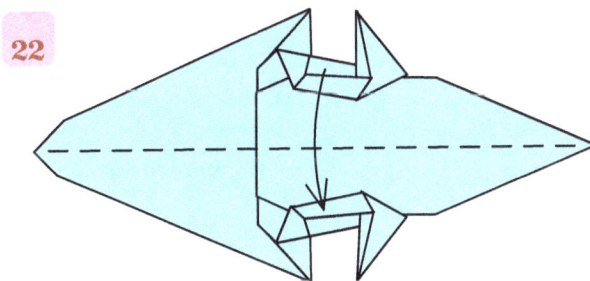

23

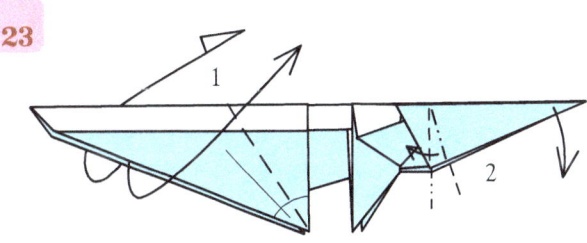

1. Outside-reverse-fold.
2. Crimp-fold.

24

1. Outside-reverse-fold.
2. Reverse-fold.
3. Squash-fold and tuck inside, repeat behind.

25

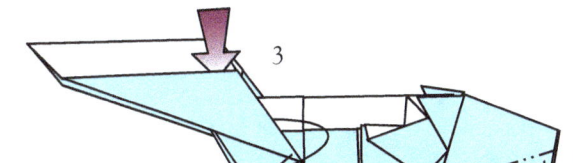

1. Fold inside.
2. Crimp-fold.
3. Unlock and unwrap the paper. Repeat behind.

Skunk 35

26

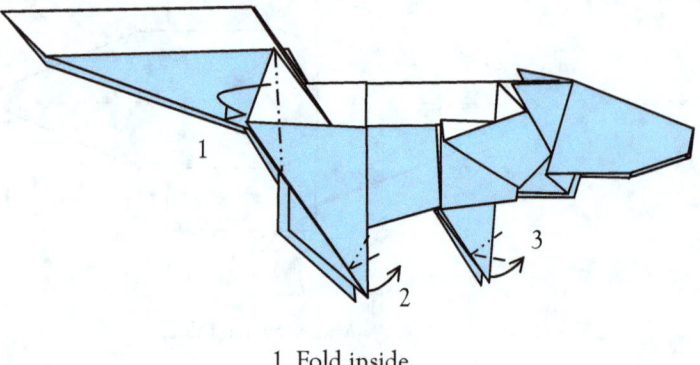

1. Fold inside.
2. Crimp-fold.
3. Crimp-fold.
Repeat behind.

27

1. Fold inside, repeat behind.
2. Reverse-fold.

28

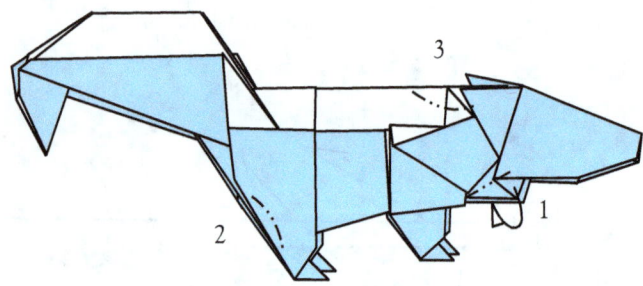

1. Fold inside, repeat behind.
2. Shape the legs, repeat behind.
3. Shape the back.

29

Skunk

Opossum

Opossums are gentle, shy animals with pink noses, round ears, and long, curly tails. In the daytime they curl up in tree holes, burrows, or under porches to nap. But when night falls, they wake up and go on quiet adventures!

At night opossums waddle through forests and backyards looking for delicious snacks like fruits, insects, and frogs. They help clean up nature's messes. If something scares them, an opossum might hiss, show its teeth or even "play dead" (lying still until the danger passes). Under the moonlight they're busy, helpful wanderers keeping the neighborhood neat while everyone else is asleep.

1. Fold and unfold.

2. Fold to the center and unfold.

3. Fold and unfold on the diagonal.

4. Fold and unfold. Rotate 180°.

5. Fold to the center and unfold.

6. Push in at the dot. Mountain-fold along the creases.

Opossum **37**

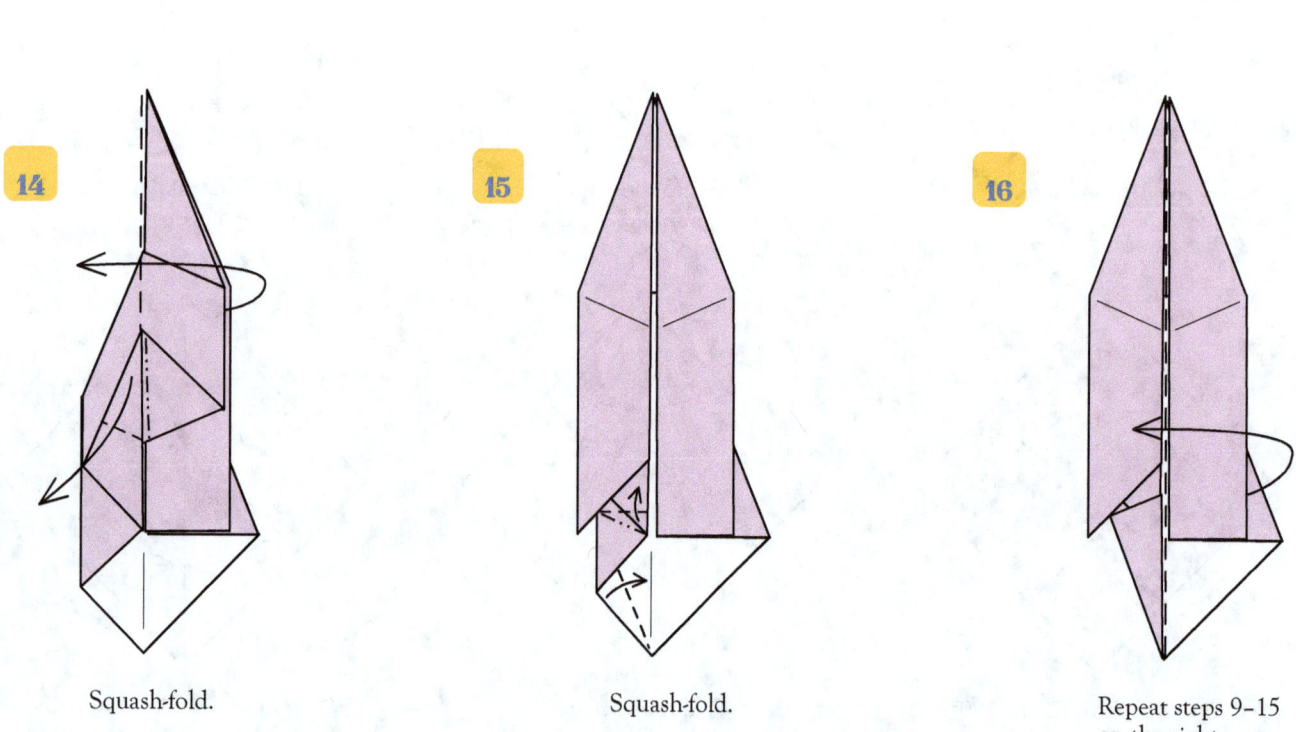

38 Origami Symphony No. 12

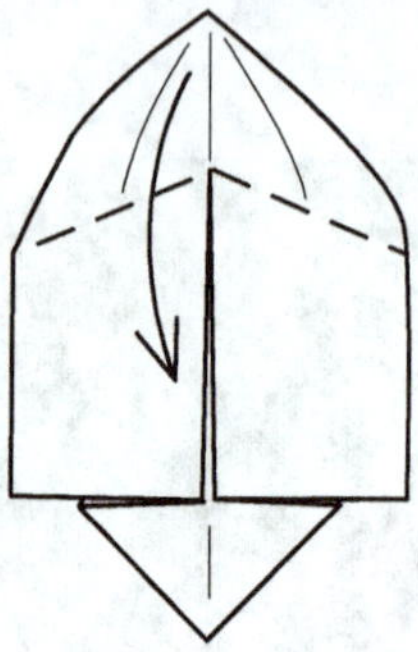

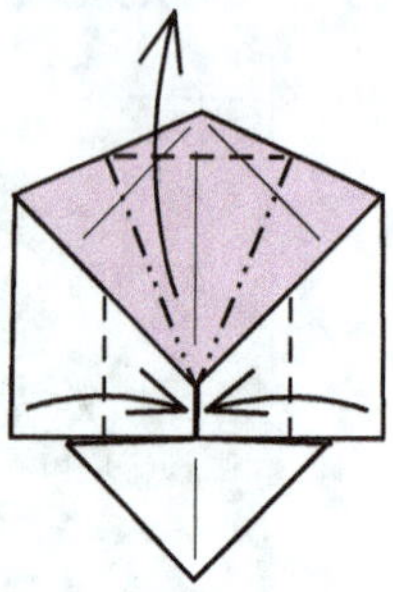

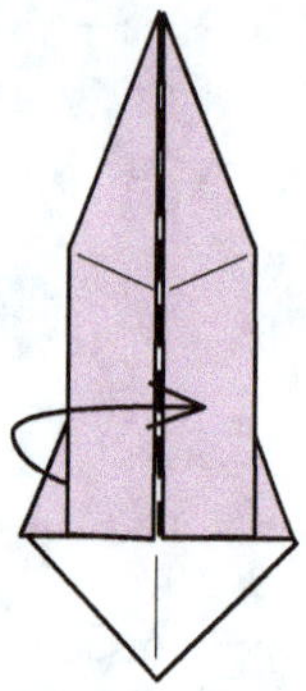

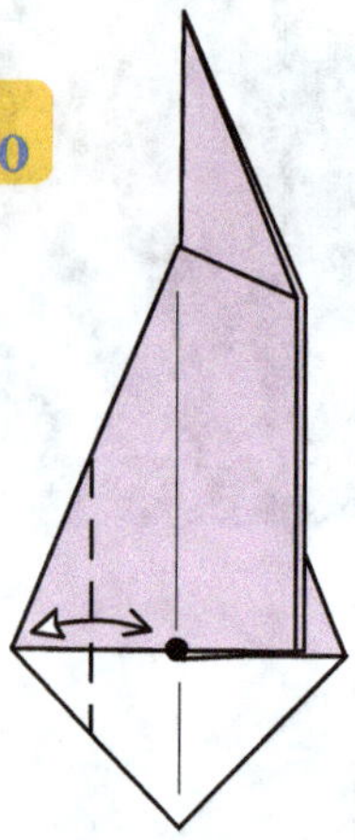

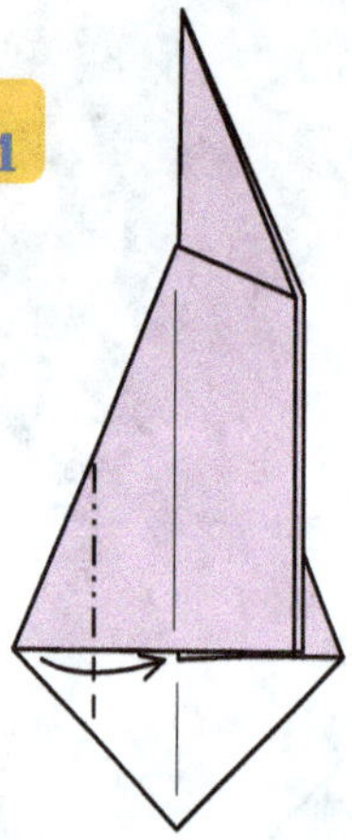

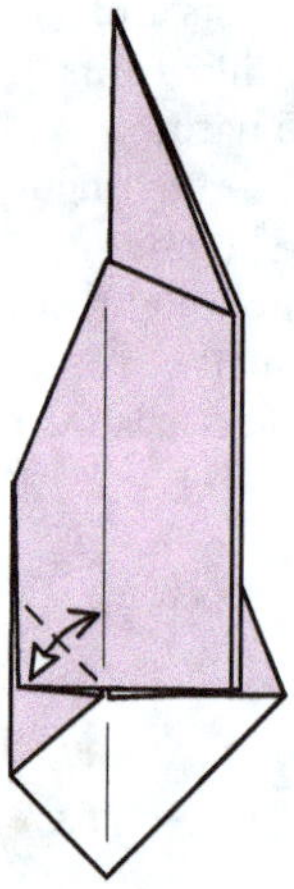

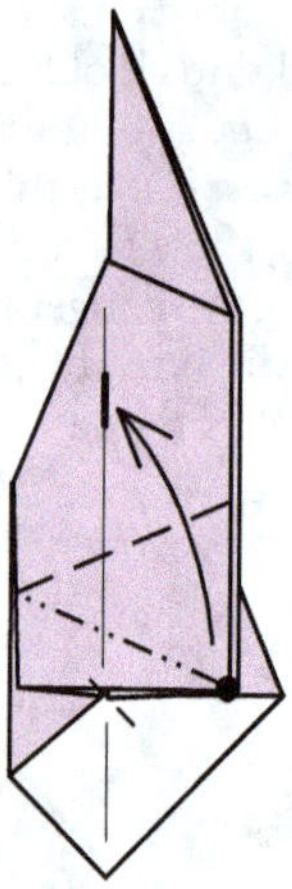

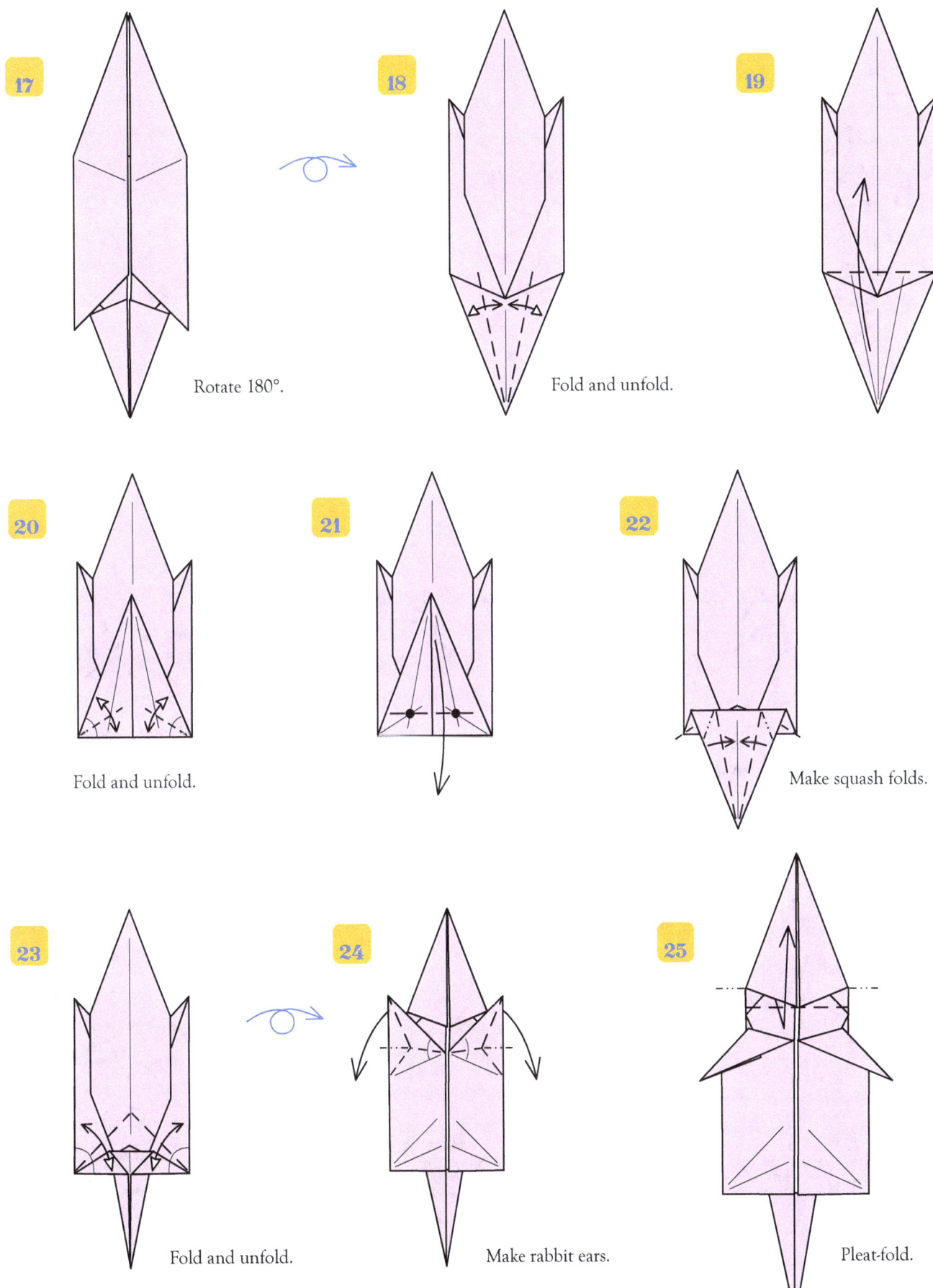

17. Rotate 180°.
18. Fold and unfold.
20. Fold and unfold.
22. Make squash folds.
23. Fold and unfold.
24. Make rabbit ears.
25. Pleat-fold.

Opossum 39

26

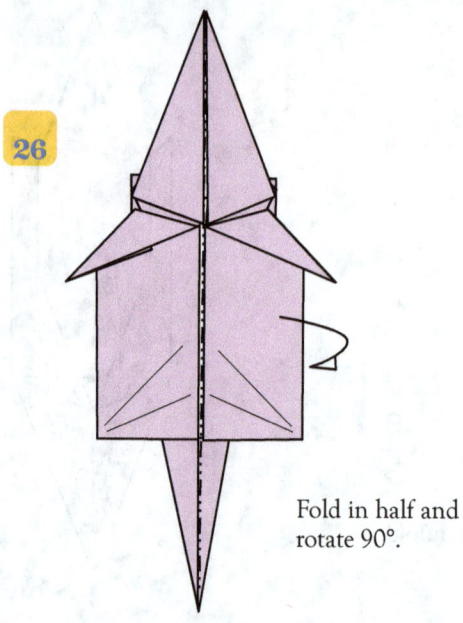

Fold in half and rotate 90°.

27

Mountain-fold along the crease for this crimp fold.

28

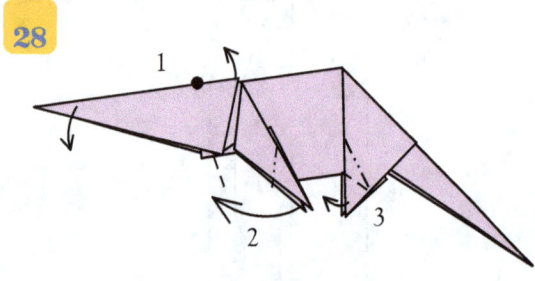

1. Pivot the head at the dot.
2. Reverse-fold, repeat behind.
3. Crimp-fold, repeat behind.

29

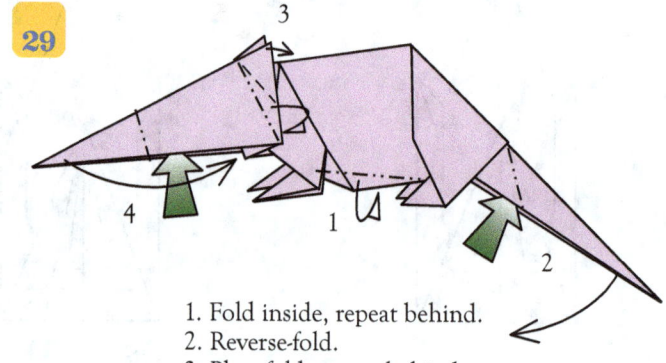

1. Fold inside, repeat behind.
2. Reverse-fold.
3. Pleat-fold, repeat behind.
4. Reverse-fold.

30

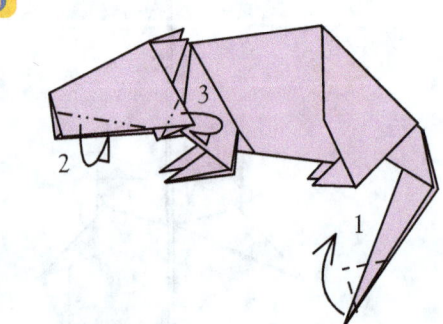

1. Make reverse folds.
2. Fold inside, repeat behind.
3. Fold inside, repeat behind.

31

Opossum

Second Movement

Andante: Nature for the Hidden Gnomes

"Hello, little wanders!" whispers a forest gnome, peeking from behind a spotted mushroom. "Welcome to our magical home, where every leaf, flower, and creature has a story. The forest comes alive at every turn—listen closely and you might hear the soft croak of a frog near the pond, or see a dragonfly shimmering like a tiny rainbow above the water." Step lightly and see the magic in every fluttering wing and spotted mushroom cap.

Butterfly

Delicate dancers of the air, butterflies remind us to move lightly and enjoy each movement. Watch their wings shimmer in the sun and how they dance from flower to flower. Follow the butterflies, as they take the scenic route.

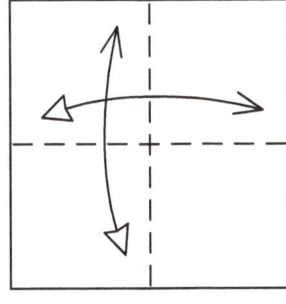

1. Fold and unfold.
2. Fold to the center.

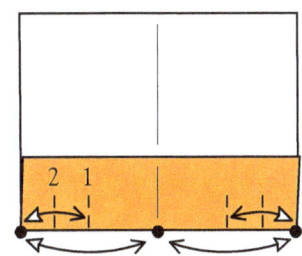

3. Fold and unfold in half, twice on the left and right.

Butterfly **41**

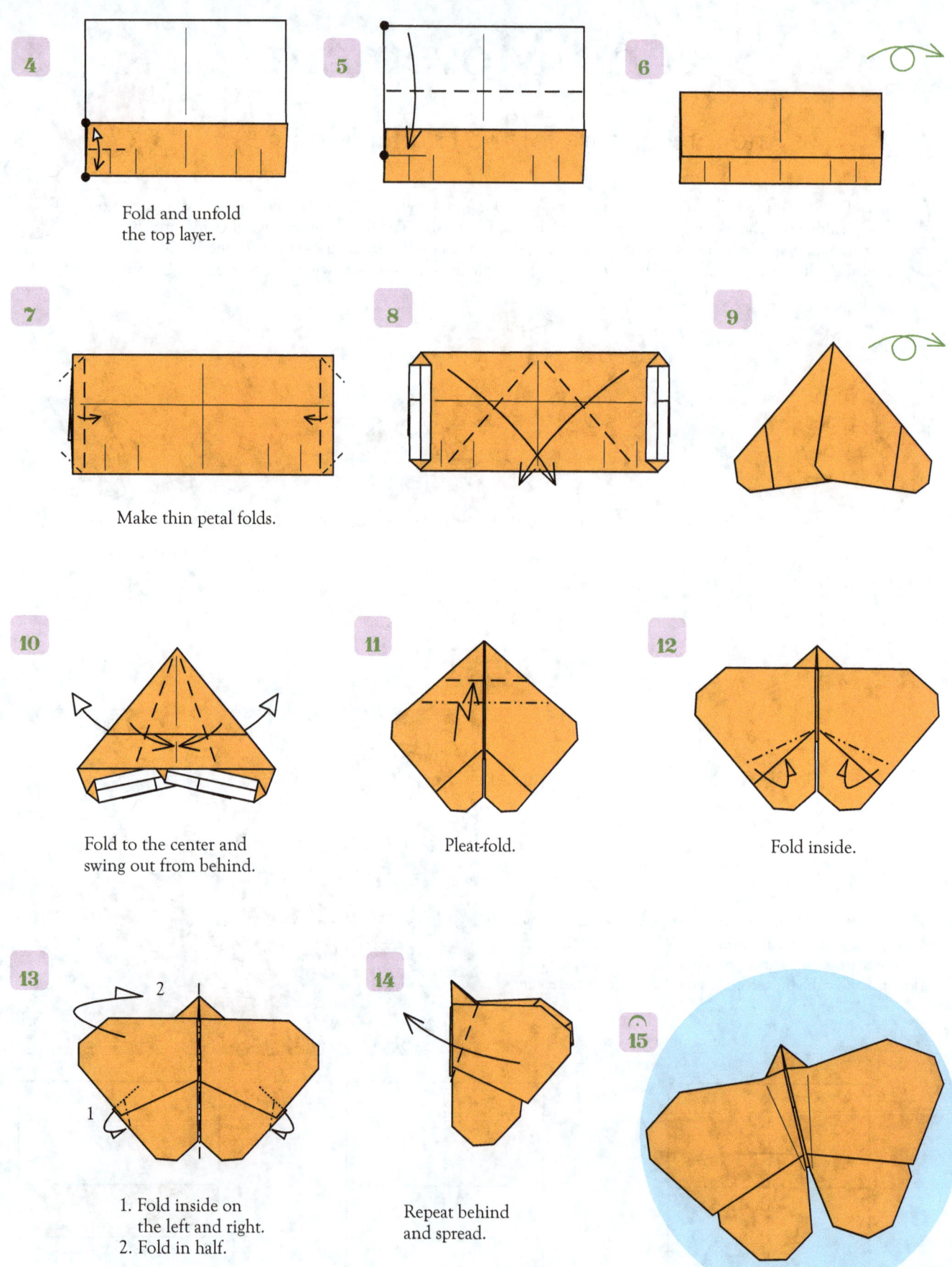

Dragonfly

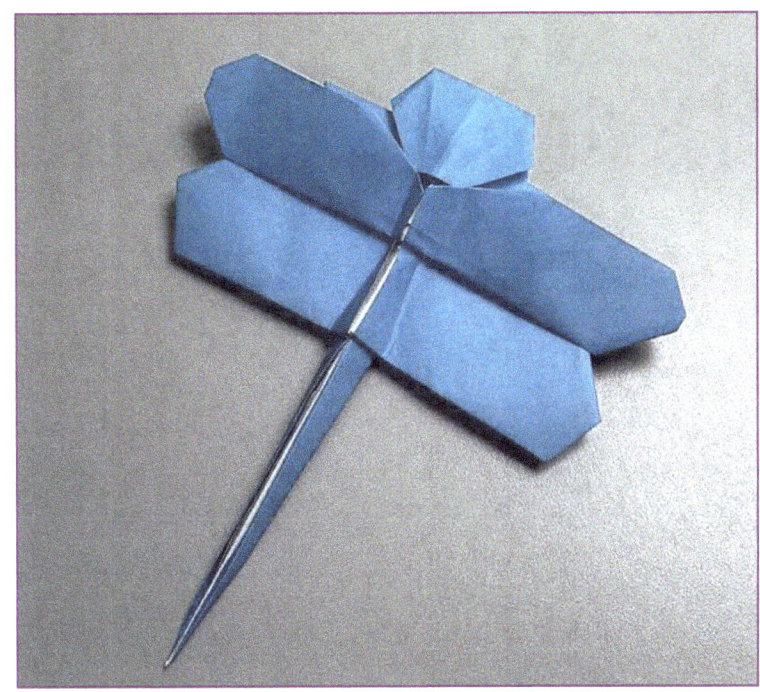

Dragonflies sparkle above the water like living jewels. They remind us to be quick, yet graceful, and to notice the small wonders around us. Follow their glimmers in the sunlight.

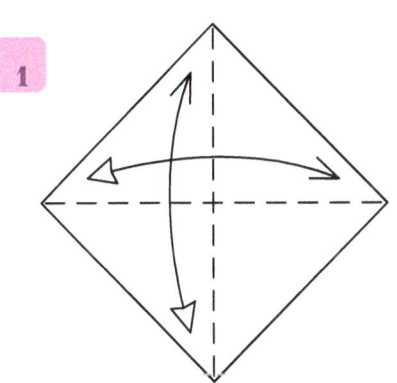

Fold and unfold.

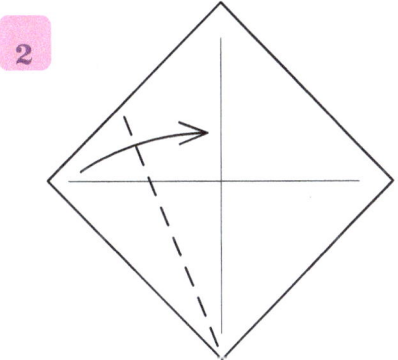

Fold to the center.

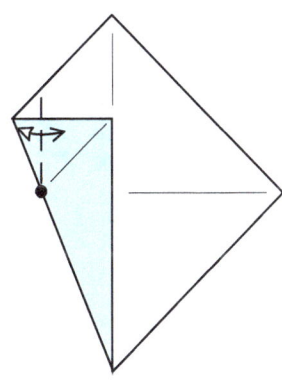

Fold and unfold.

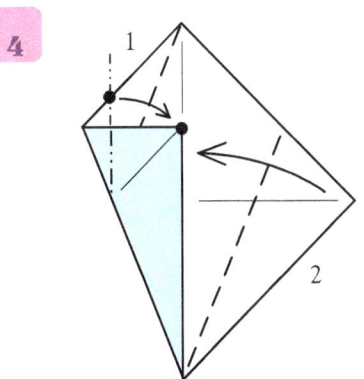

1. This is similar to a reverse fold.
2. Repeat steps 2-4 on the right.

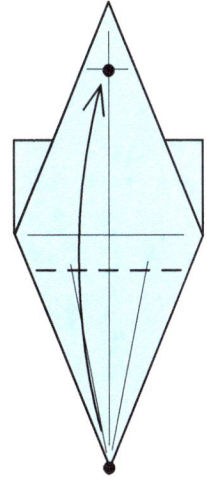

1. Fold and unfold.
2. Fold to the center and unfold.

Dragonfly 43

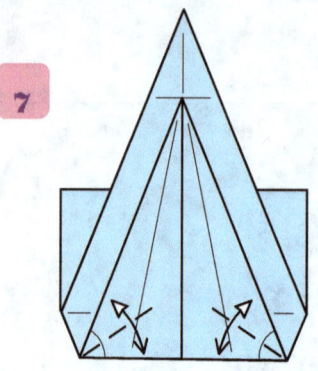
7

Fold and unfold.

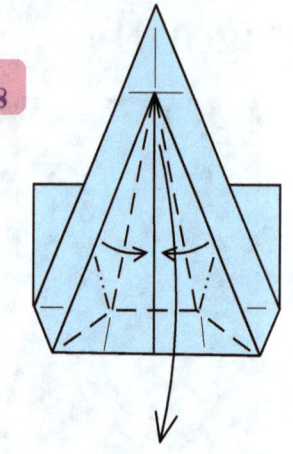
8

Fold along the creases.

9

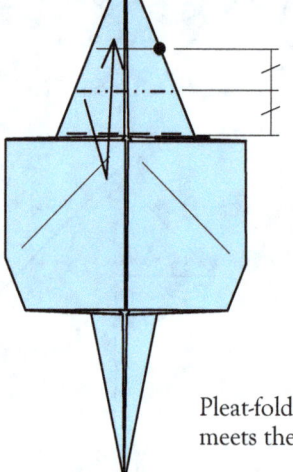
10

Pleat-fold so the dot meets the bold line.

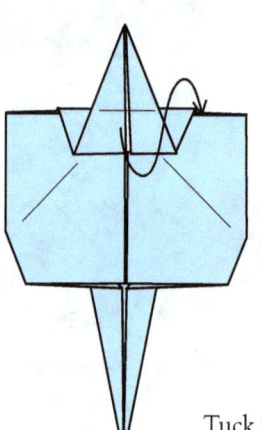
11

Tuck inside.

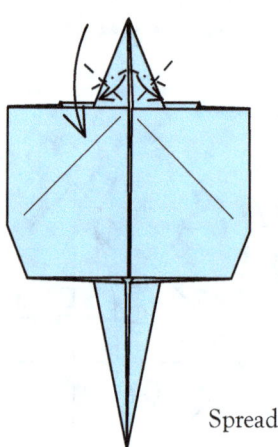
12

Spread.

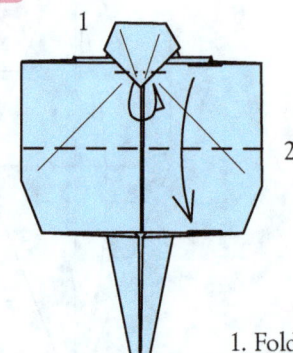
13

1. Fold inside.
2. Fold down.

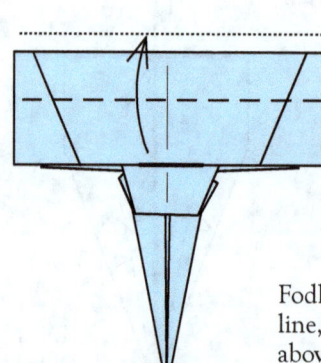
14

Fodl up to the dotted line, which is slightly above the top.

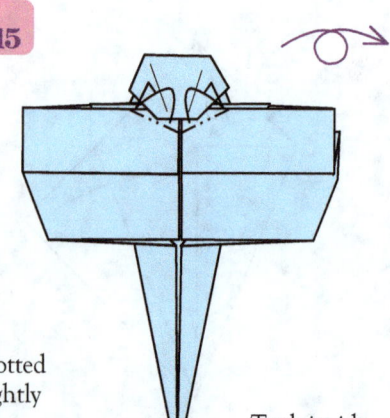
15

Tuck inside.

44 *Origami Symphony No. 12*

16

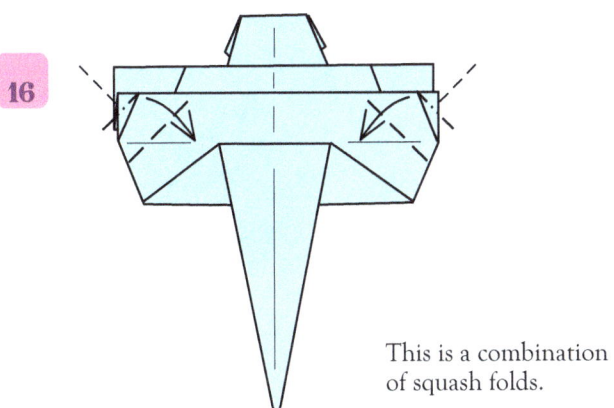

This is a combination of squash folds.

17

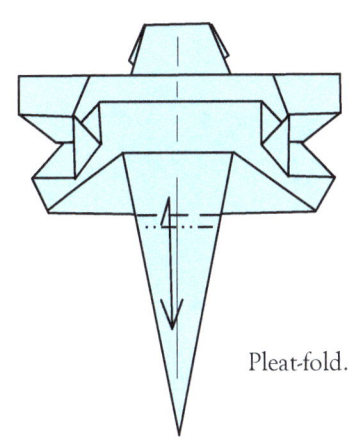

Pleat-fold.

18

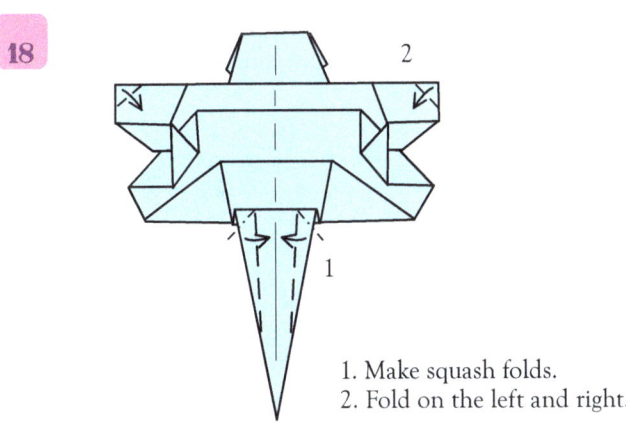

1. Make squash folds.
2. Fold on the left and right.

19

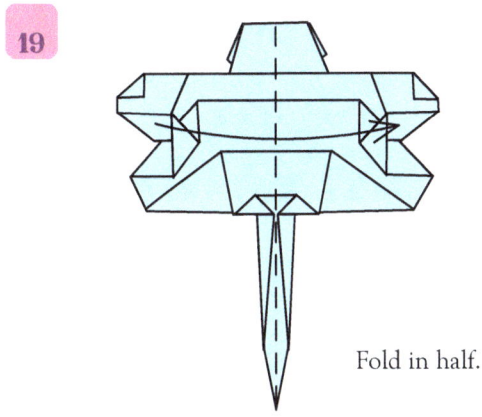

Fold in half.

20

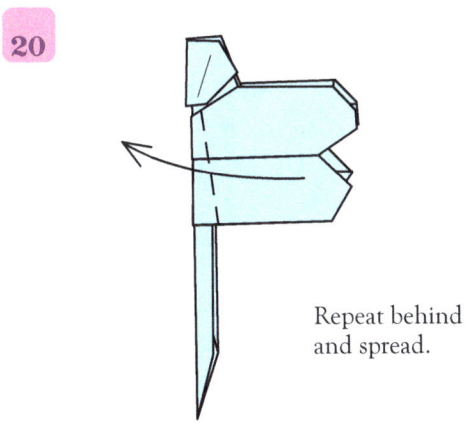

Repeat behind and spread.

21

Dragonfly

Frog

Frogs sing songs by the pond at night. Their secret is: they only croak when the time is right. Watch them jump, hop, and splash as we enjoy the quiet music of the forest.

1 Fold and unfold.

2 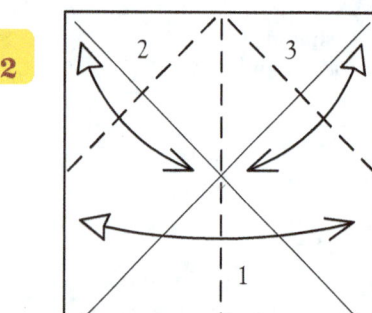 Fold and unfold at 1, 2, and 3.

3 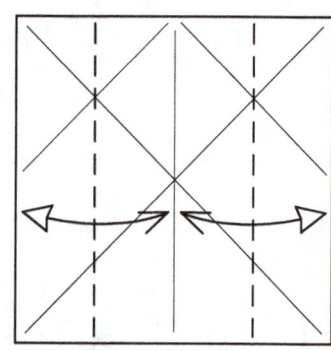 Fold to the center and unfold.

4 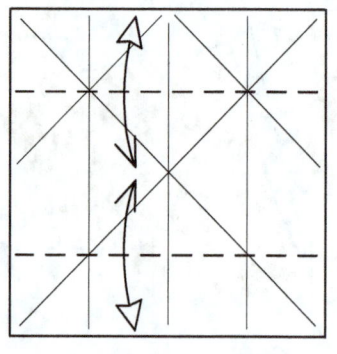 Fold and unfold.

5 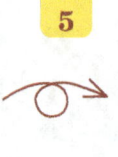 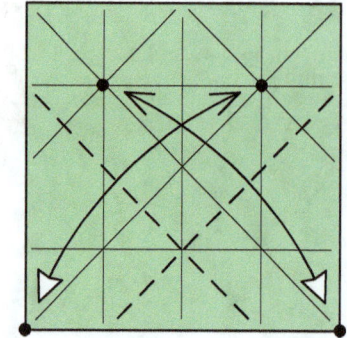 Fold and unfold.

6 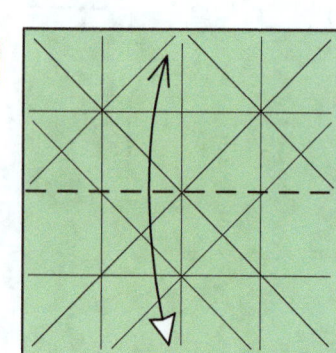 Fold and unfold.

46   Origami Symphony No. 12

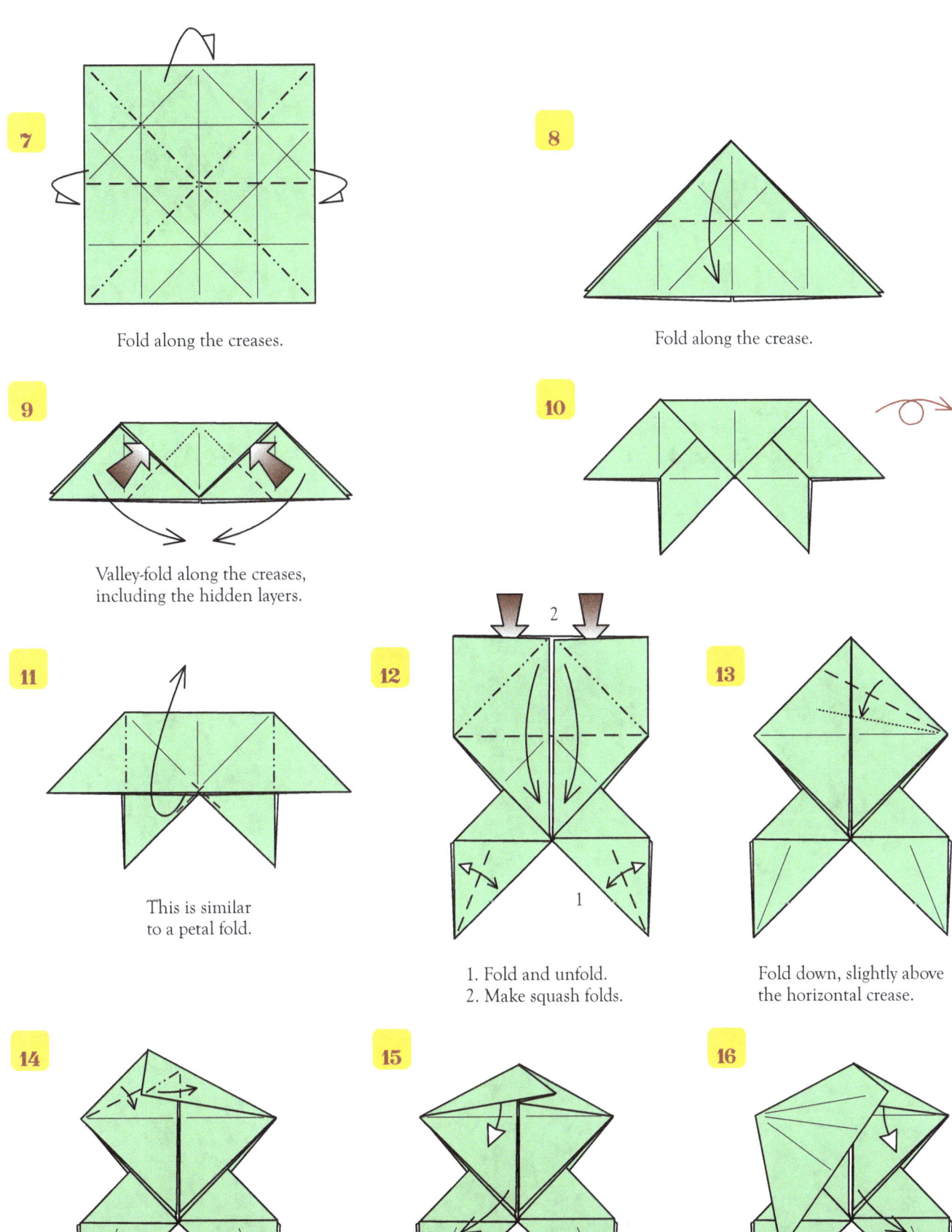

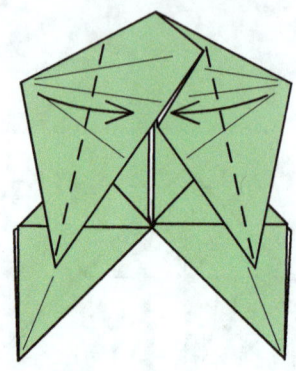

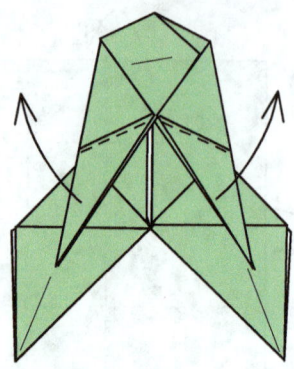

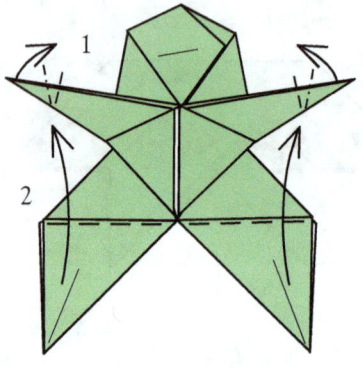

1. Make squash folds.
2. Fold up.

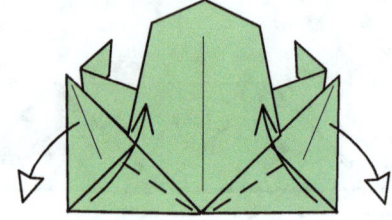

Fold up and swing out from behind.

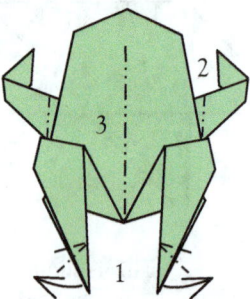

Moutain-fold along the creases for these squash folds.

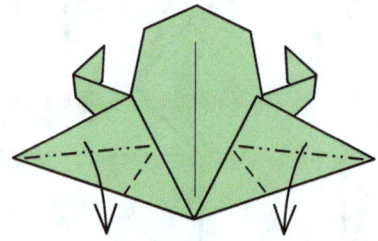

1. Make squash folds.
2. Bend the arms.
3. Bend in half so the Frog is sitting.

Frog

48 Origami Symphony No. 12

Turtle

Turtles carry their homes on their backs as they take their time to enjoy the forest. Pause to notice the moss on the rocks, the sunlight on the leaves, and the tiny treasures hidden along the path.

 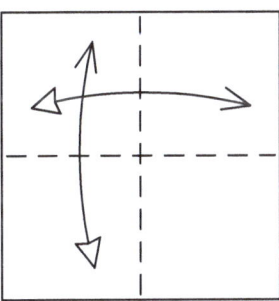

Fold and unfold.

 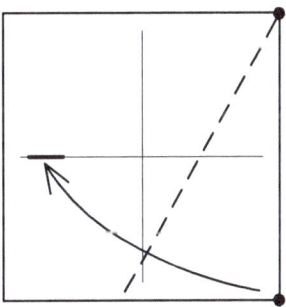

Bring the lower dot to the line.

 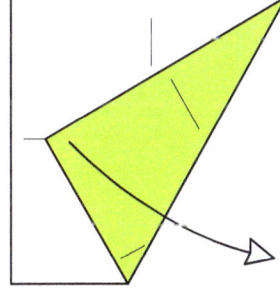

Unfold.

 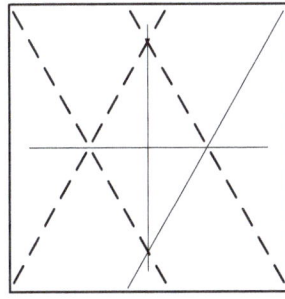

Fold and unfold three more times.

 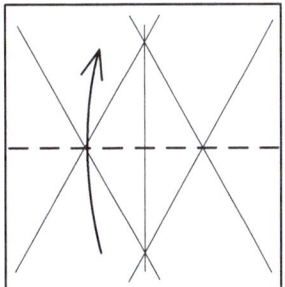

 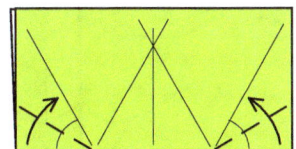

Turtle 49

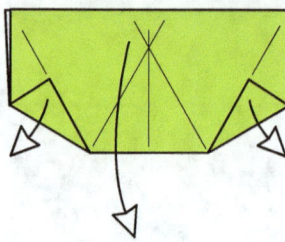

Unfold everything.

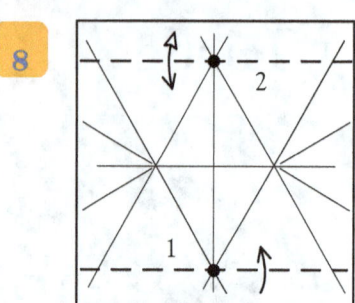

1. Fold up.
2. Fold and unfold.

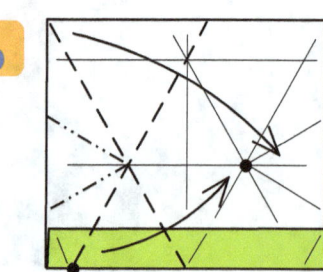

Fold along the creases.

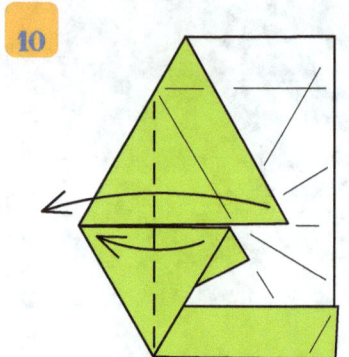

Fold along a hidden crease.

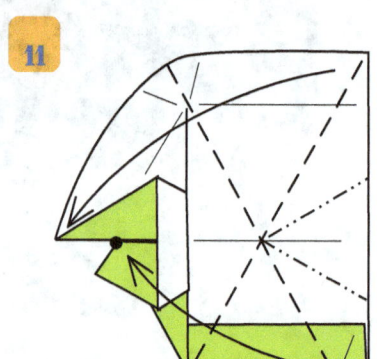

The top ot 3C. Repeat steps 9–10 on the right and flatten.

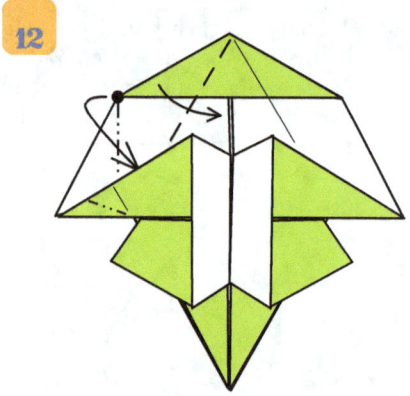

Tuck inside at the dot.

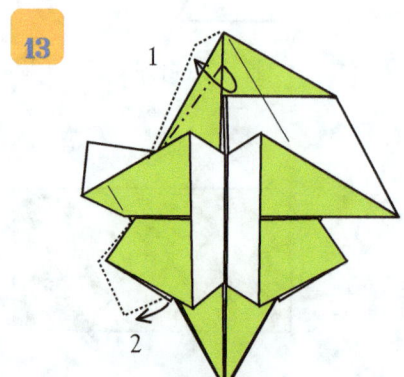

1. Slide out the top flap.
2. Slide out the hidden white paper.

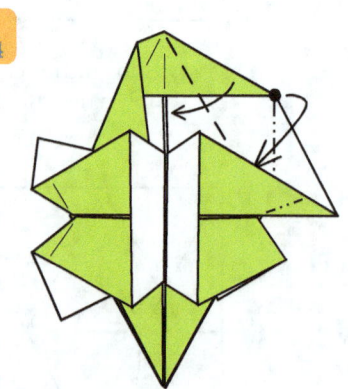

Repeat steps 12–113 on the right.

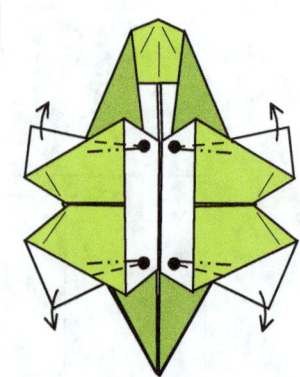

Pivot at the dots, folding on the dark paper which is hidden, to move the feet.

50 Origami Symphony No. 12

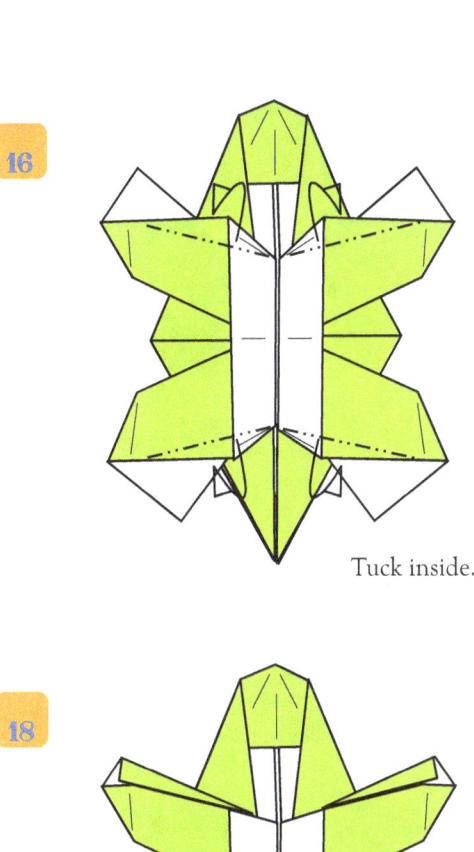

Tuck inside.

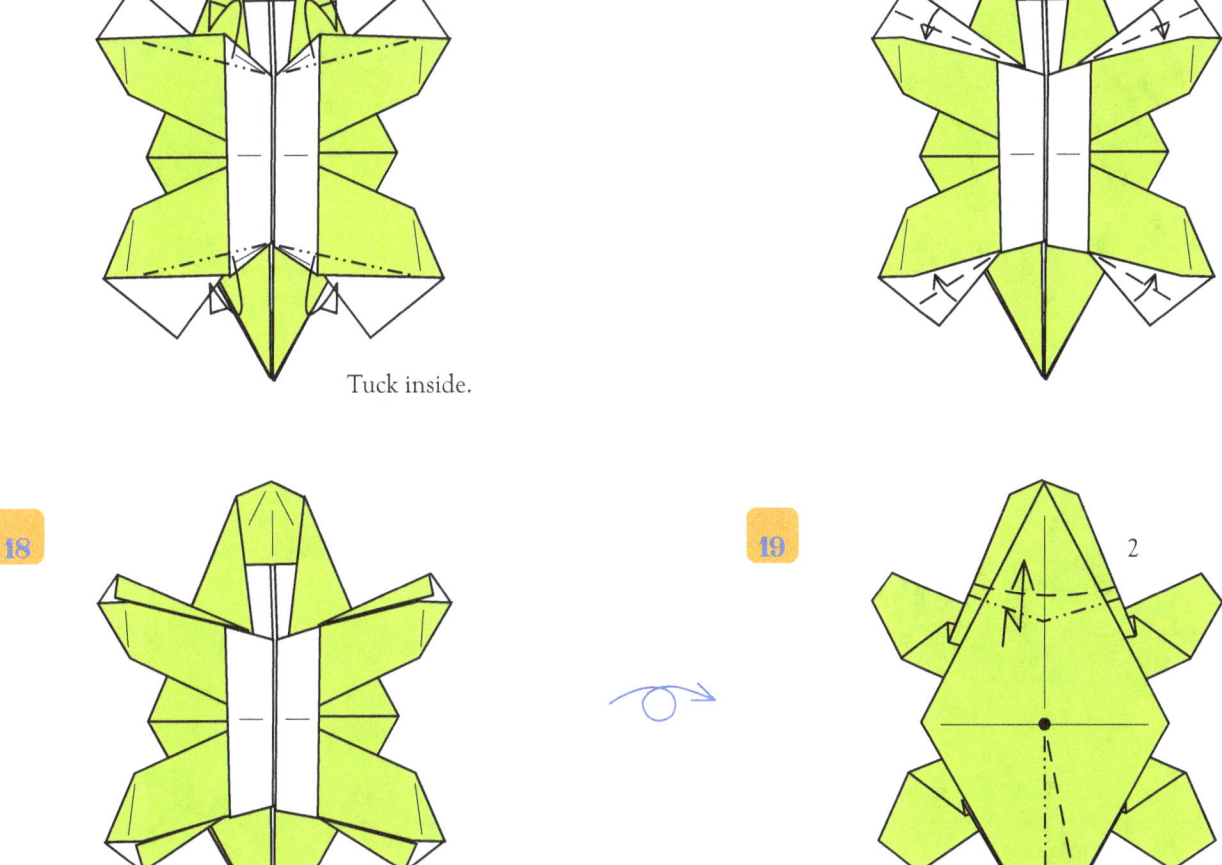

1. Puff out at the dot so the shell becomes 3D. Mountain-fold along the crease.
2. This is similar to a pleat fold.

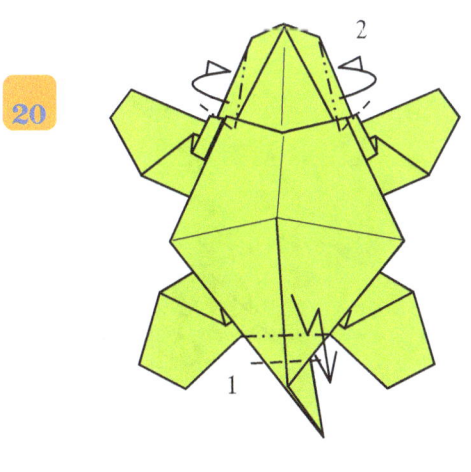

1. Pleat-fold.
2. Make thin squash folds.

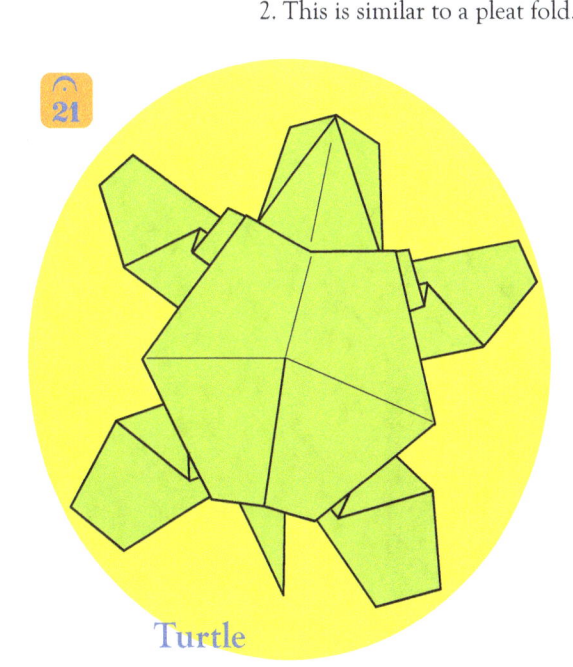

Turtle

Robin

The robin greets each morning with a cheerful song, a reminder to start the day in a happy way as you hop around. When a robin is pecking in the leaves, it is looking for joy in simple, ordinary places.

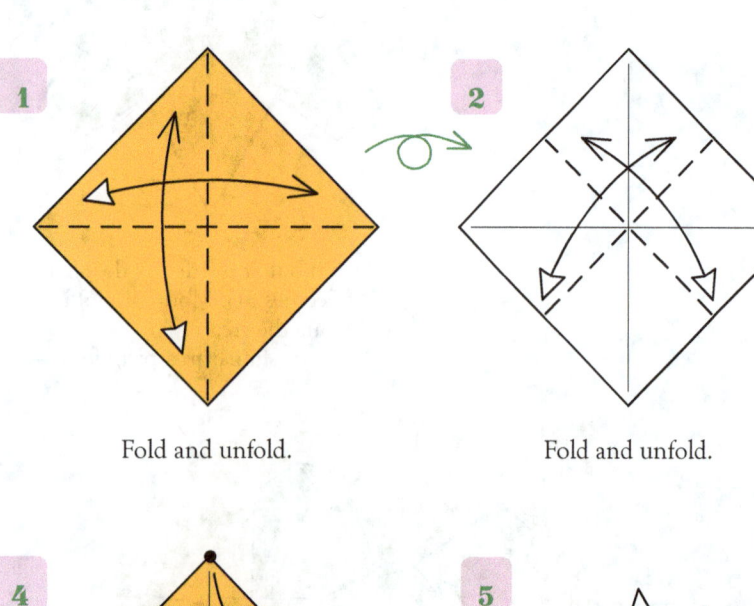

1. Fold and unfold.
2. Fold and unfold.
3. Fold and unfold.

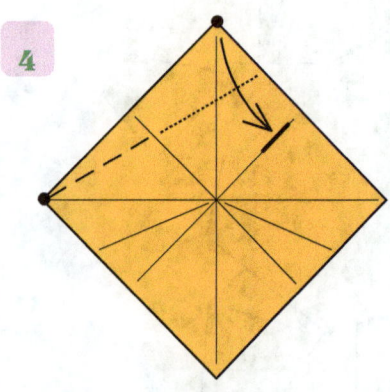
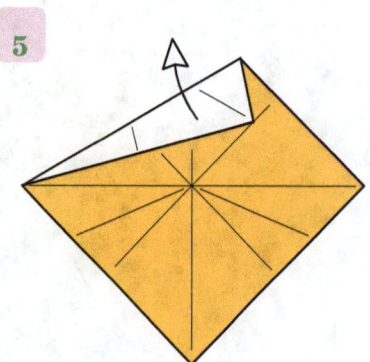
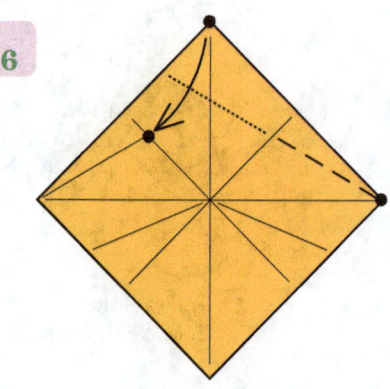

4. Bring the upper dot to the line.
5. Unfold.
6. Repeat steps 4–5 on the right.

52 *Origami Symphony No. 12*

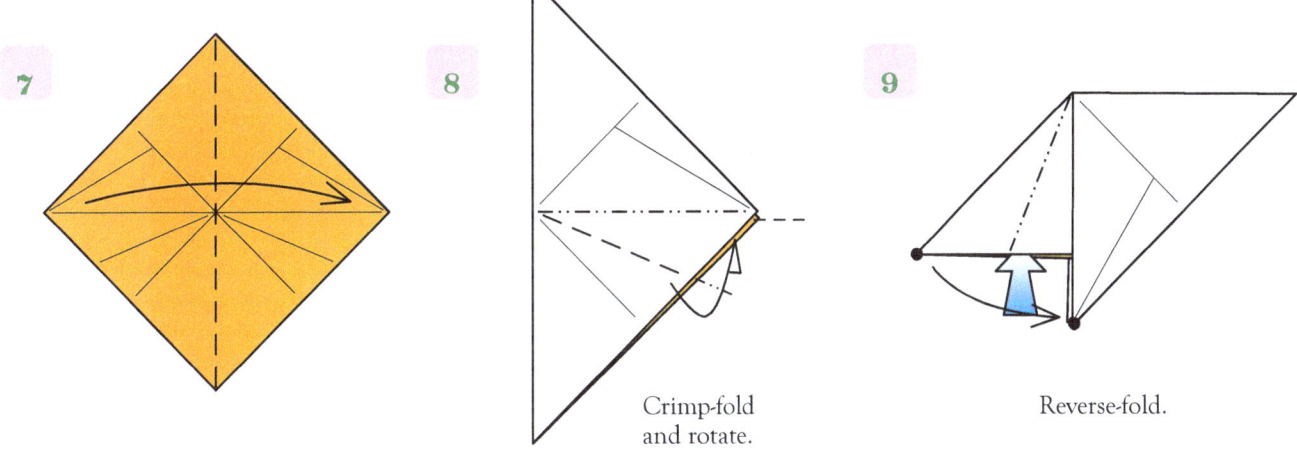

7

8
Crimp-fold and rotate.

9
Reverse-fold.

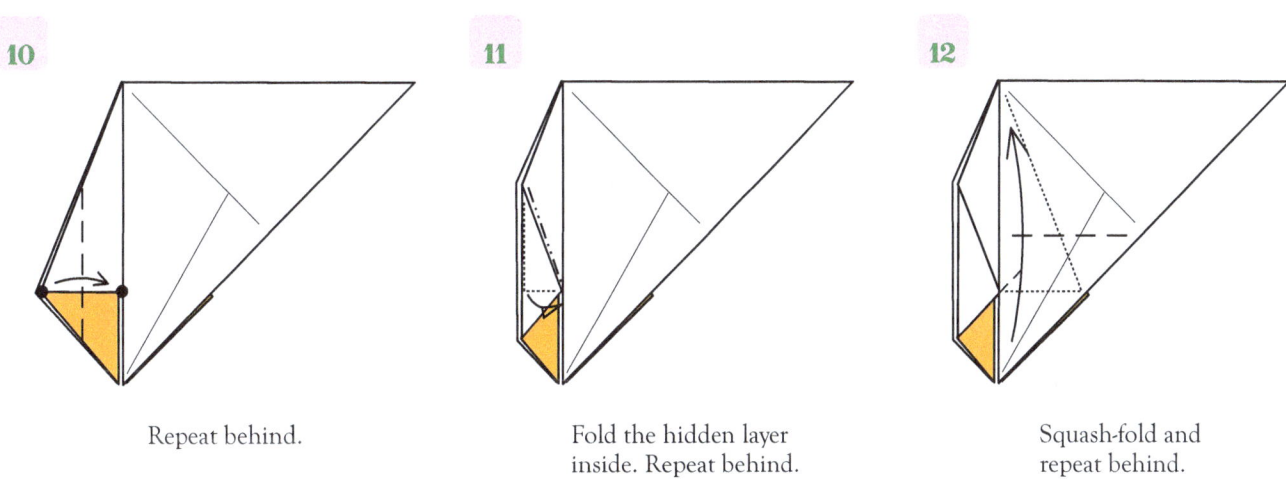

10
Repeat behind.

11
Fold the hidden layer inside. Repeat behind.

12
Squash-fold and repeat behind.

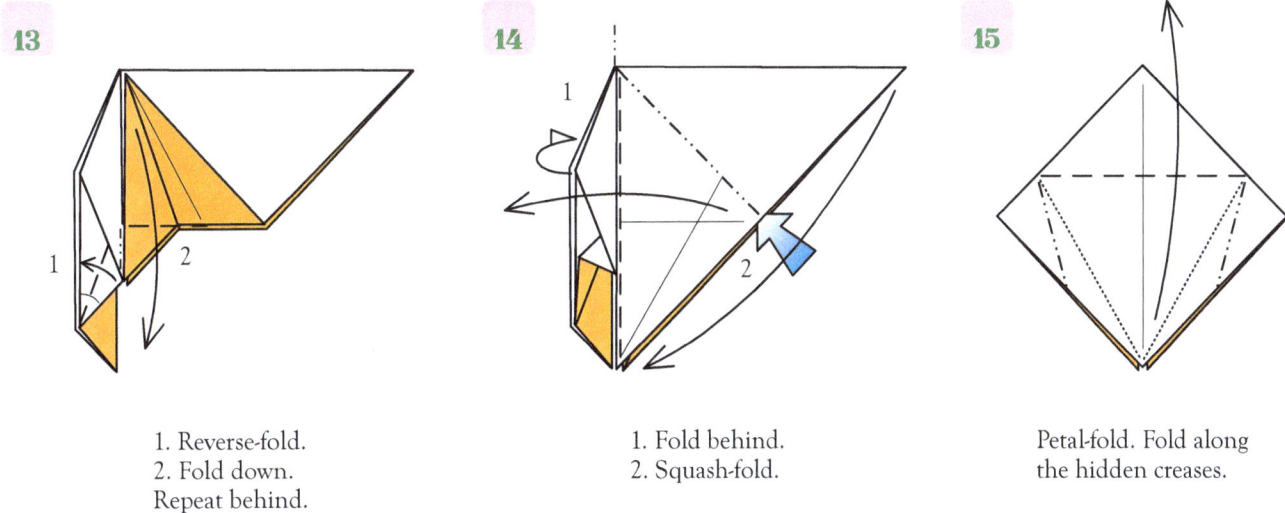

13
1. Reverse-fold.
2. Fold down.
Repeat behind.

14
1. Fold behind.
2. Squash-fold.

15
Petal-fold. Fold along the hidden creases.

Robin 53

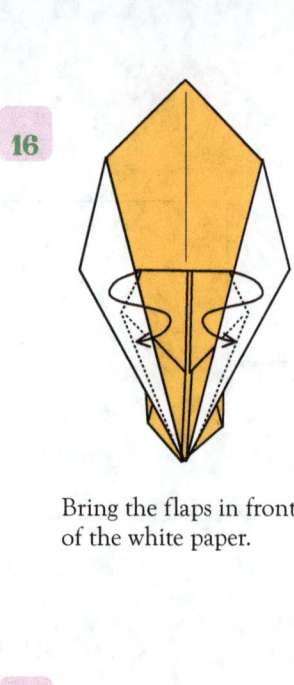

Bring the flaps in front of the white paper.

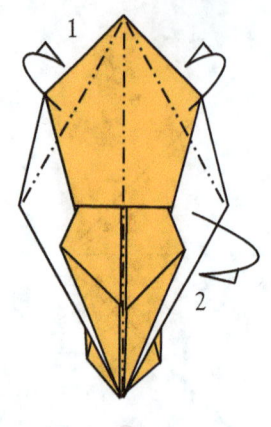

1. Fold behind on the left and right.
2. Fold in half.
Rotate.

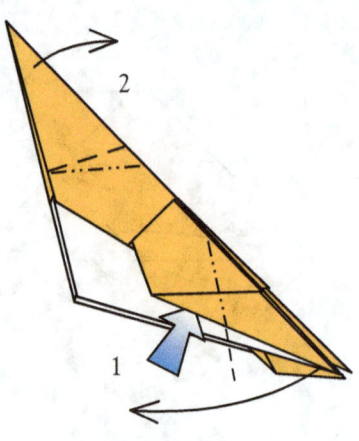

1. Reverse-fold, repeat behind.
2. Crimp-fold.

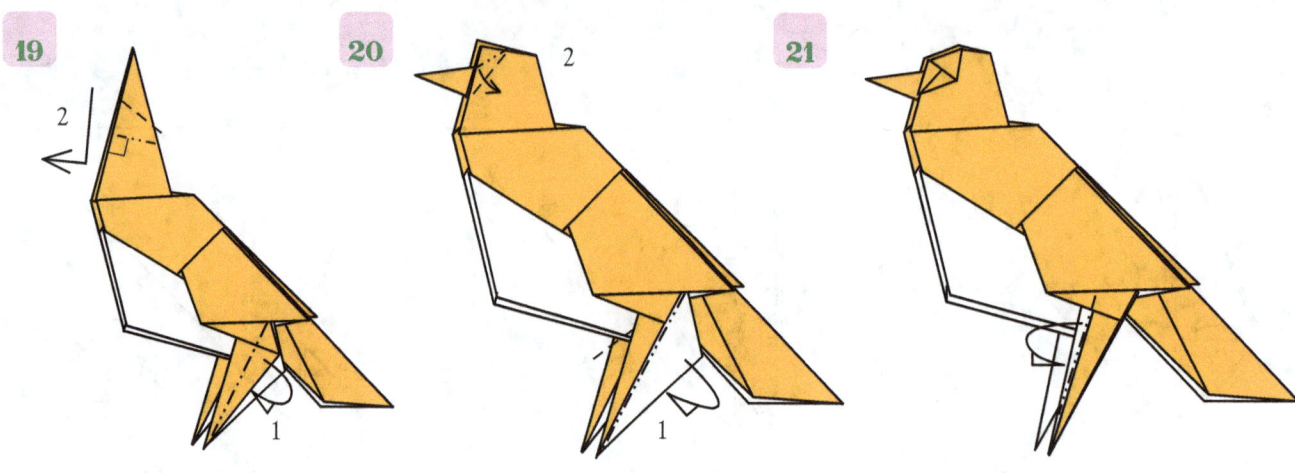

1. Fold inside, repeat behind.
2. Crimp-fold.

1. Reverse-fold.
2. Squash-fold.
Repeat behind.

Reverse-fold, repeat behind.

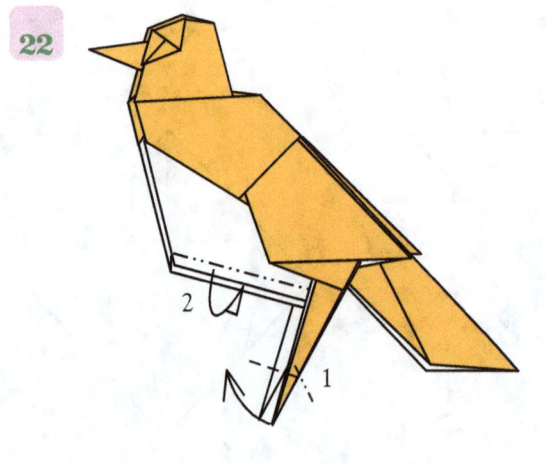

1. Crimp-fold.
2. Fold inside.
Repeat behind.

Robin

54 Origami Symphony No. 12

Cardinal

The cardinal flashes bright red through the trees like a little lantern. It whispers to stand out, be brave, and bring color to a quiet day.

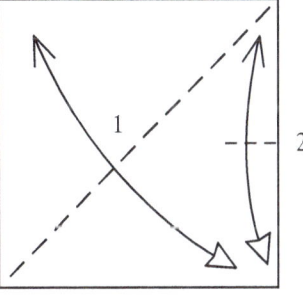

1. Fold and unfold.
2. Fold and unfold on the right.

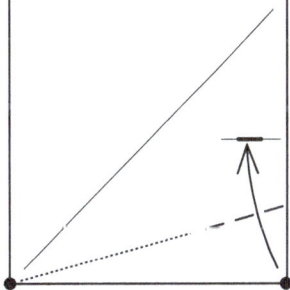

Bring the corner to the line.

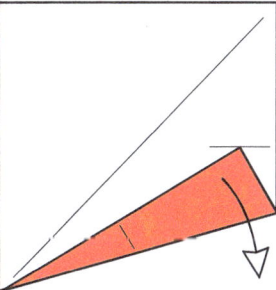

Unfold.

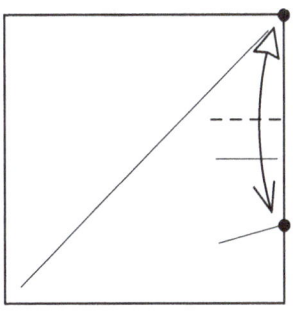

Fold and unfold.

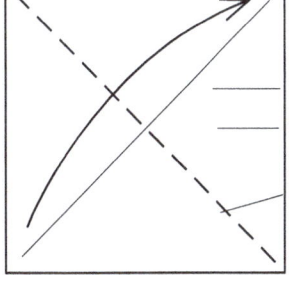

Rotate.

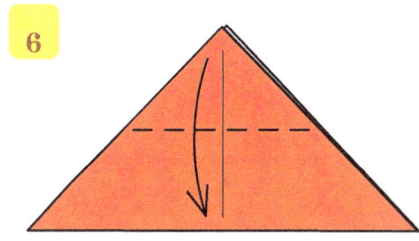

Fold the top layer.

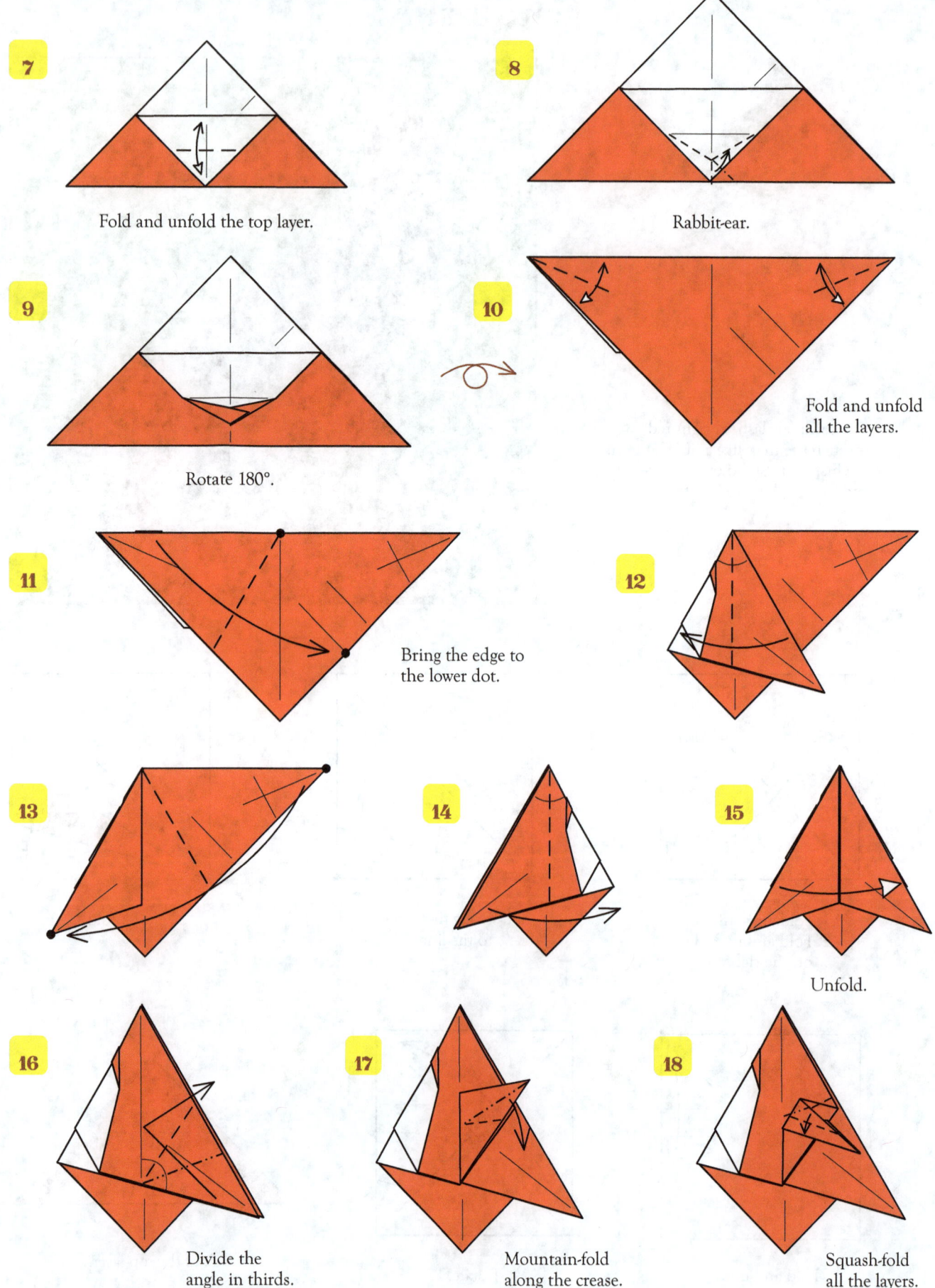

56 Origami Symphony No. 12

19

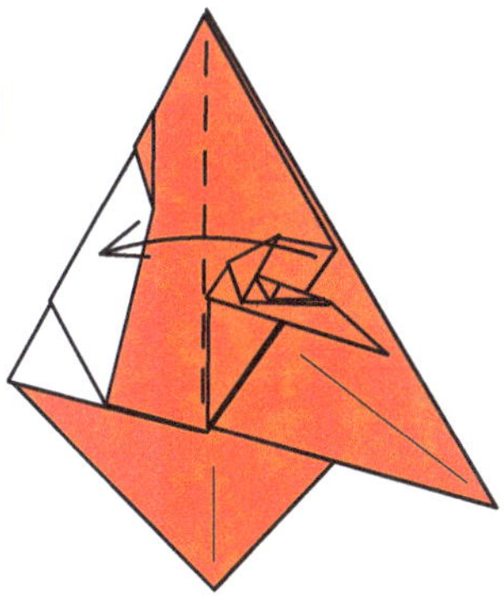

20 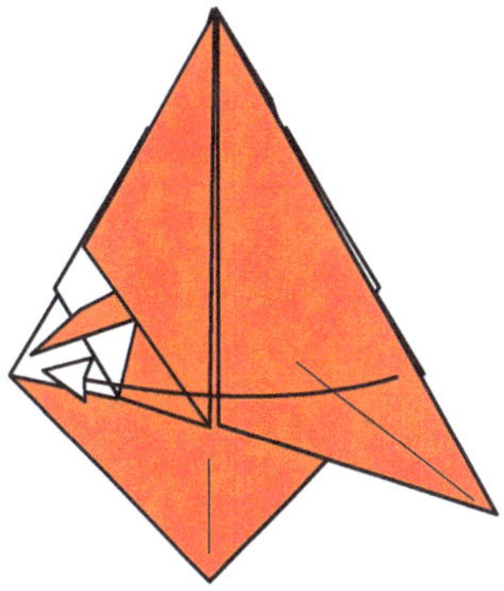 Repeat steps 15–19 on the right.

21 Fold in half and rotate.

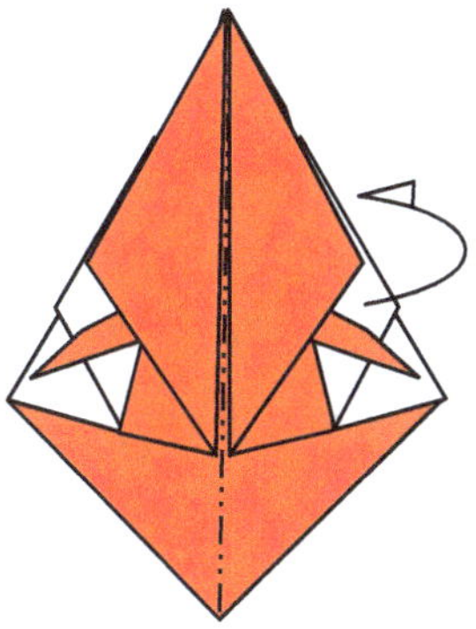

22 
1. Crimp-fold.
2. Reverse-fold, repeat behind.

23 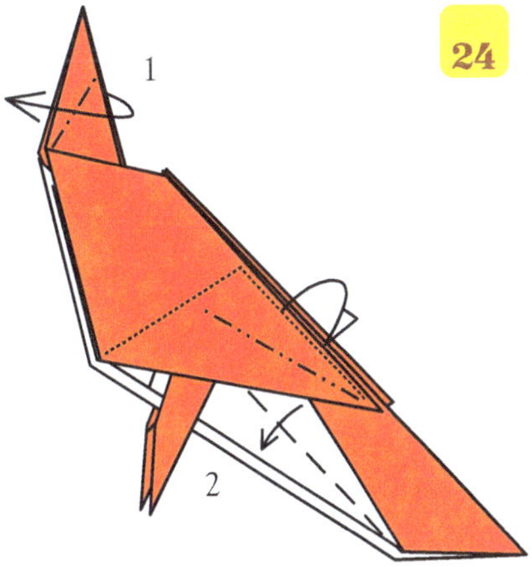
1. Pull out the top layers.
2. Reverse-fold.
Repeat behind.

24 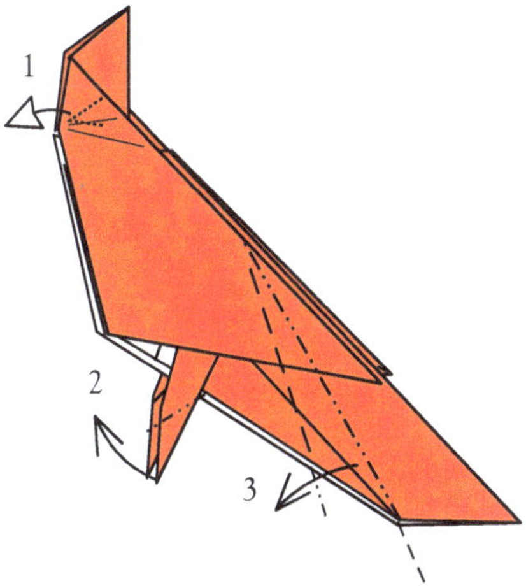
1. Pull out the hidden beak.
2. Reverse-fold, repeat behind.
3. Crimp-fold.

25 
1. Fold along the creases with soft folds. Repeat behind.
2. Reverse-fold.

26

Cardinal

Cardinal **57**

Rabbit

Rabbits dart, hop, and hide among the leaves, showing us to stay alert and explore playfully. They are quick, clever, and always ready for a surprise adventure. Even small feet can leave big impressions if you move with care and curiosity.

1 Fold and unfold.

2 Fold and unfold.

3 Bring the corner to the line.

4 Unfold and rotate 180°.

5 Repeat steps 3–4.

6 Make rabbit ears.

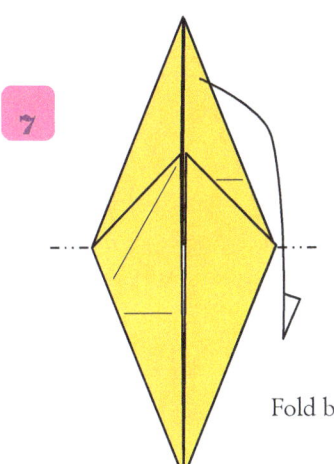

7

Fold behind.

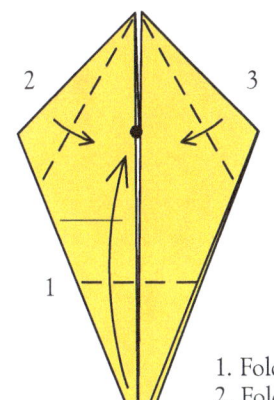

8

1. Fold the top flap.
2. Fold along the crease.
3. Fold along the hidden crease on the back.

9

1. Fold down.
2. Fold up from behind.

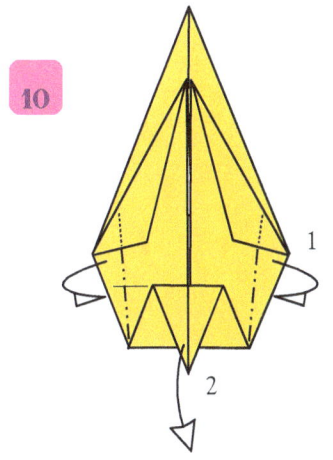

10

1. Fold inside.
2. Unfold.

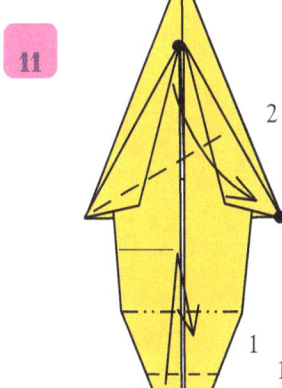

11

1. Fold inside along the creases.
2. Fold the flap on the left.

12

1. Rabbit-ear so the flap goes to the top.
2. Fold the flap on the right.

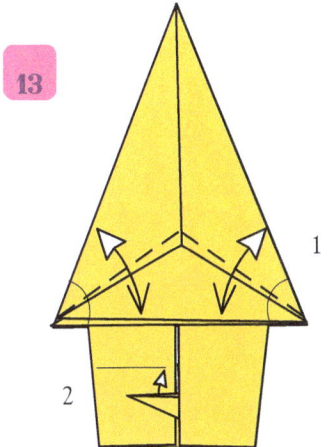

13

1. Fold and unfold.
2. Pull out on both sides.

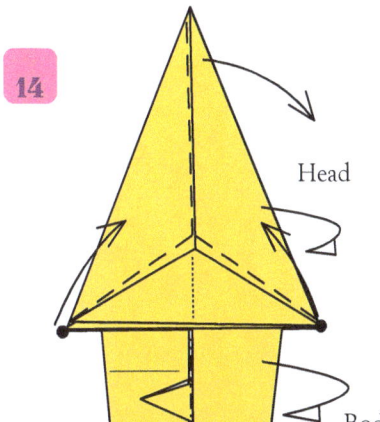

14

Fold the head and body in half while lifting the ears up, shown at the dots. Rotate.

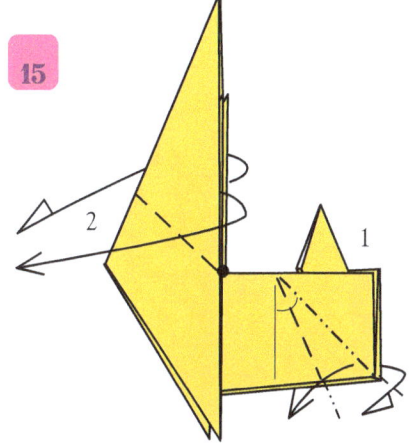

15

1. Crimp-fold.
2. Outside-reverse-fold.

Rabbit **59**

16

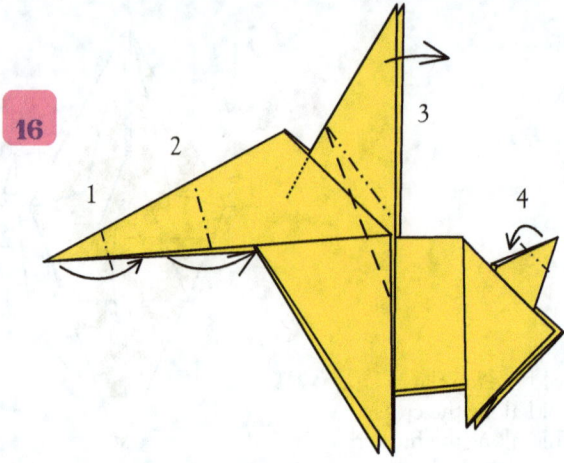

1. Reverse-fold.
2. Reverse-fold.
3. Pleat-fold, repeat behind.
4. Reverse-fold.

17

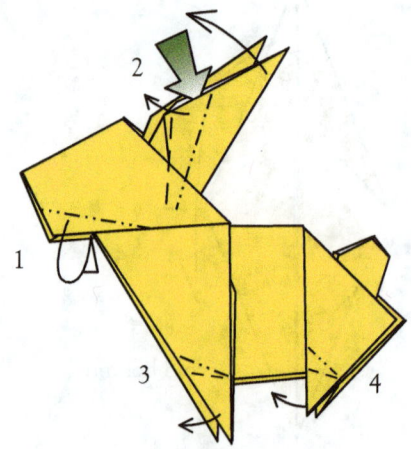

1. Fold inside.
2. Squash-fold.
3. Crimp-fold.
4. Crimp-fold.
Repeat behind.

18

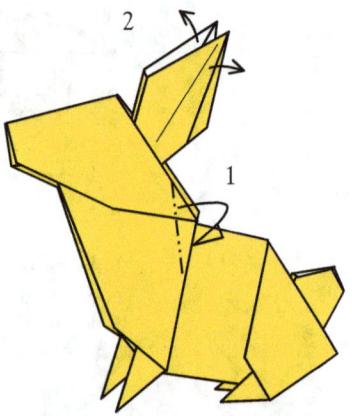

1. Fold inside, repeat behind.
2. Spread the ears.

19

Rabbit

60 Origami Symphony No. 12

Squirrel

Squirrels gather nuts and prepare for the seasons ahead, teaching us to plan, save, and enjoy things along the way. They leap from branch to branch with courage and curiosity.

1
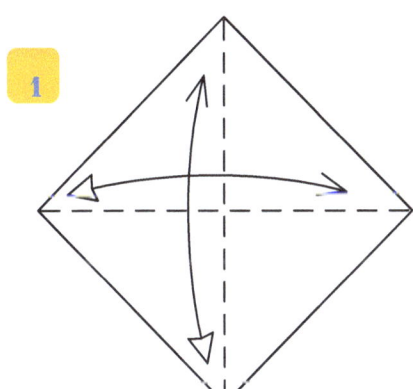
Fold and unfold.

2
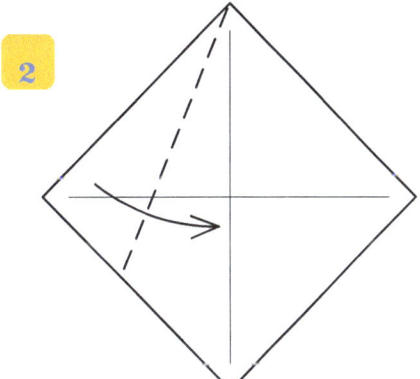
Fold to the center.

3
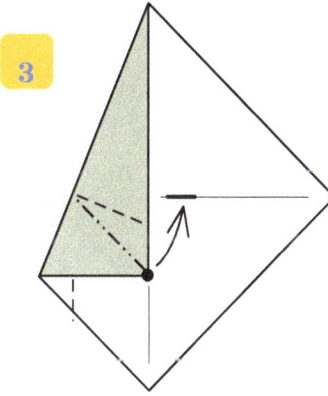
Squash-fold so the dot meets the line.

4
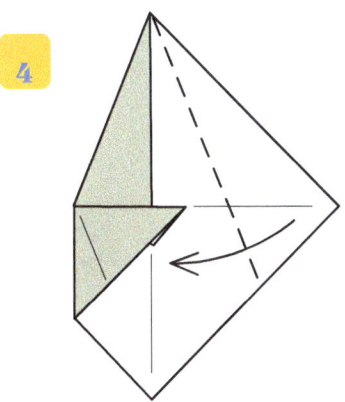
Repeat steps 2–3 on the right.

5
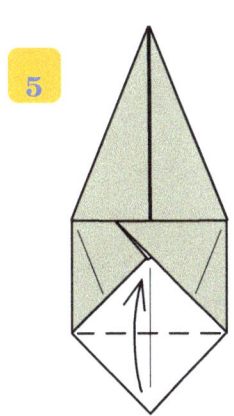

6

Fold to the center.

Squirrel 61

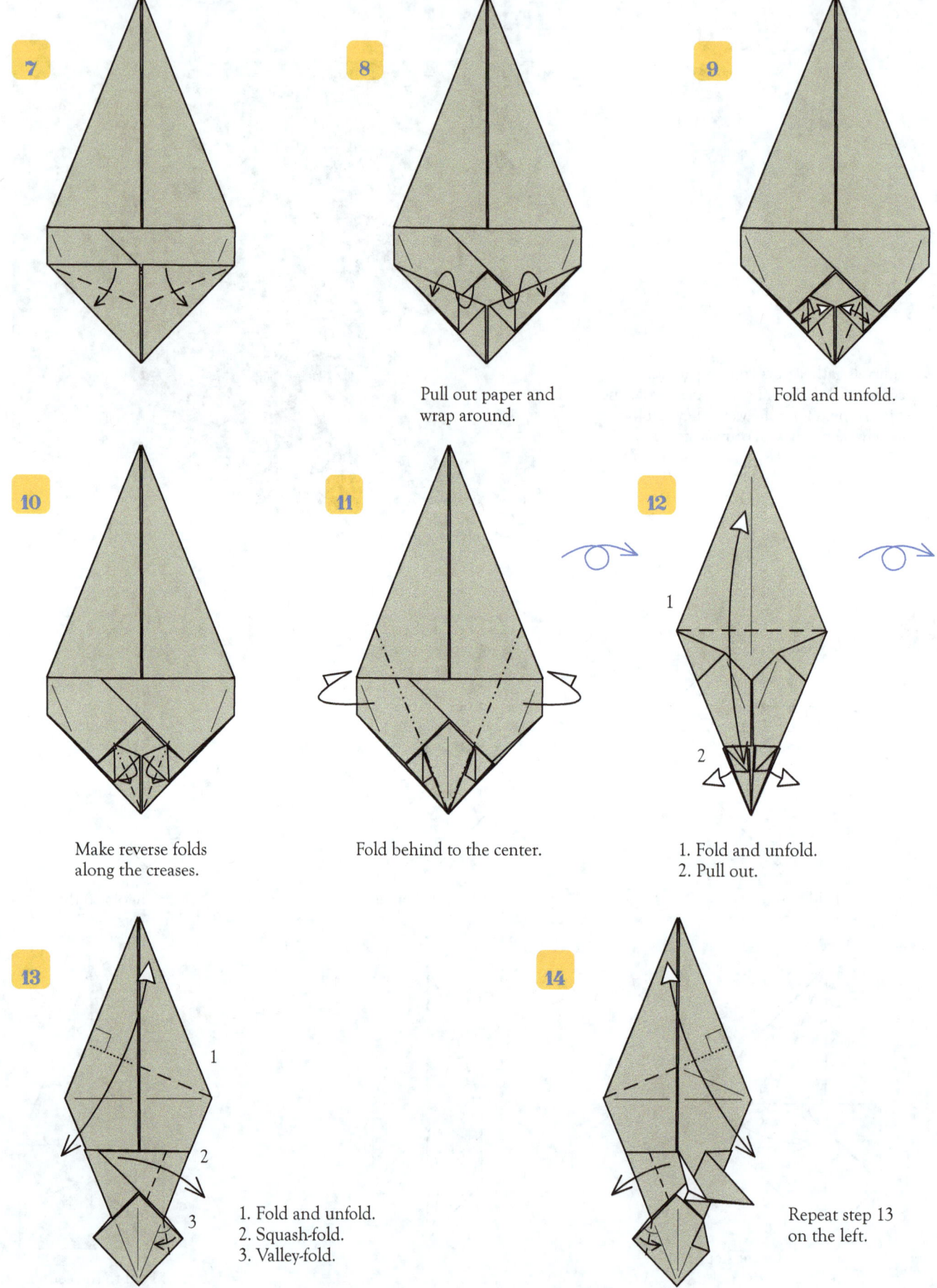

62 Origami Symphony No. 12

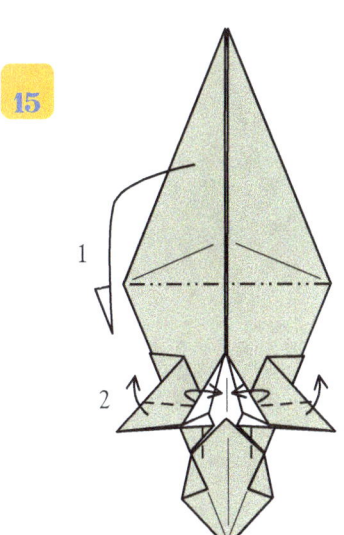

1. Fold behind.
2. Fold up with small squash folds.

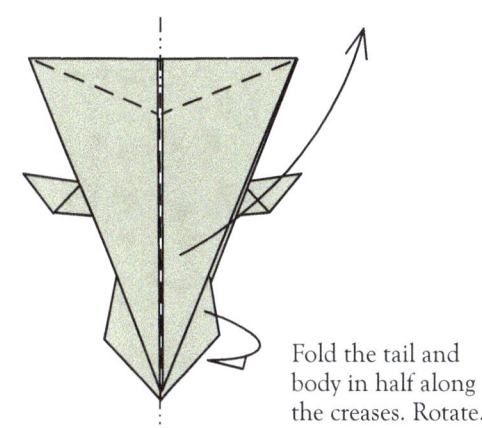

Fold the tail and body in half along the creases. Rotate.

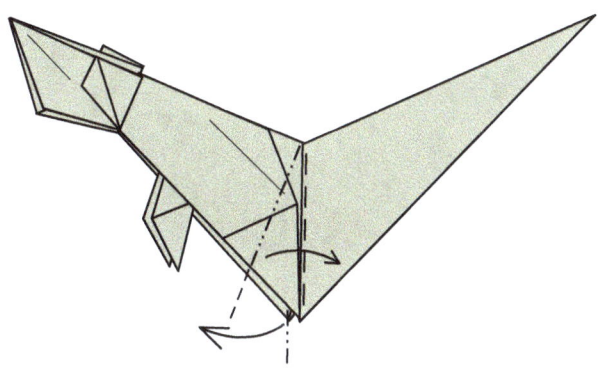

Crimp-fold.

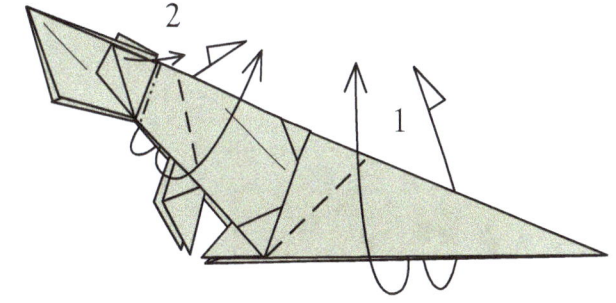

1. Outside-reverse-fold.
2. Crimp-fold at the ears.

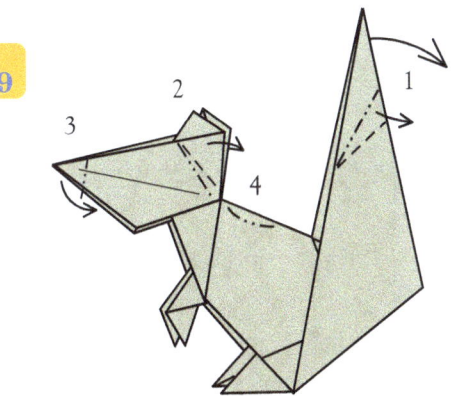

1. Outside-reverse-fold and spread.
2. Pleat-fold, repeat behind.
3. Reverse-fold.
4. Shape the back.

Squirrel

Mushroom

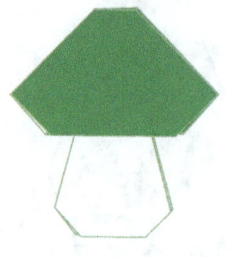

Mushrooms take time to grow, but when they appear, they bring delight. These little umbrellas of the forest floor pop up after the rain, bringing tiny surprises. Gnomes snuggle in cozy mushroom houses where the wide cap acts as a roof.

1.
1. Fold and unfold.
2. Fold and unfold on the left.

2. Bring the corner to the line.

3. Unfold.

4. Fold and unfold.

5. Fold and unfold.

6.
1. Fold behind along the crease.
2. Fold and unfold.

64 Origami Symphony No. 12

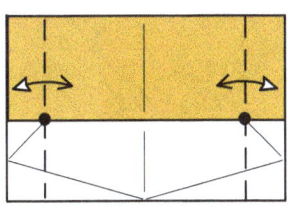
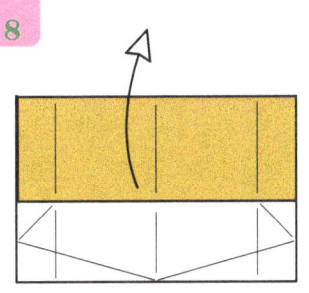
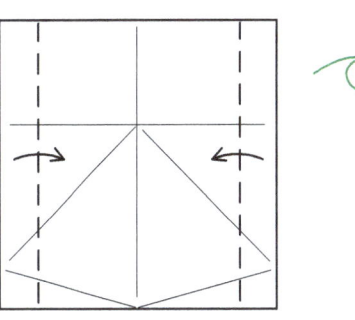

Fold and unfold.

Unfold.

Fold along the creases.

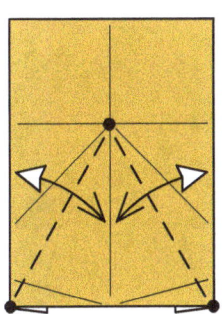
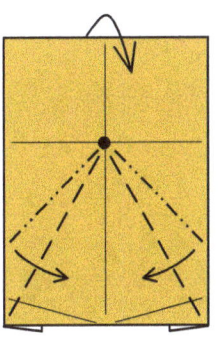
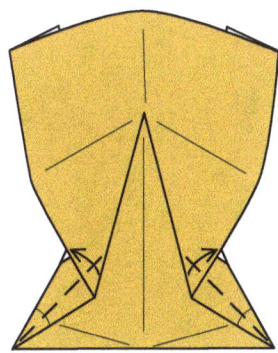

Fold and unfold, including the layers at the bottom.

Push in at the dot.

This is 3D. Fold the top layers.

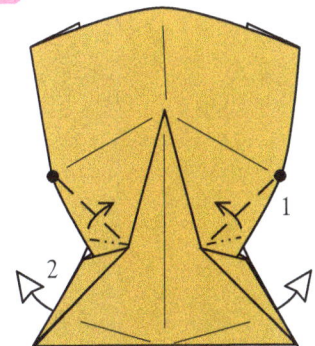
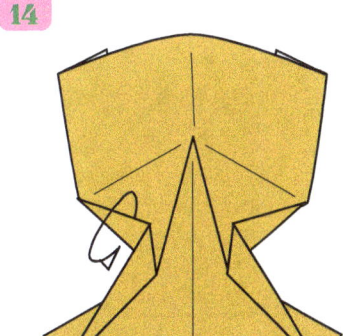
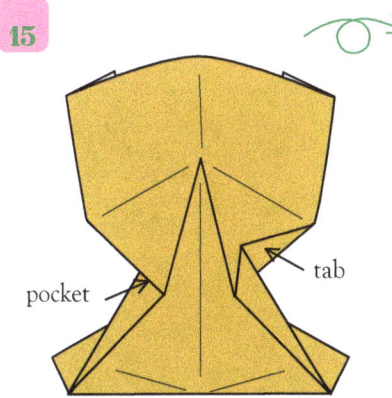

1. Pull out.
2. Unfold from behind.

Wrap around.

Note the tab and pocket. Later, the tab will tuck inside the pocket.

Mushroom **65**

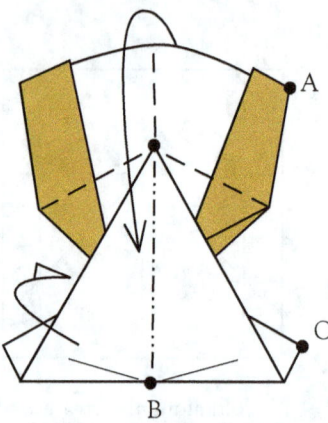

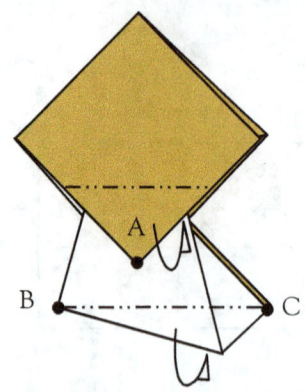

Push in at the center dot and bring the top flap down while folding the bottom triangle in half. Follow dots A, B, and C into the next step.

1. Fold inside.
2. Fold inside.
Repeat behind.

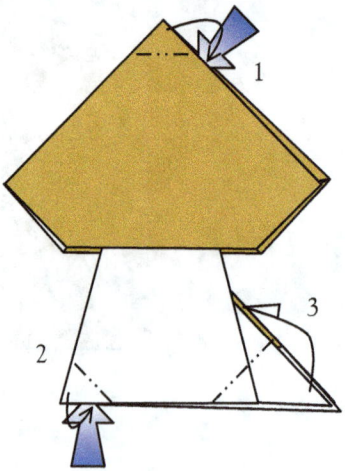

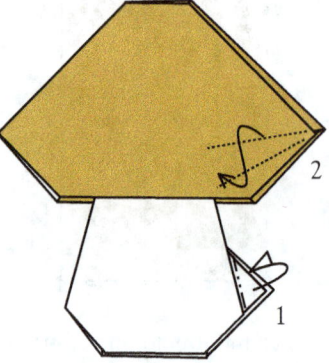

1. This is a combination of a reverse fold and sink.
2. Reverse-fold.
3. Fold inside, repeat behind.

1. Fold inside, repeat behind.
2. Tuck the tab inside the pocket to lock the model. See step 15.
The Mushroom can stand.

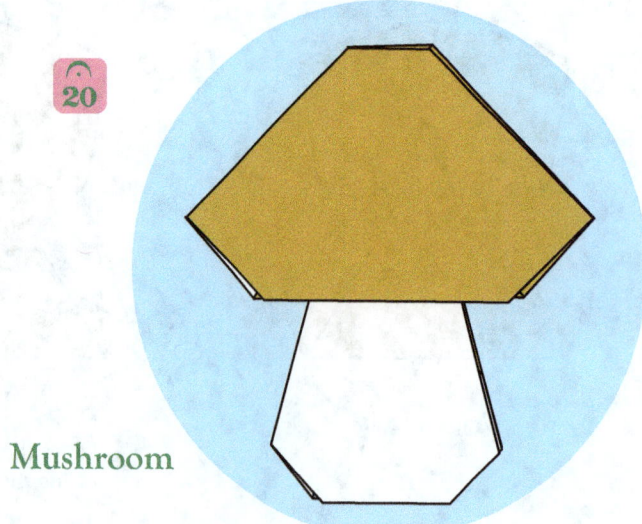

Mushroom

Spotted Mushroom

Spotted mushrooms make perfect hiding spots for tiny insect and mischievous gnomes. Gnomes hold tea parties on the mushroom caps. Spotted mushroom villages bring new adventures every day.

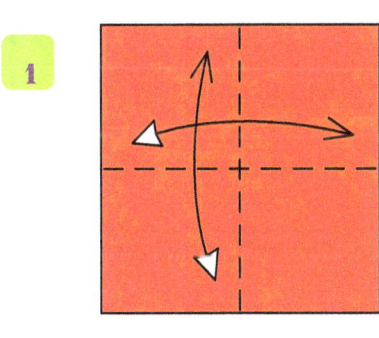

Fold and unfold.

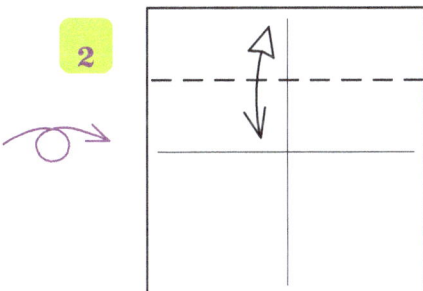

Fold and unfold.

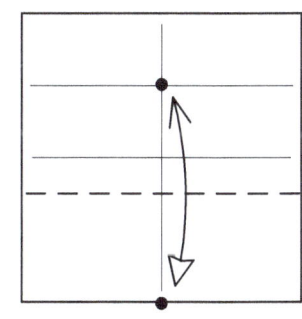

Fold and unfold.

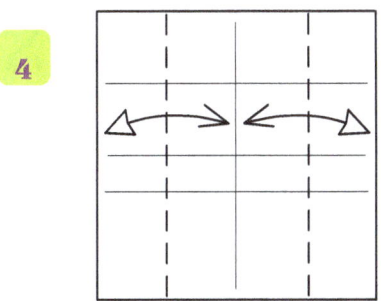

Fold to the center and unfold.

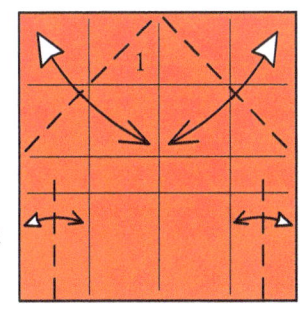

1. Fold and unfold to the center.
2. Fold and unfold on the left and right.

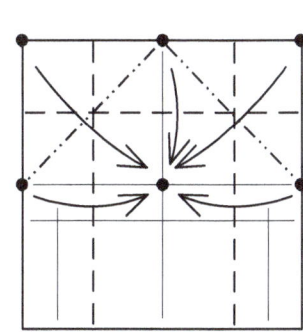

Fold along the creases. All the dots will meet in the center.

Spotted Mushroom **67**

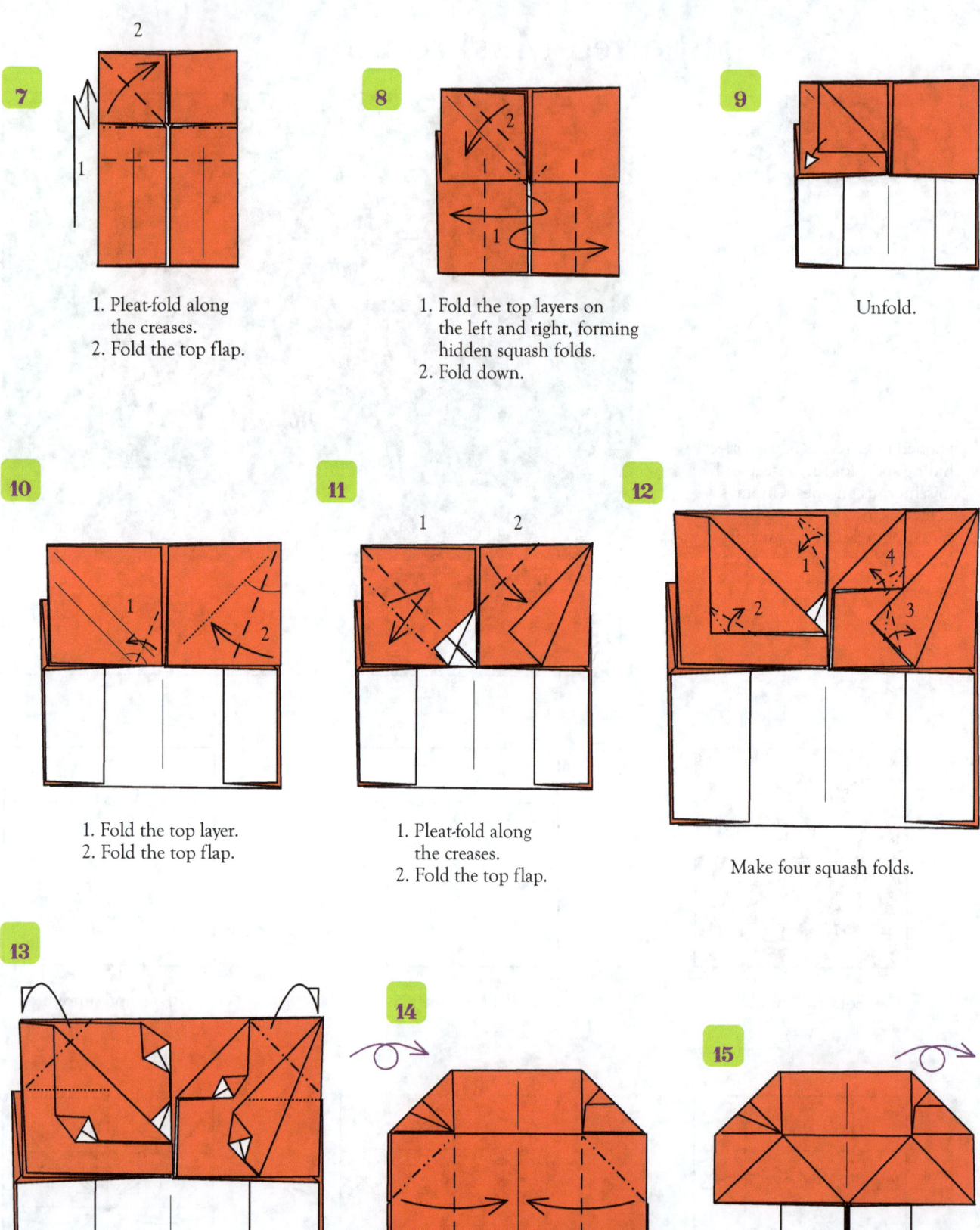

16

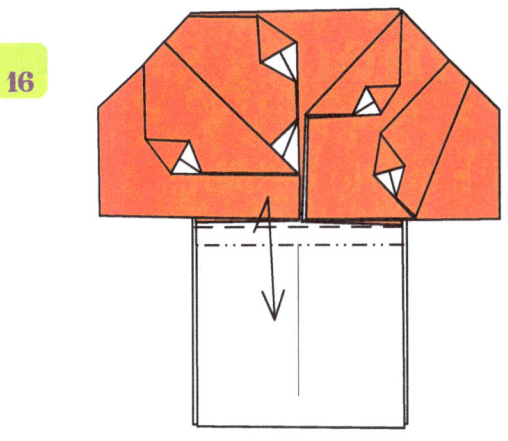

Pleat-fold.

17

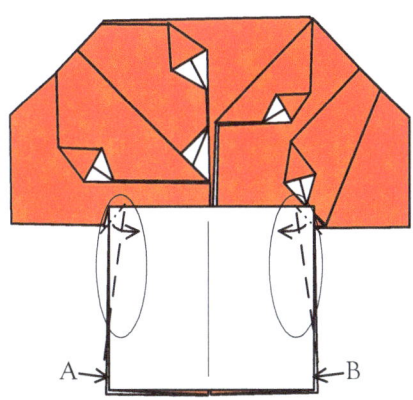

Make squash fold on the hidden layers A and B.

18

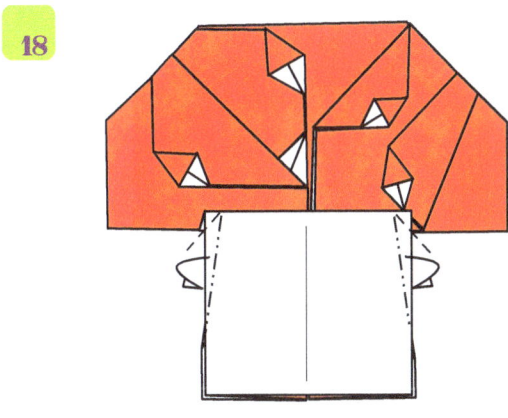

Fold inside.

19

Tuck inside.

20

1. Fold behind.
2. Fold inside, repeat behind. Spread at the bottom so the Mushroom can stand.

21

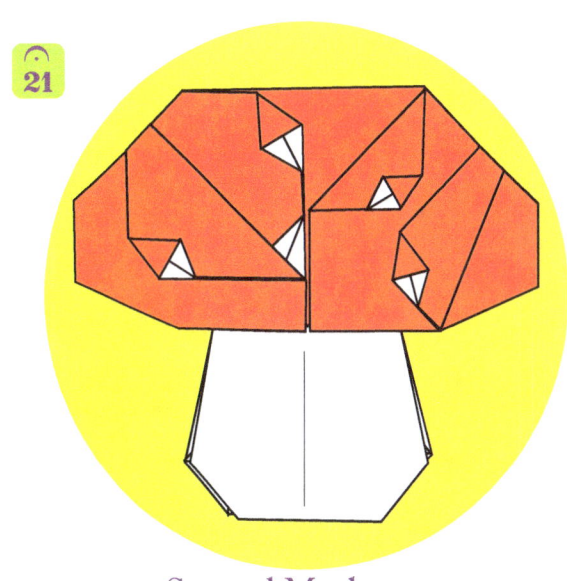

Spotted Mushroom

Spotted Mushroom **69**

Third Movement

Minuet of Flying Saucers with a Trio of Gems

Hidden in the labs of their caves, the tinker gnomes worked endlessly on flying saucers. Their project was to build flying saucers of every shape. From triangular and square saucers that zoomed like little lanterns of light, to pentagonal and hexagonal ones that twirled among mushrooms, all the way to heptagonal and octagonal ones, they saw that no matter the shape, with careful tinkering and a bit of courage can make anything fly.

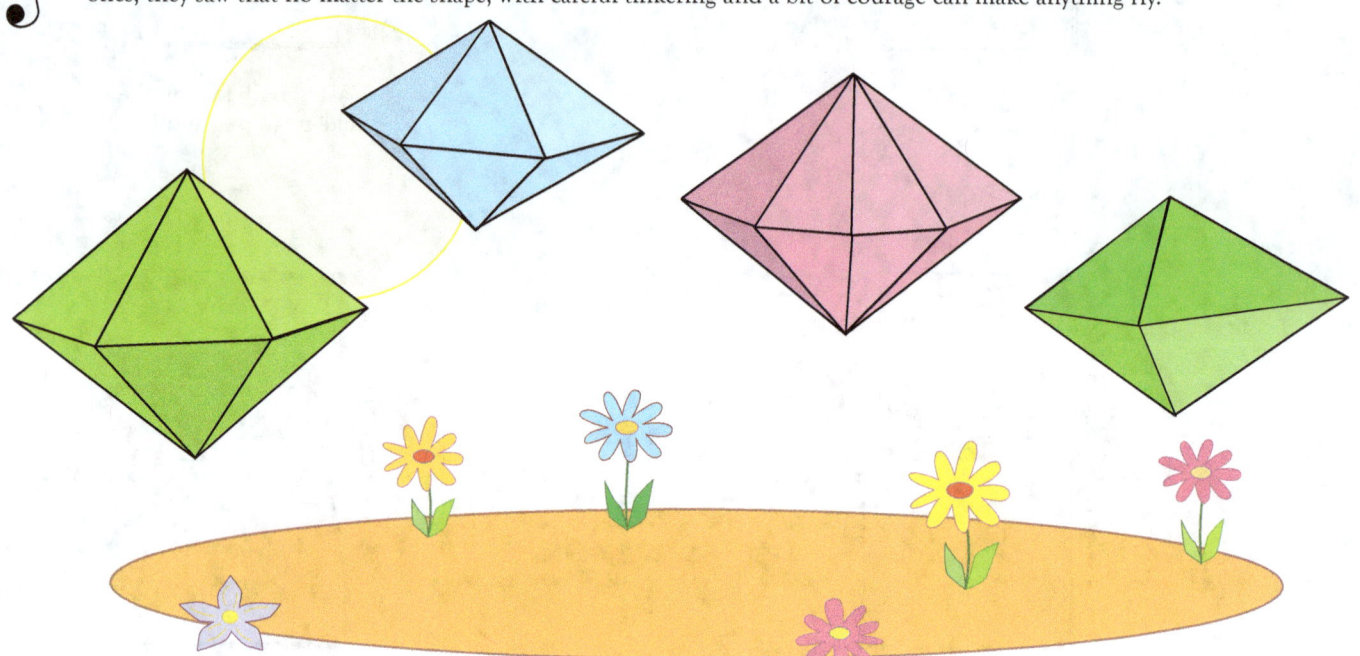

Triangular Flying Saucer

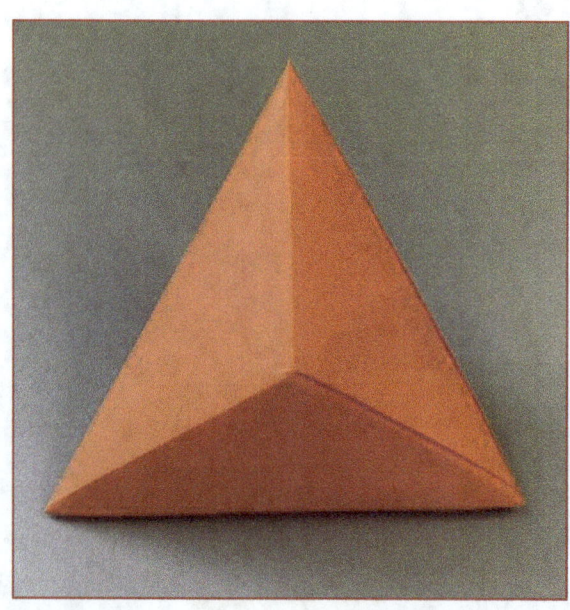

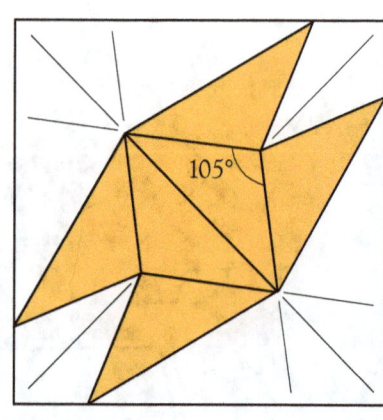

Deep beneath the roots of an ancient oak, the tinkers are hard at work! Sparks fly, gears spin, and they are building something very special: a triangular flying saucer. With twinkling gem lights, the saucer is ready to fly. Triangles can fly faster than circles if you treat them kindly.

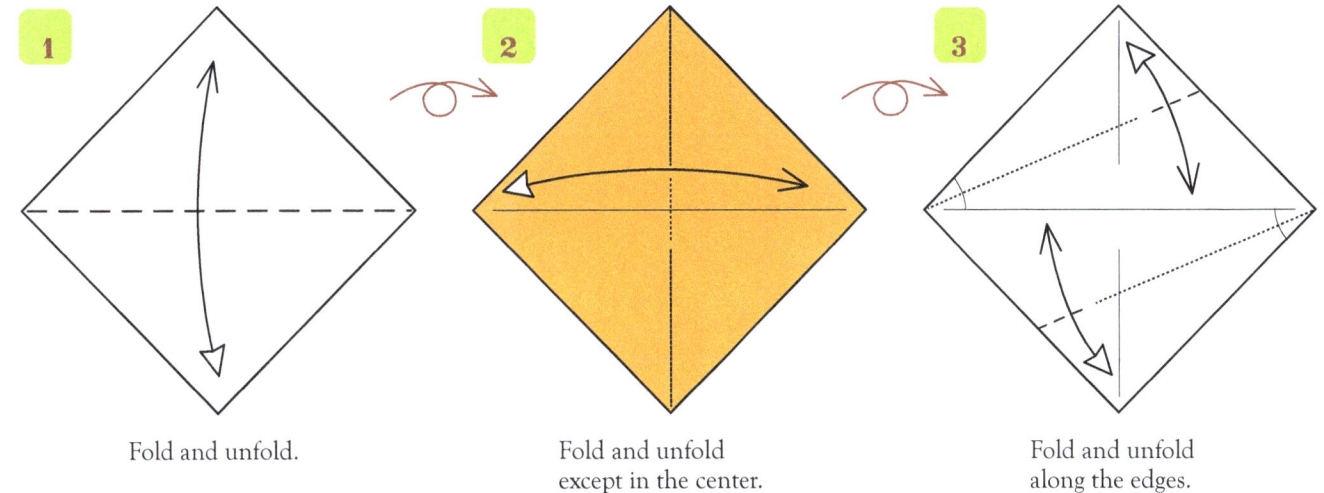

1. Fold and unfold.
2. Fold and unfold except in the center.
3. Fold and unfold along the edges.

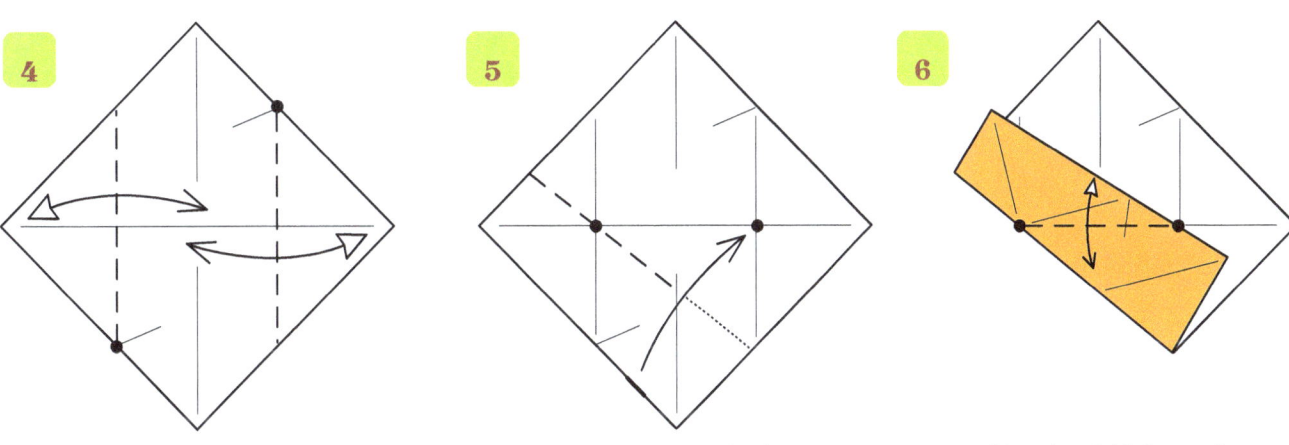

4. Fold and unfold.
5. Bring the edge to the dot.
6. Fold and unfold the top layer along a hidden crease.

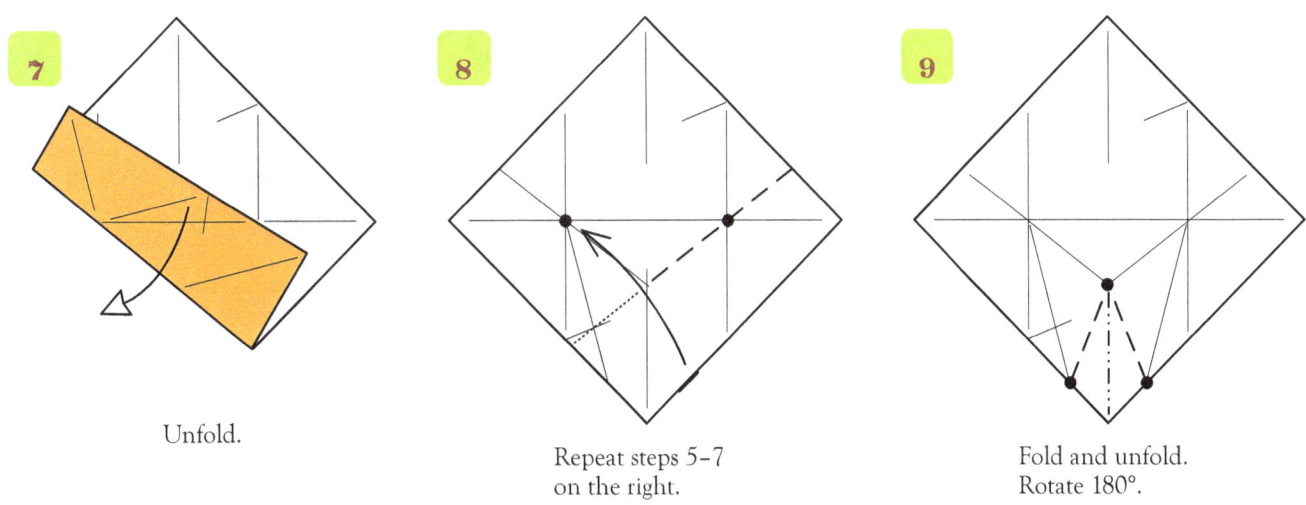

7. Unfold.
8. Repeat steps 5–7 on the right.
9. Fold and unfold. Rotate 180°.

Trianglular Flying Saucer **71**

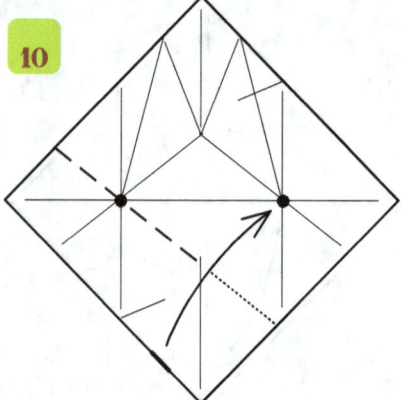

Repeat steps 5-9.

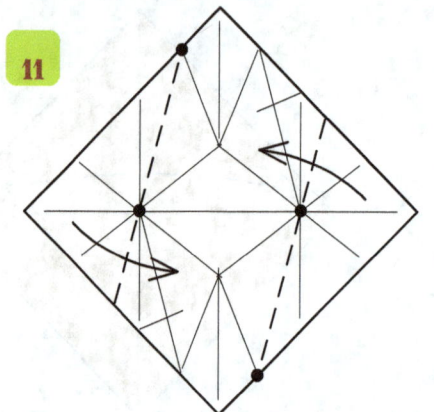

Fold along the creases by the dots, extending them.

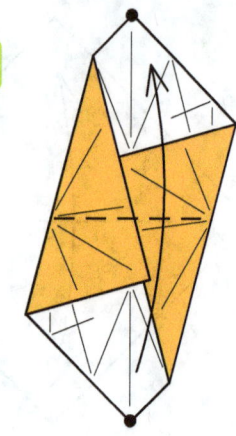

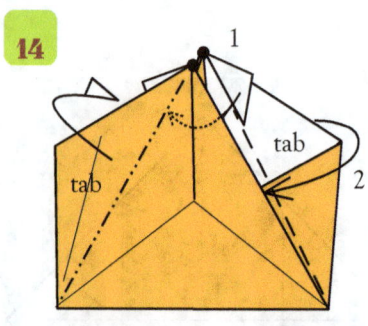

Puff out at the dot.
Turn over and repeat.

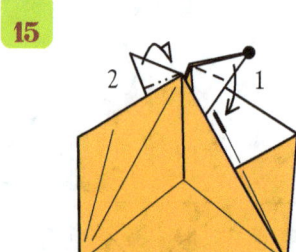

1. Fold to the crease.
2. Turn over and repeat.

1. The two dots at the top will meet as the top flaps spiral inward to lock it.
2. Tuck the tabs inside.

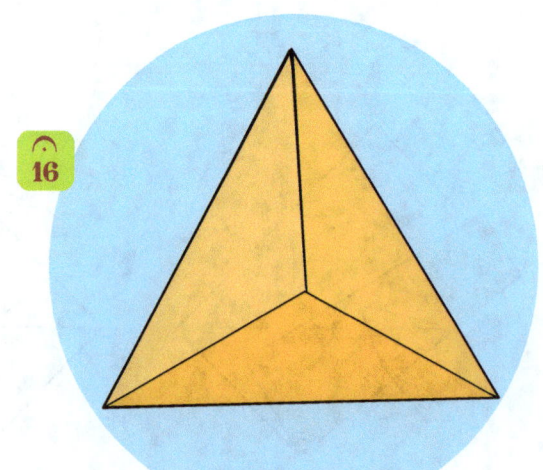

Triangular Flying Saucer

72 Origami Symphony No. 12

Square Flying Saucer

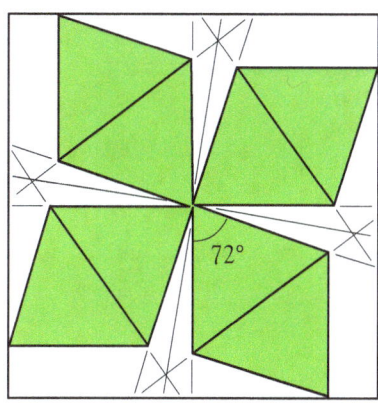

Deep in a root-filled workshop, Gimble Tinker was busy at work creating a square flying saucer. He climbed aboard, and whoosh... it lifted into the sky. It wobbled a little, then zipped through the forest leaving trails of glittering light.

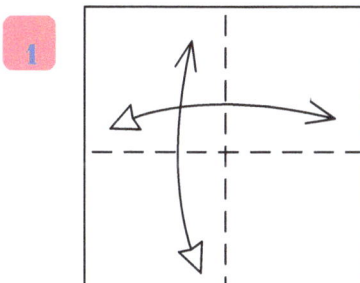

1. Fold and unfold.

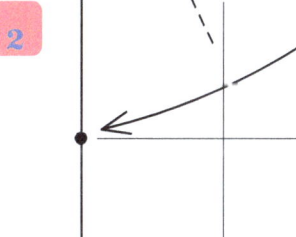

2. Fold and unfold at the top.

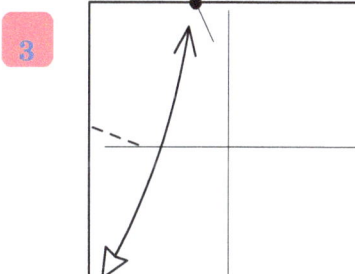

3. Fold and unfold on the left.

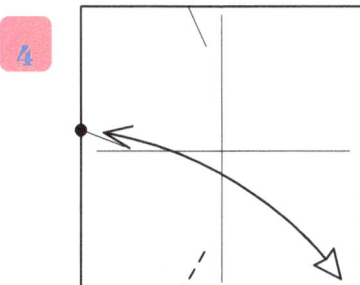

4. Fold and unfold on the bottom. Rotate 180°.

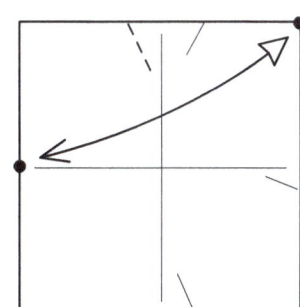

5. Repeat steps 2–4.

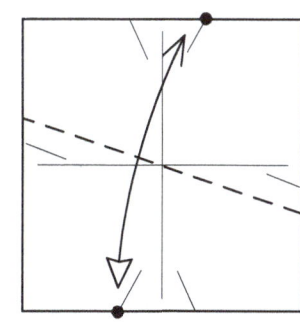

6. Fold and unfold.

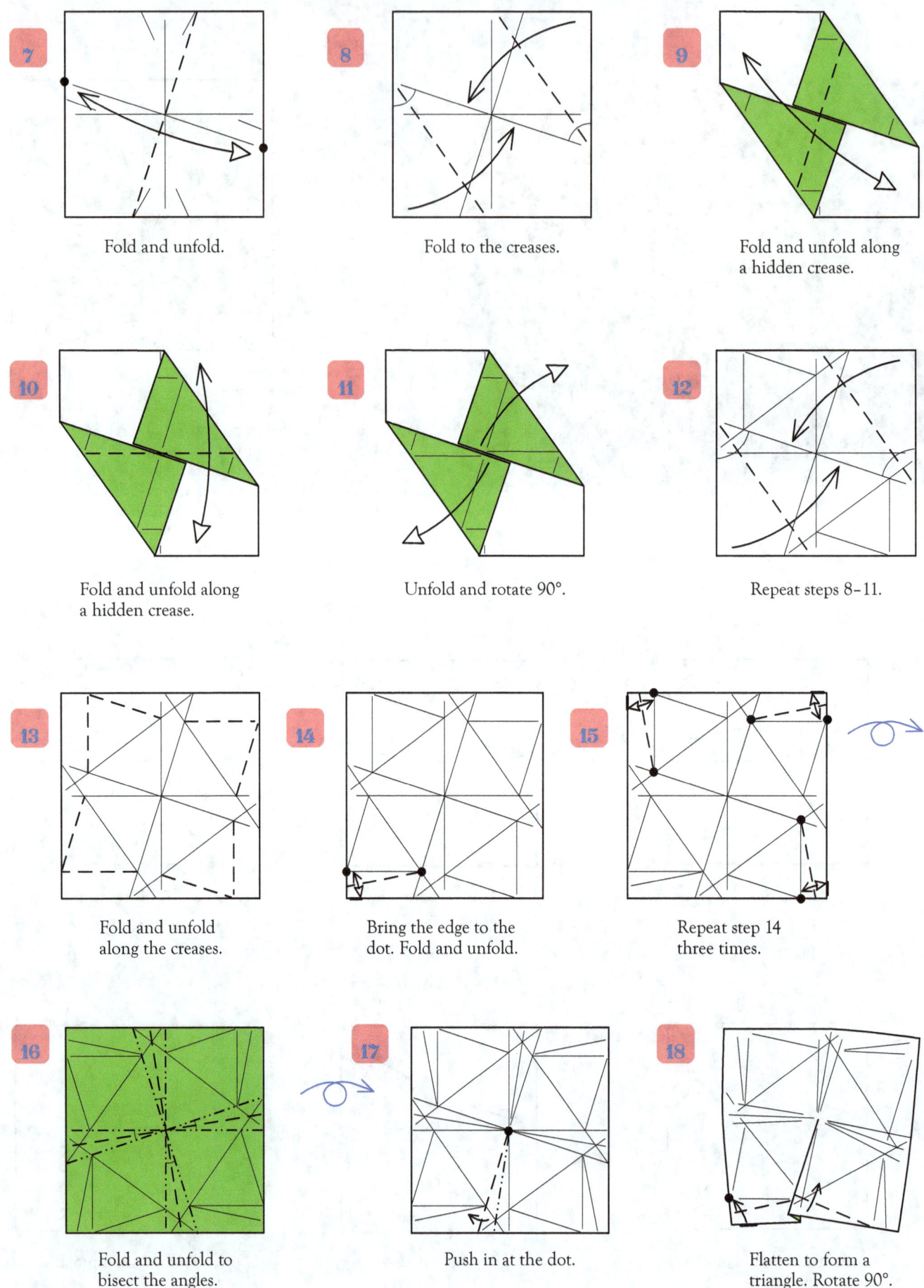

74 *Origami Symphony No. 12*

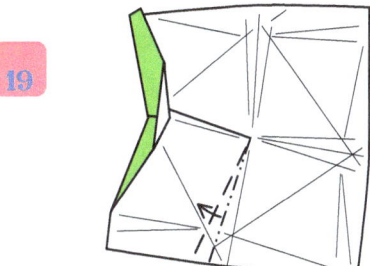

Repeat steps 17–18 three times. Rotate to view the outside.

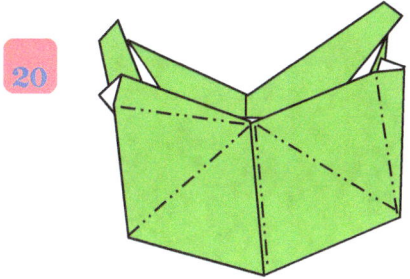

Fold and unfold on the edges all around.

Tuck the tab behind region A and continue all around. The four dots will meet at the top. The tabs will spiral inward to lock the model.

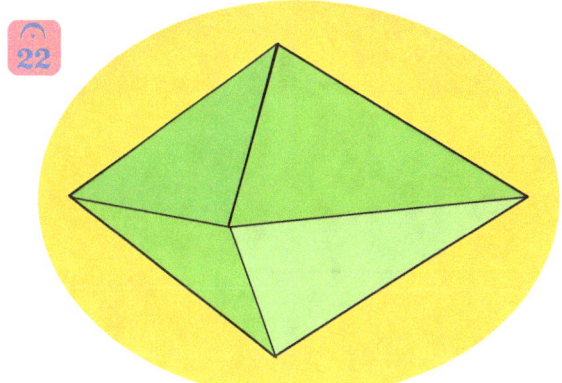

Square Flying Saucer

Pentagonal Flying Saucer

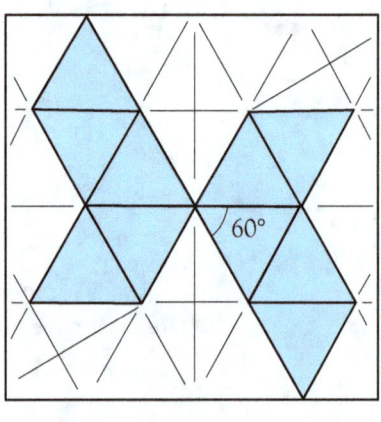

PentaGlimmer Tinker is an expert in odd shapes. He built a pentagonal flying saucer. As he said: "Five side, five times the fun!" Balance each corner and you'll soar smoother than ever.

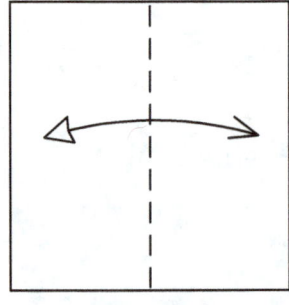

1

Fold and unfold.

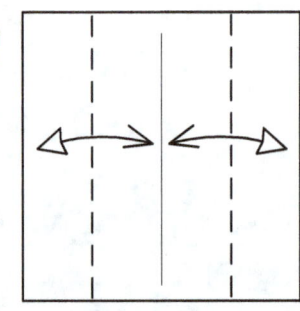

2

Fold and unfold.

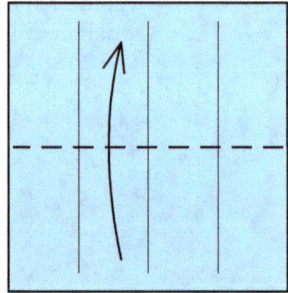

3

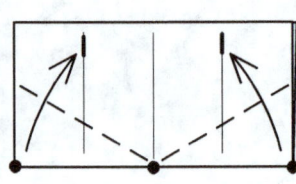

4

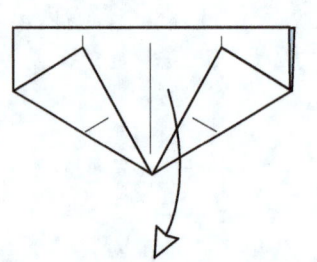

5

Unfold and rotate 90°.

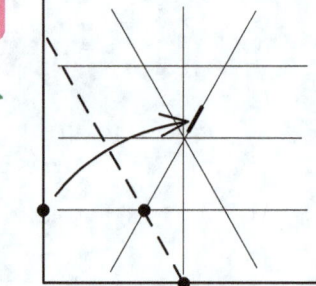

6

Fold and unfold.

76 *Origami Symphony No. 12*

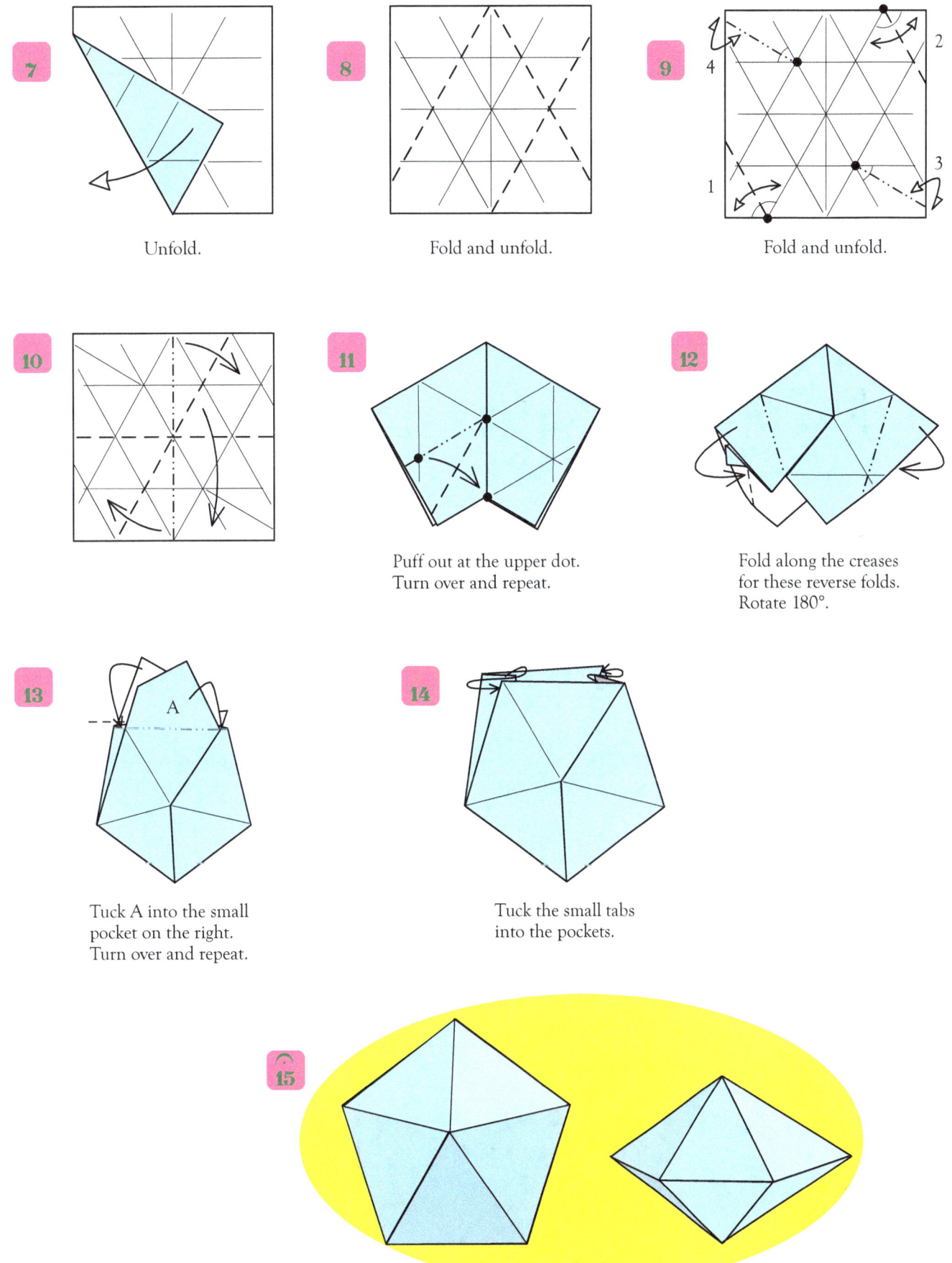

Pentagonal Flying Saucer

Hexagonal Flying Saucer

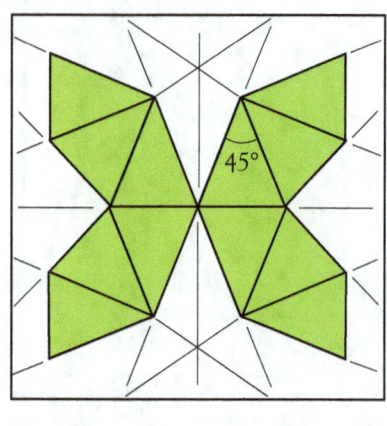

HexaWibble Tinker polished 12 shining panels for the top and bottom panels of his hexagonal flying saucer. The saucer zipped across the night sky, weaving through mushrooms and dancing with dragonflies.

 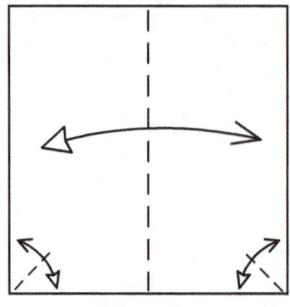
Fold and unfold.

  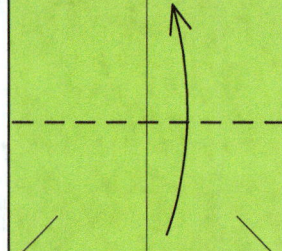

 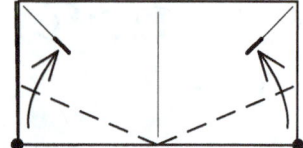

 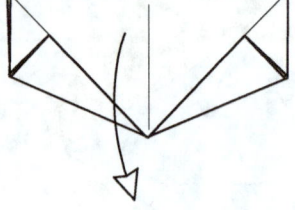
Unfold everything.

Fold and unfold along the creases. Rotate 90°.

 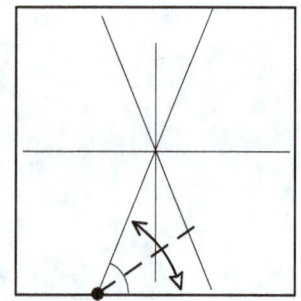
Fold and unfold to bisect the angle.

78 Origami Symphony No. 12

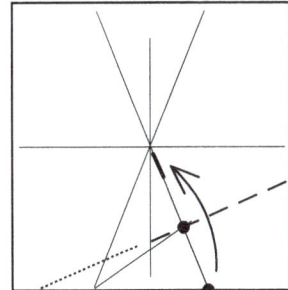
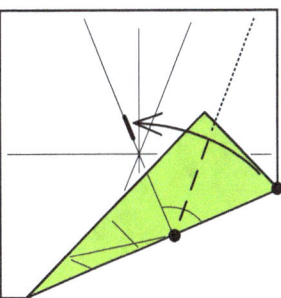

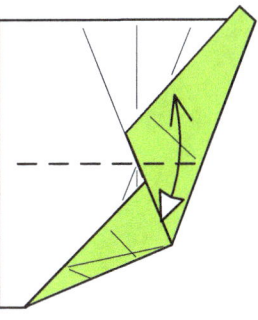

Bisect the angle.

Fold and unfold along a partially hidden crease.

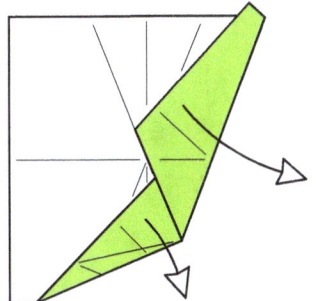
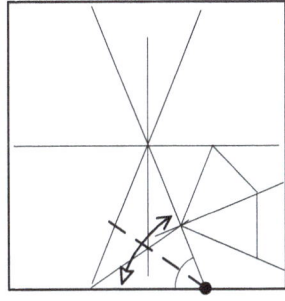
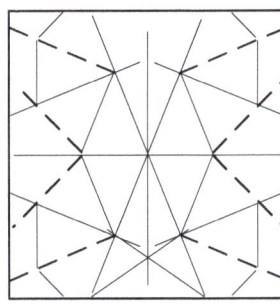

Unfold everything.

Repeat steps 6–10 three times, in the opposite direction and at the top.

Fold and unfold along the creases, extending some of them.

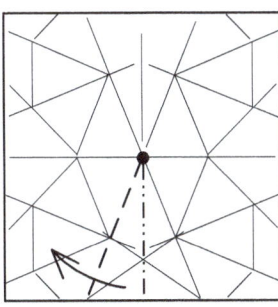
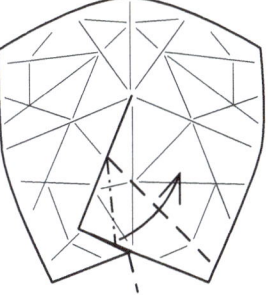
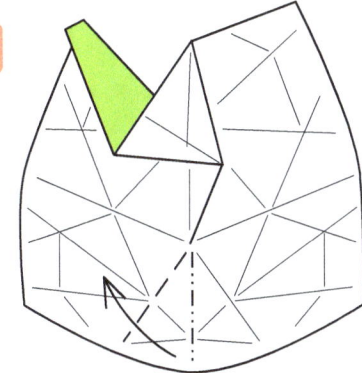

Push in at the dot.

Valley-fold along the crease for this squash fold. Rotate 180°.

Repeat steps 13–14. Then flatten.

Hexagonal Flying Saucer **79**

16

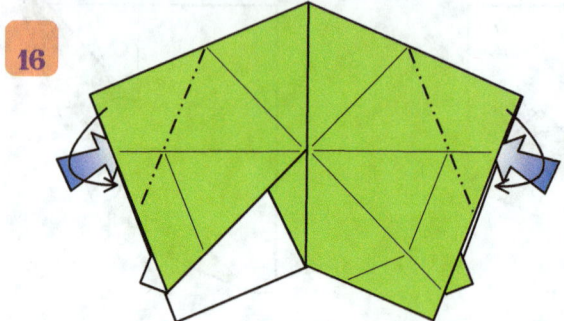

Make reverse folds.

17

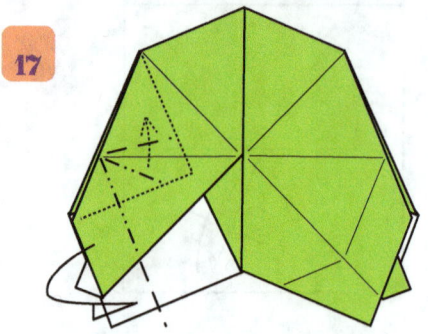

Fold the inside layers together for this spine-lock fold. Turn over and repeat.

18

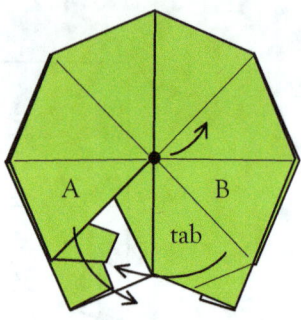

Lift up at the dot. Fold the tab under A. Turn over and repeat.

19

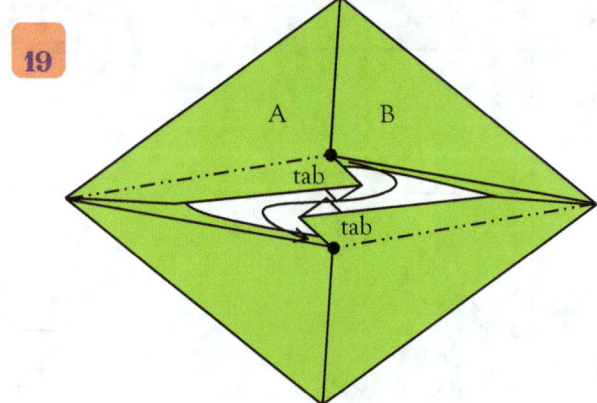

Tuck the two tabs into each other so the dots meet.

20

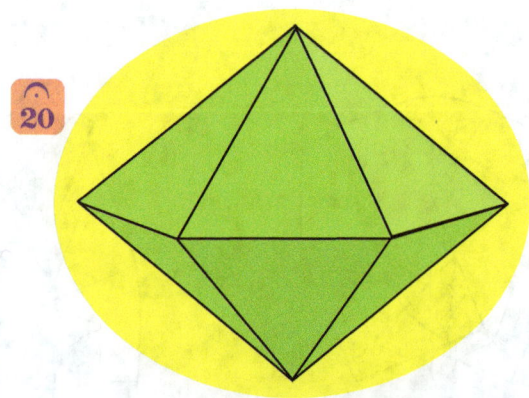

Hexagonal Flying Saucer

80 Origami Symphony No. 12

Heptagonal Flying Saucer

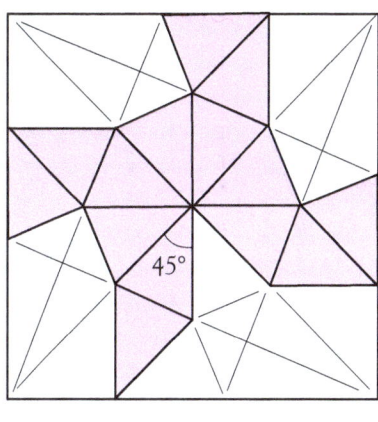

As HeptaPepta Tinker finished building his heptagonal flying saucer, he wondered if the seven corners would offer seven ways to soar. With a soft hum, the saucer lifted, wobbling at first, then spinning like a top. HeptaPepta realized that each extra side brings new adventures and surprises.

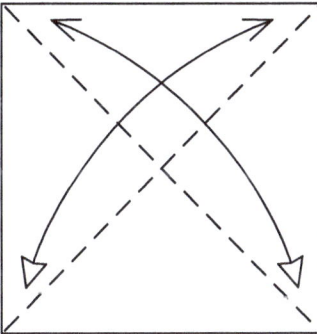

Fold and unfold.

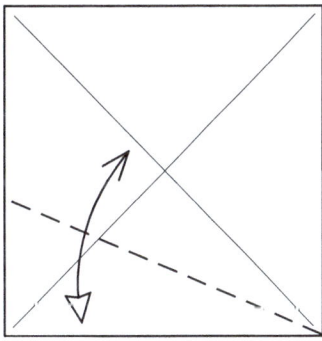

Fold and unfold. Rotate 90°.

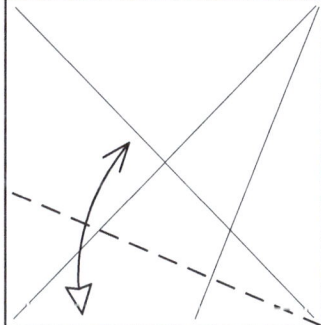

Repeat step 2 three times.

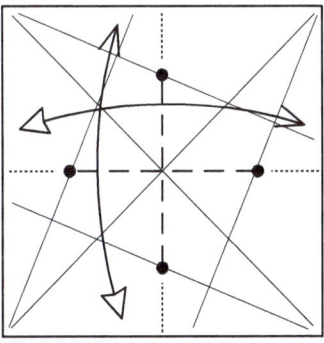

Fold and unfold in half, creasing in the center.

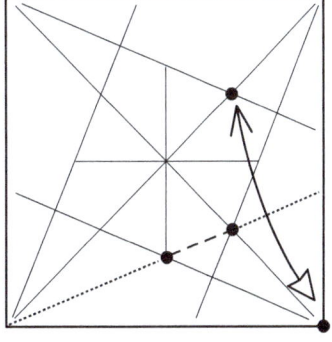

Fold and unfold in the center.

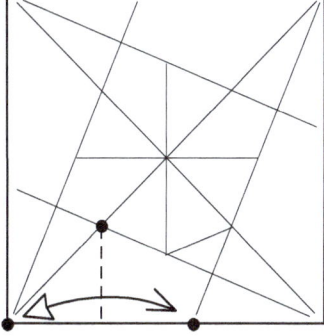

Fold and unfold.

Heptagonal Flying Saucer **81**

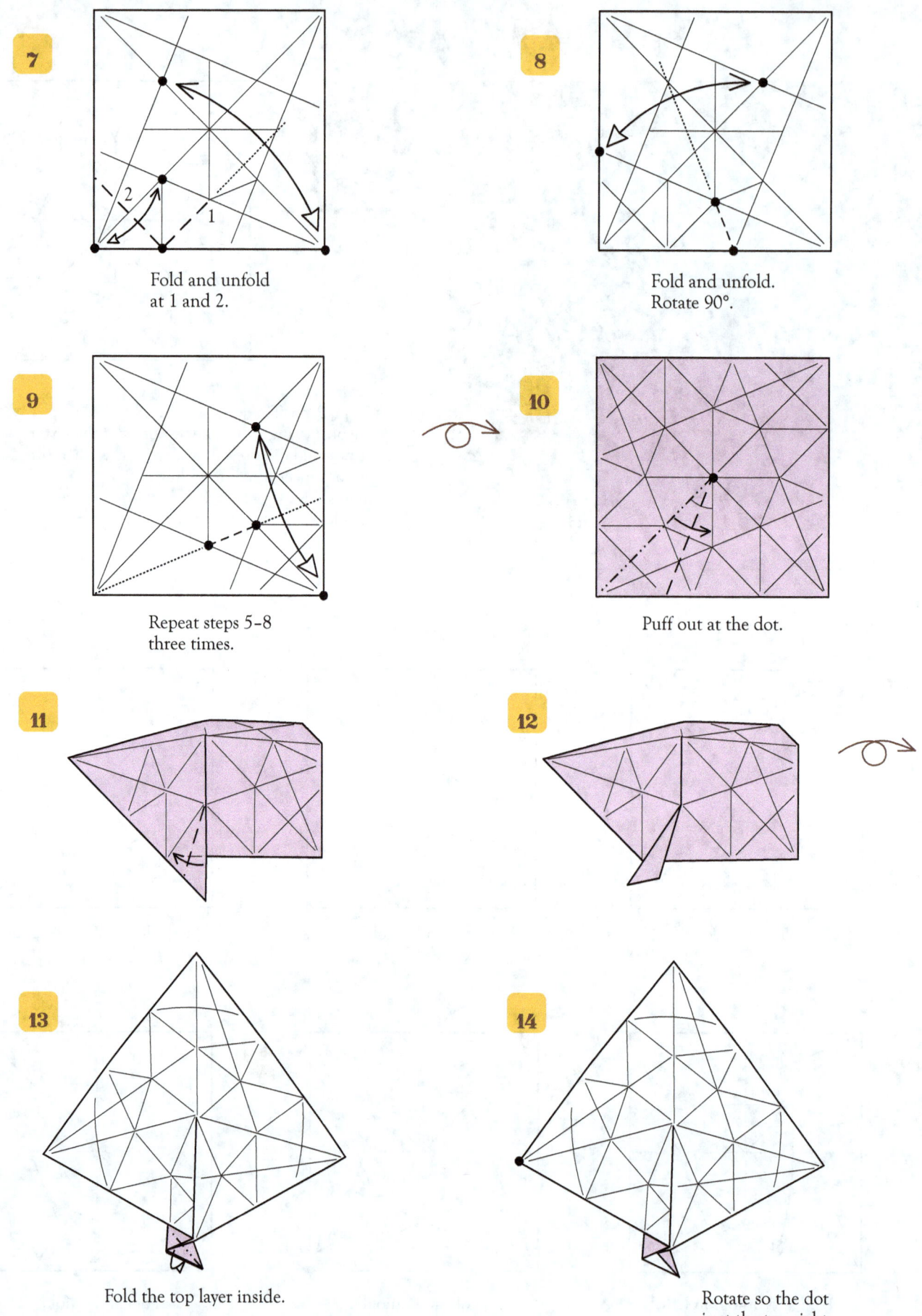

82 Origami Symphony No. 12

15.

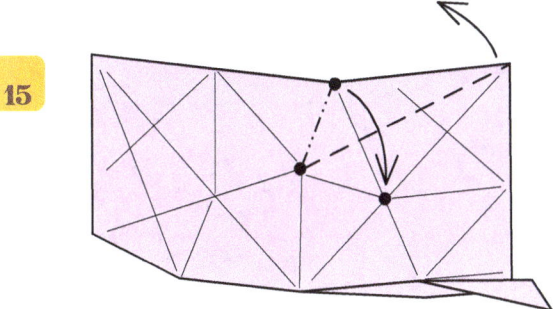

Puff out at the left dot.

16.

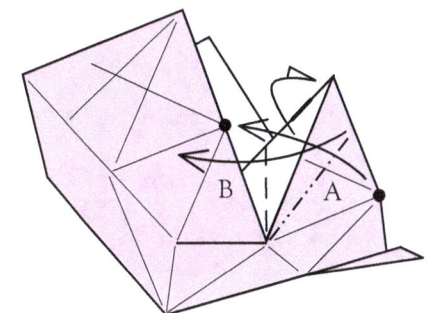

A will cover part of B. The dots will meet, and the bold edge will also meet the dots.

17.

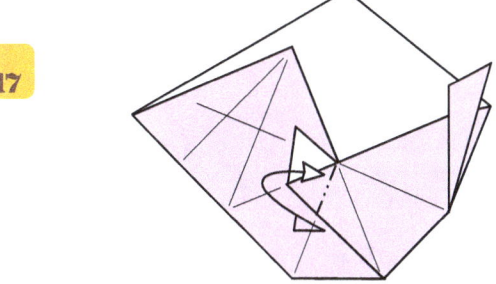

Fold and unfold along the crease.

18.

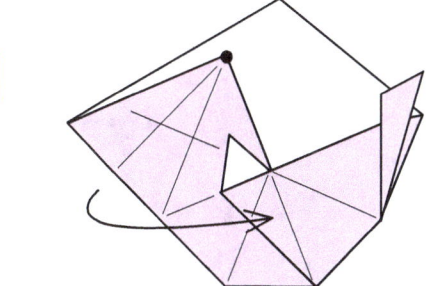

Rotate the dot to the right and let the model spread a little.

19.

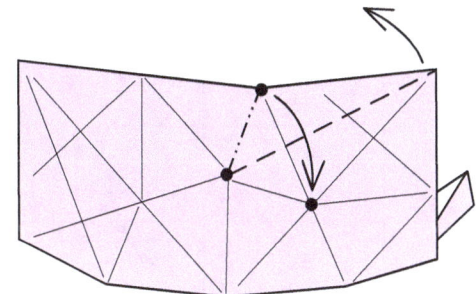

Repeat steps 15–18 two times.

20.

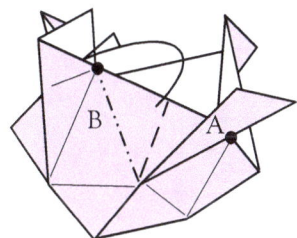

Note the different corner is on the right. Tuck most of region A under B so the dots meet.

21.

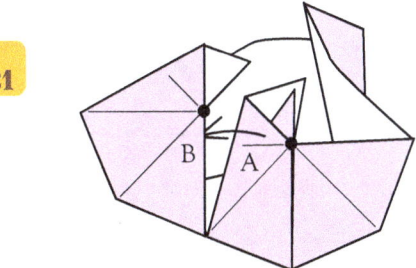

Tuck tab A under region B so the dots meet. Continue going around for this three-way spiral lock.

22.

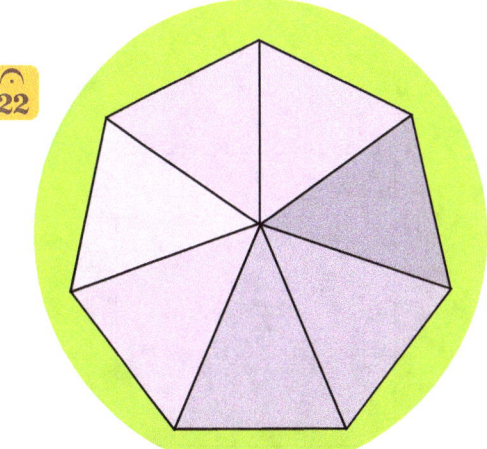

Heptagonal Flying Saucer

Heptagonal Flying Saucer **83**

Octagonal Flying Saucer

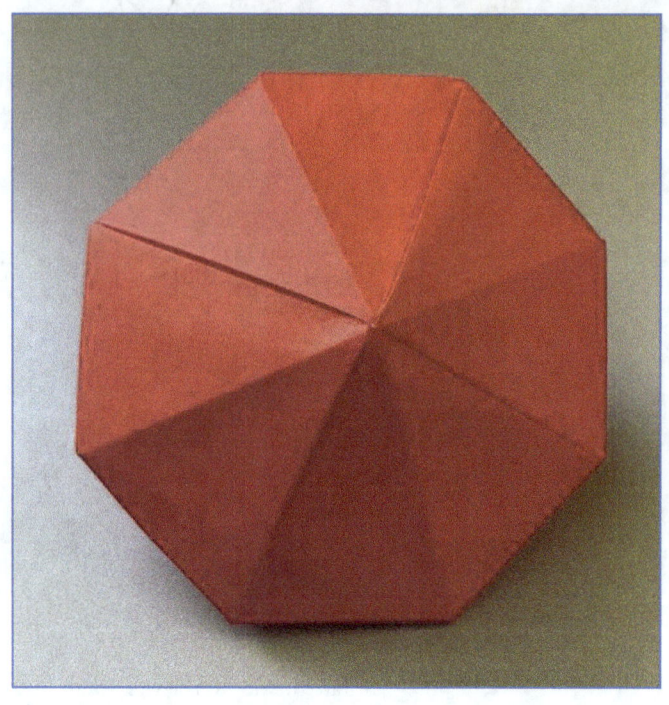

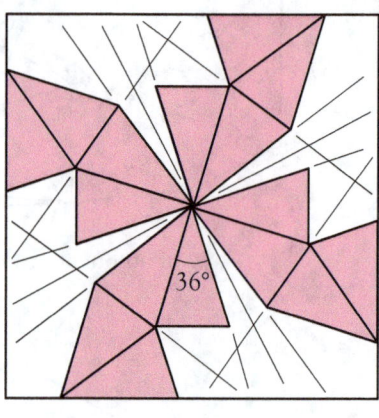

OctoBeam Tinker's saucer has eight edges, shining like lanterns in the dark. Eight sides make eight chances for magic. The octagonal saucer flew above treetops and looped around owls.

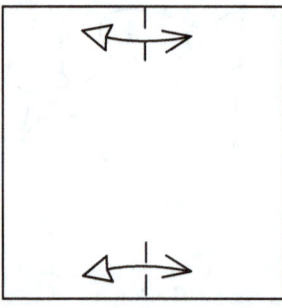

1. Fold and unfold on the edges.

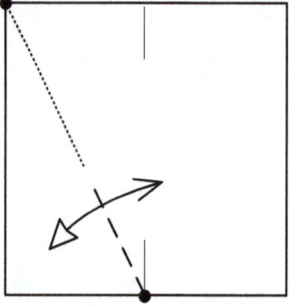

2. Fold and unfold creasing lightly on the bottom half.

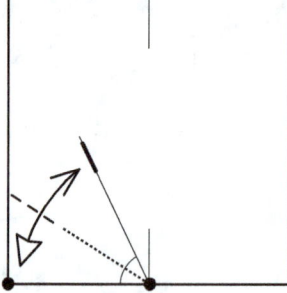

3. Fold and unfold on the edges to bisect the angles.

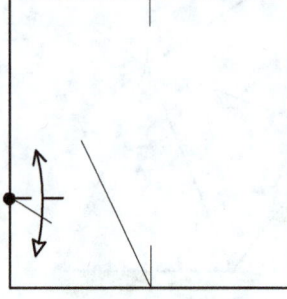

4. Fold and unfold on the left.

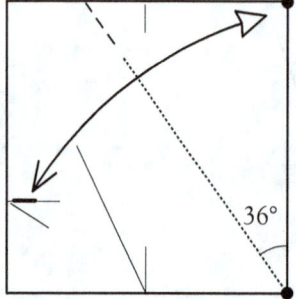

5. Bring the corner to the crease. Fold and unfold on the top.

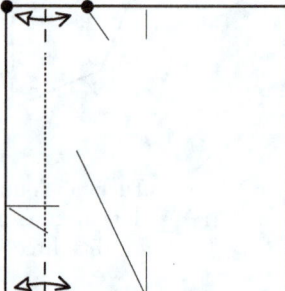

6. Fold and unfold on the top and bottom. Rotate 180°.

84 Origami Symphony No. 12

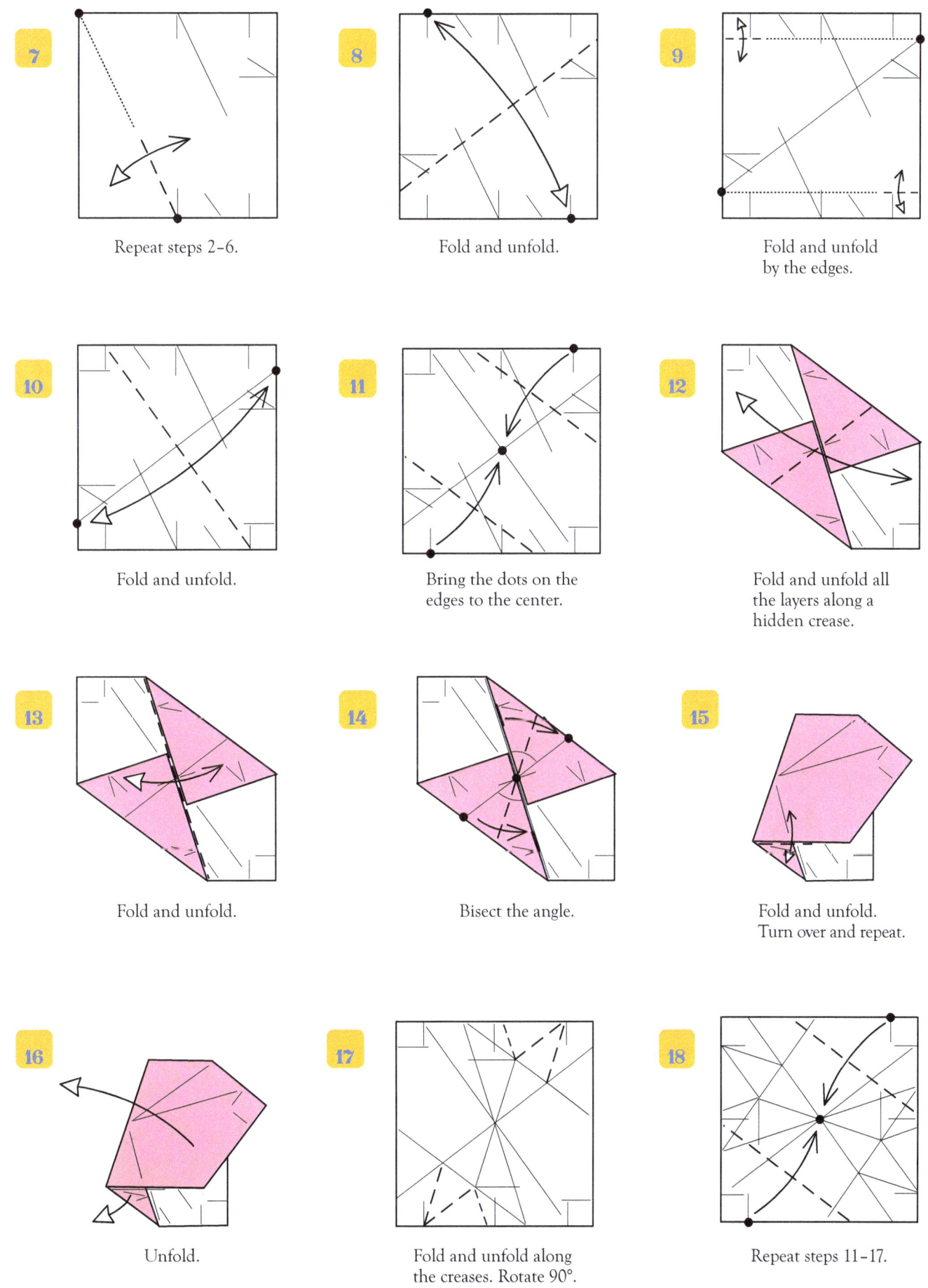

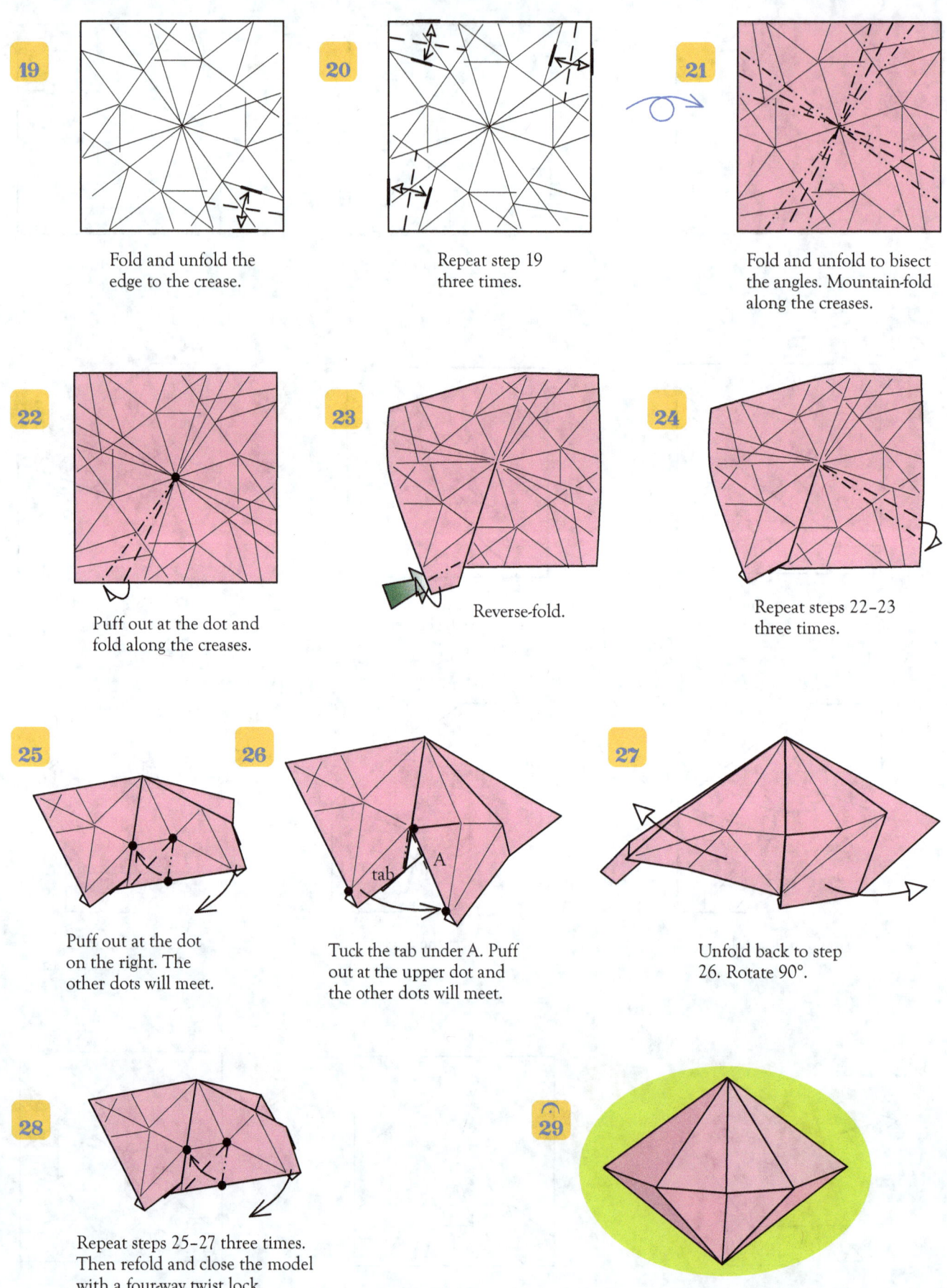

Octagonal Flying Saucer

Trio of Gems

 Mountain gnomes are busy at work in tiny stone workshops hidden in cliffs and caves. These gnomes specialize in crafting dipyramid gems with square, pentagonal, and hexagonal bases. Each shape has its own magic. Corners, edges, and faces must meet just right for the sparkle to shine. Through this, the gnomes learn that a dash of creativity can turn ordinary stones into treasures that sparkle with dreams.

Square Dipyramid

High in the mountains, Gimble Gem was busy at work in his tiny stone workshop. His project was to make a square dipyramid, a gem with two perfect pyramids joined at the base. To make it takes patience, steady hands, and a sparkle of joy. Even the smallest gem can hold the biggest dreams.

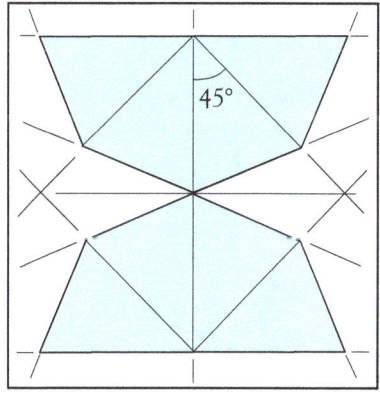

 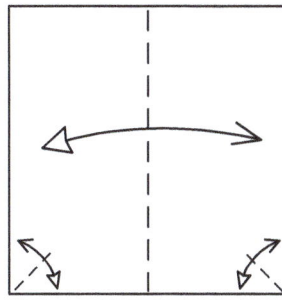

Fold and unfold.

  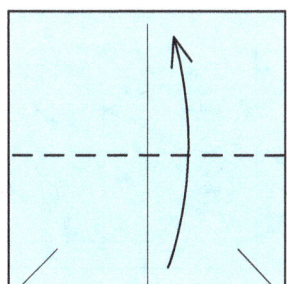

 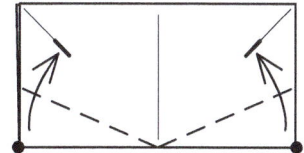

Square Dipyramid **87**

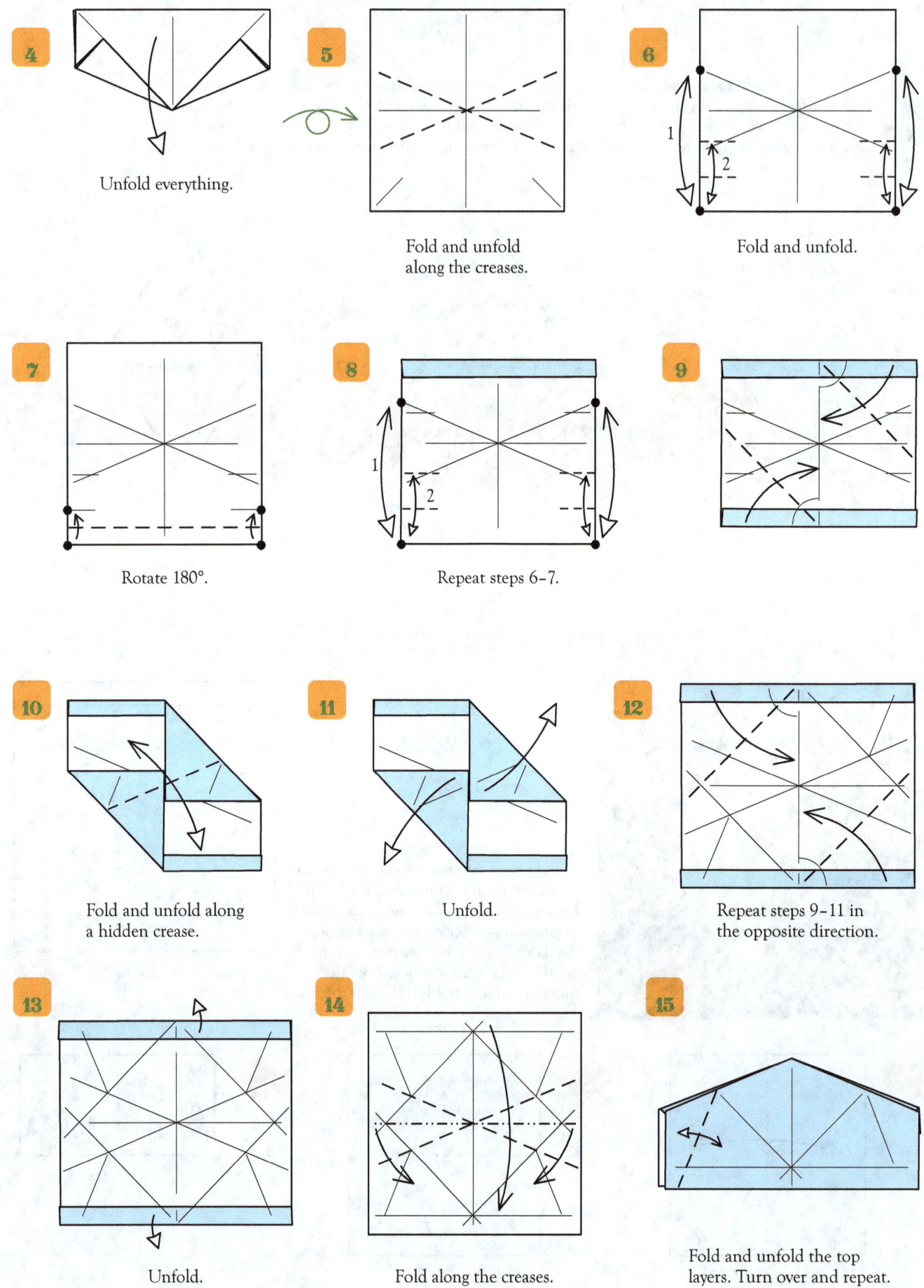

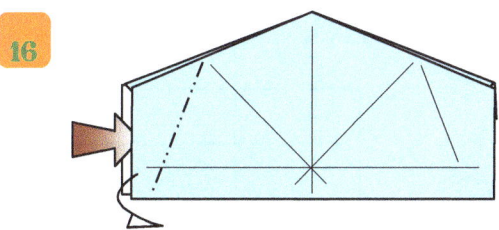

Reverse-fold. Turn over and repeat.

 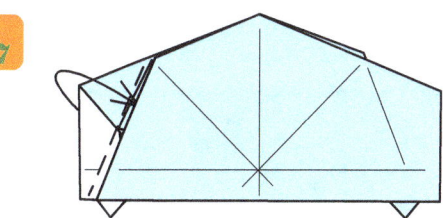

Tuck inside. Turn over and repeat.

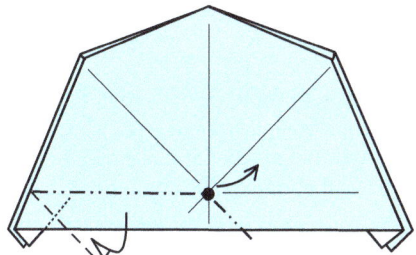

Lift up at the dot and reverse-fold on the left. Turn over and repeat.

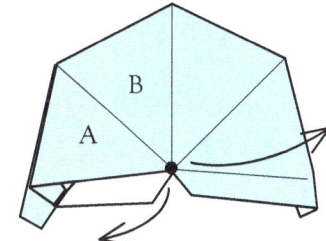

Open and bring the dot to the right.

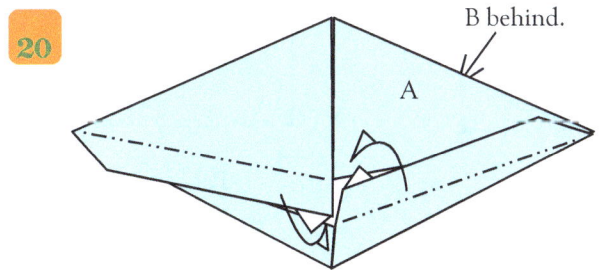

B behind.

Interlock the tabs.

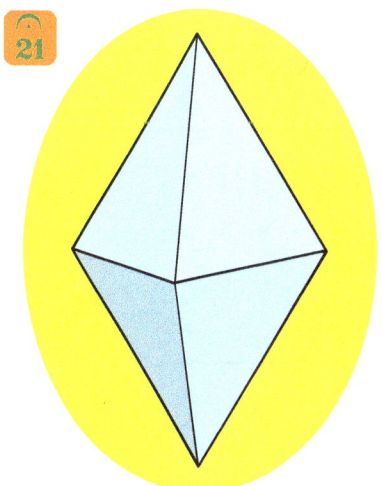

Square Dipyramid

Square Dipyramid **89**

Pentagonal Dipyramid

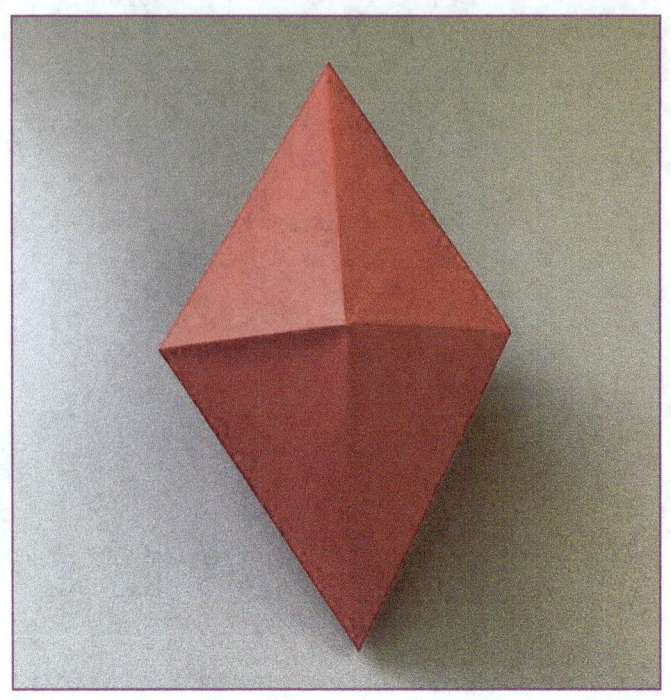

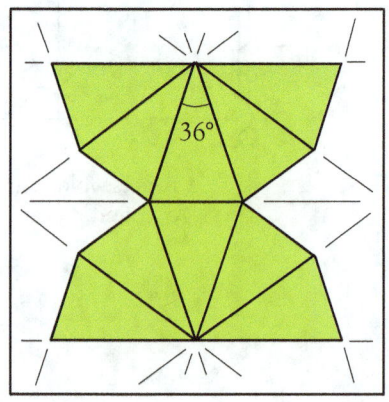

For more fun, Gimble Gem wanted to make a pentagonal dipyramid gem. When finished, Gimble watched it make radiant rainbows as it shone in the sunlight.

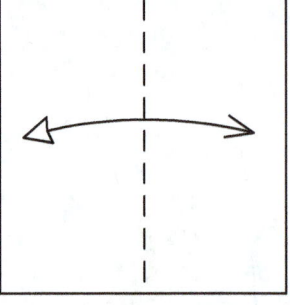

1. Fold and unfold.

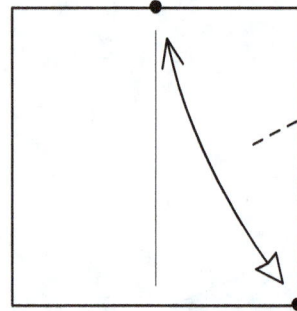

2. Fold and unfold on the right.

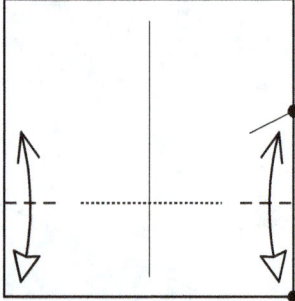

3. Fold and unfold on the edges.

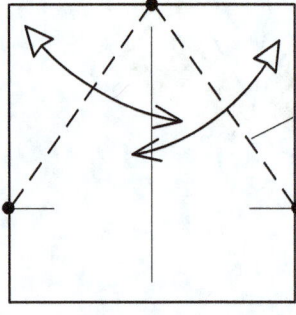

4. Fold and unfold. Rotate 180°.

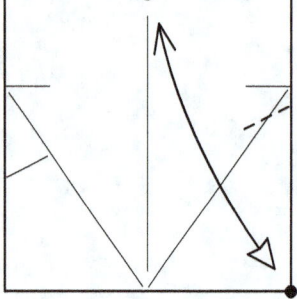

5. Repeat steps 2-4. Rotate 90°.

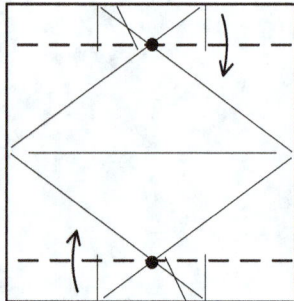

6.

90   *Origami Symphony No. 12*

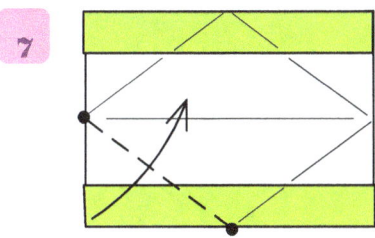

Fold along the crease.

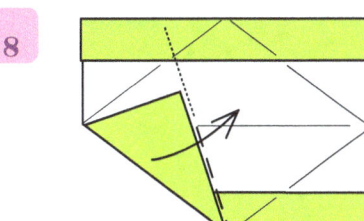

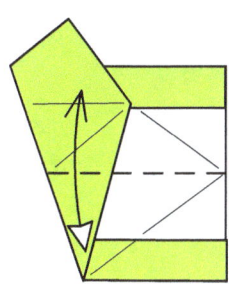

Fold and unfold.

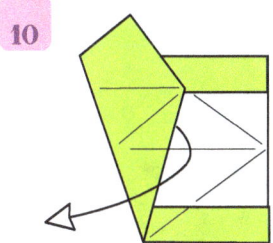

Unfold.

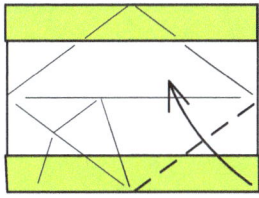

Repeat steps 7–10 on the three other corners.

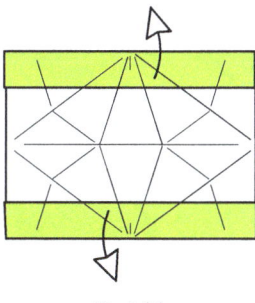

Unfold.

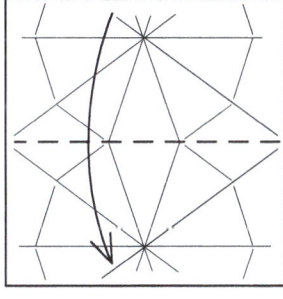

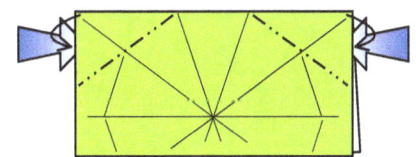

Reverse-fold.

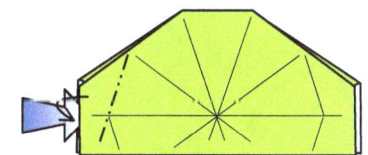

Reverse-fold. Turn over and repeat.

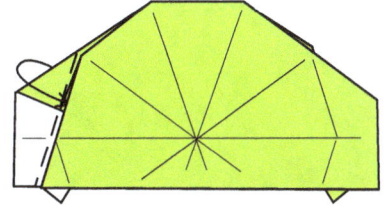

Tuck inside. Turn over and repeat.

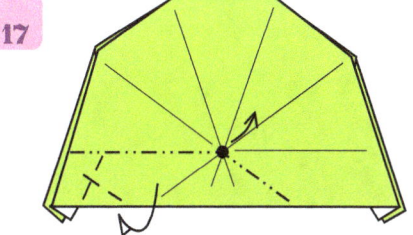

Lift up at the dot and reverse-fold on the left. Turn over and repeat.

Pentagonal Dipyramid

18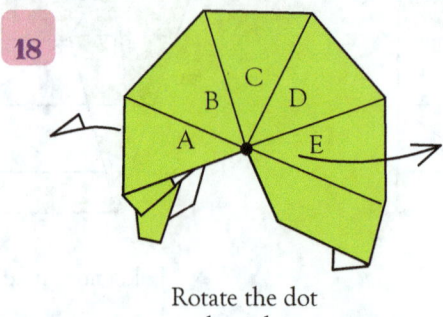

Rotate the dot to the right.

19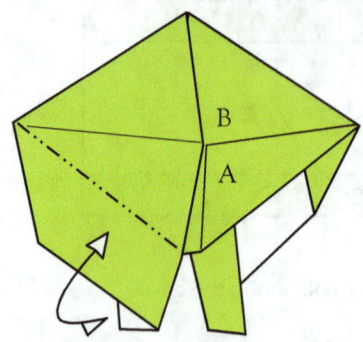

Fold and unfold several layers. Turn over and repeat.

20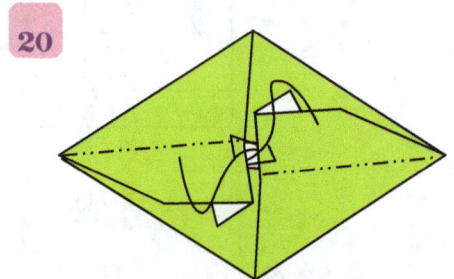

Tuck and interlock the tabs.

21

Pentagonal Dipyramid

92   Origami Symphony No. 12

Hexagonal Dipyramid

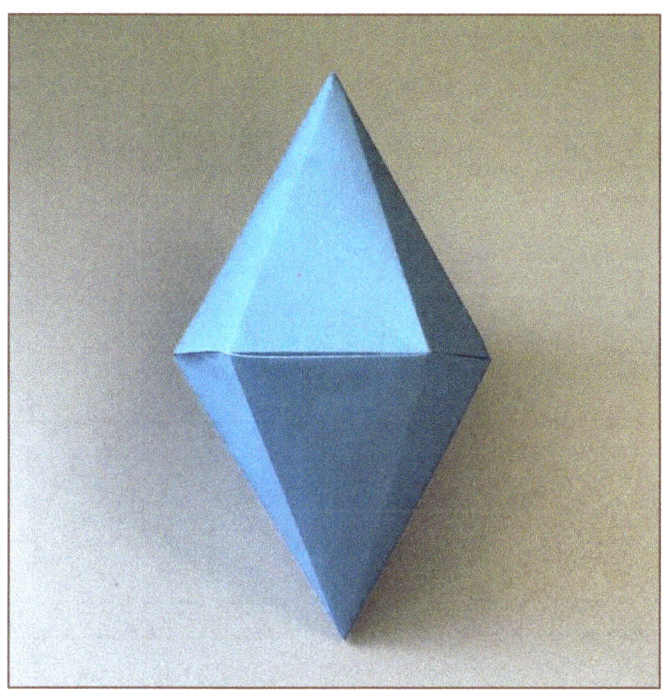

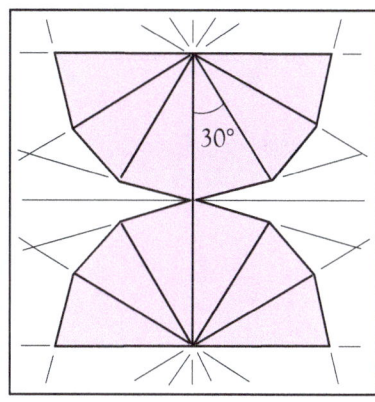

Working tirelessly in his mountain workshop, Hobble Gem created a hexagonal dipyramid. Under sunlight, it glowed brighter than gold. Its glow was seen far beyond the mountains.

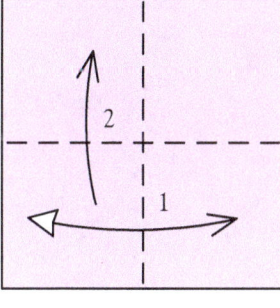

1. Fold and unfold.
2. Fold up.

Fold and unfold the top layer.

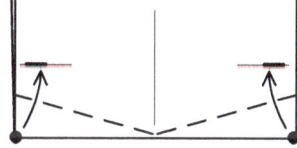

Bring the dots to the creases.

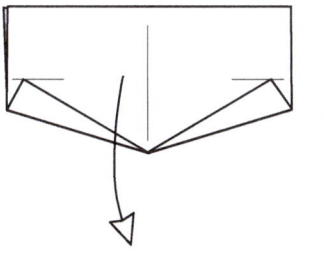

Unfold everything.

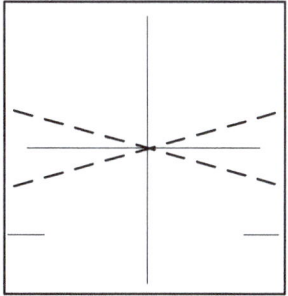

Fold and unfold along the creases

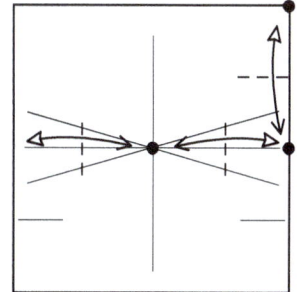

Fold to the center and unfold.

Hexagonal Dipyramid 93

7	8	9
		Fold and unfold.

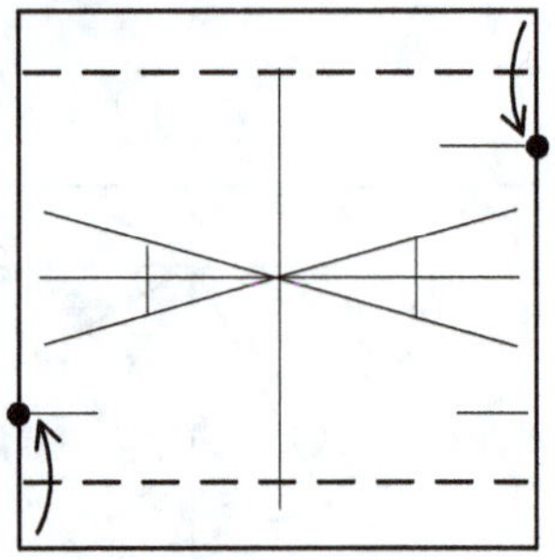

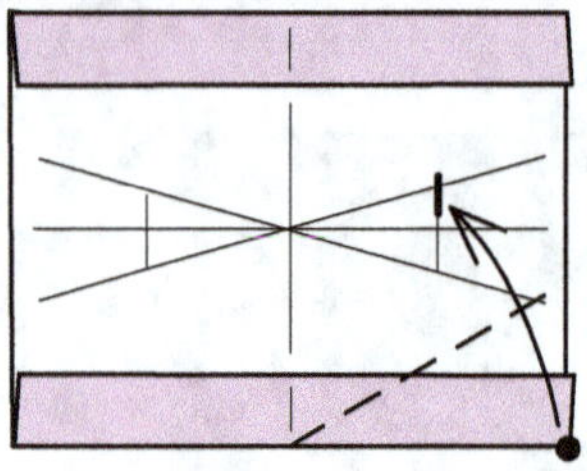

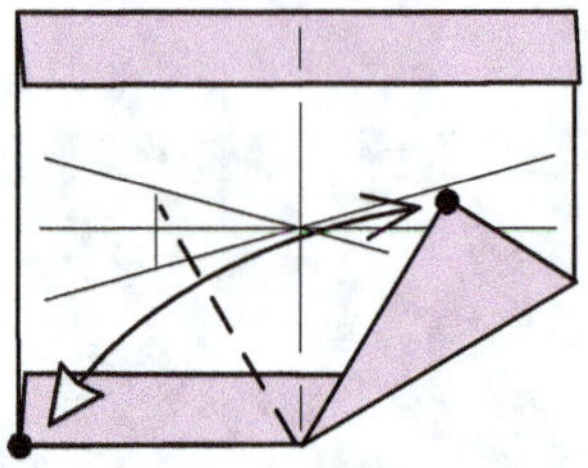

10	11	12
Unfold.	Repeat steps 8–10 on the three other corners.	Unfold.

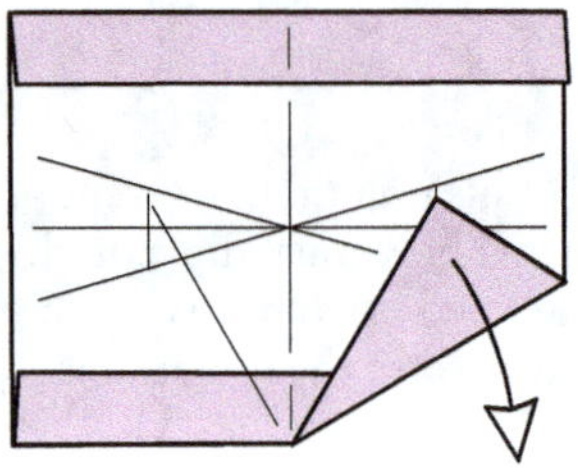

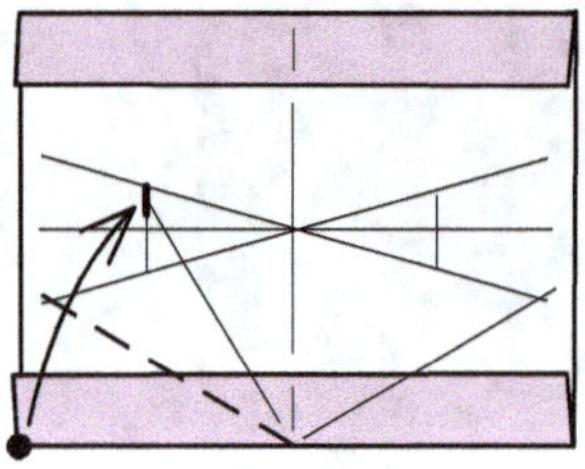

13	14	15
Fold along the crease.	Squash-fold.	Fold and unfold.

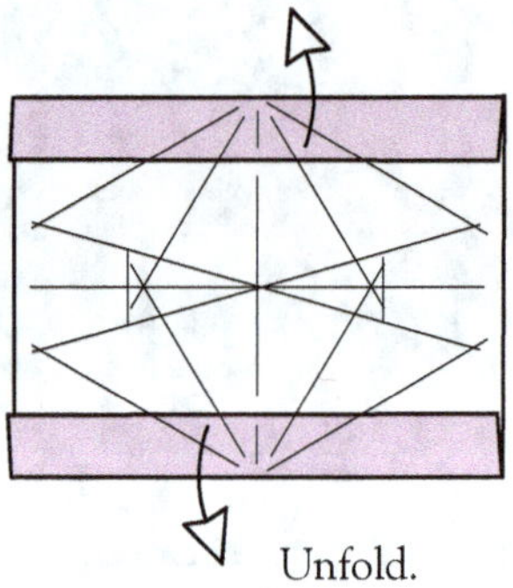

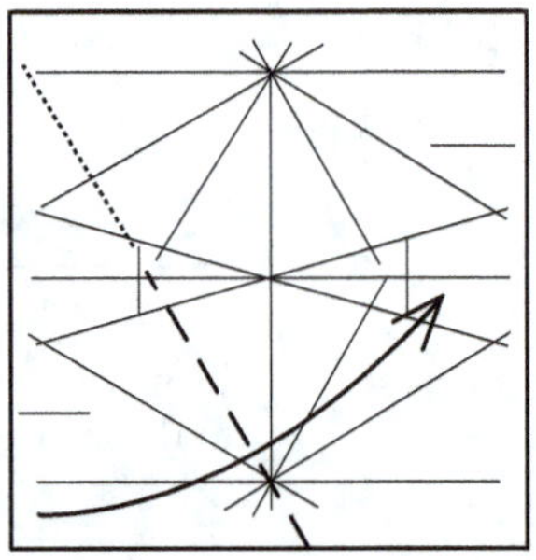

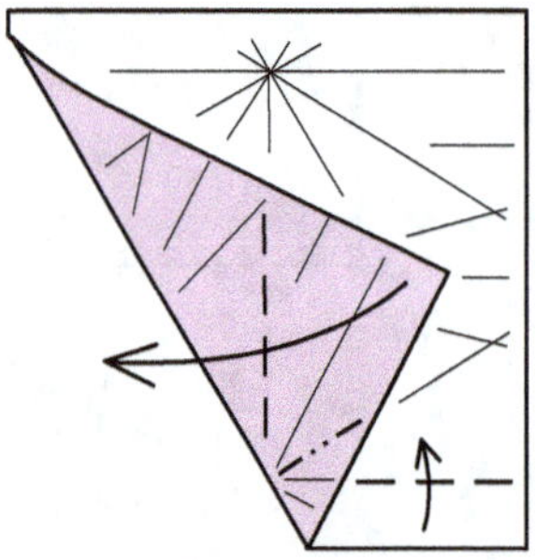

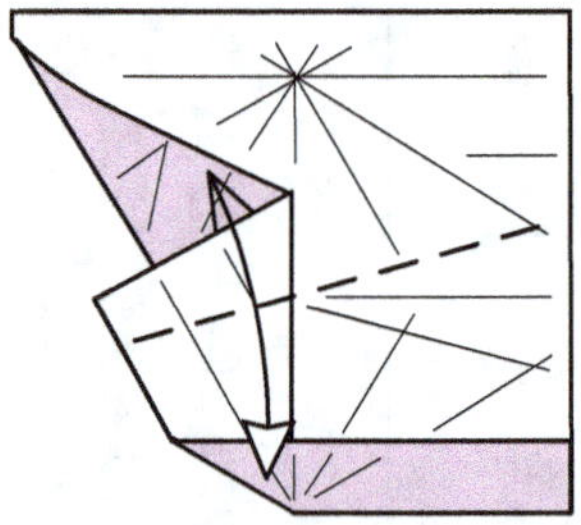

16	17	18
Unfold.	Repeat steps 13–16 on the three other corners.	Fold and unfold.

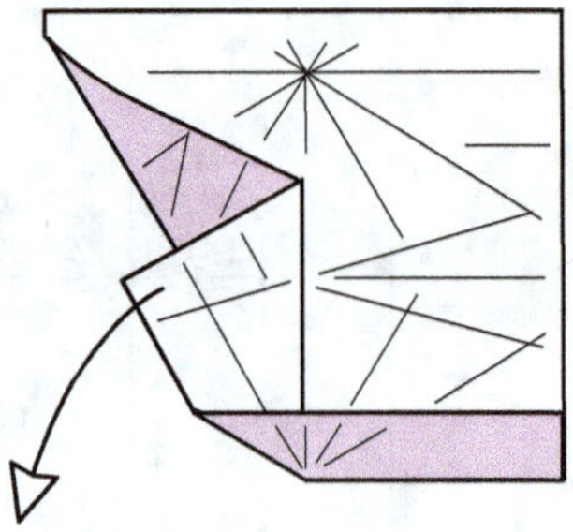

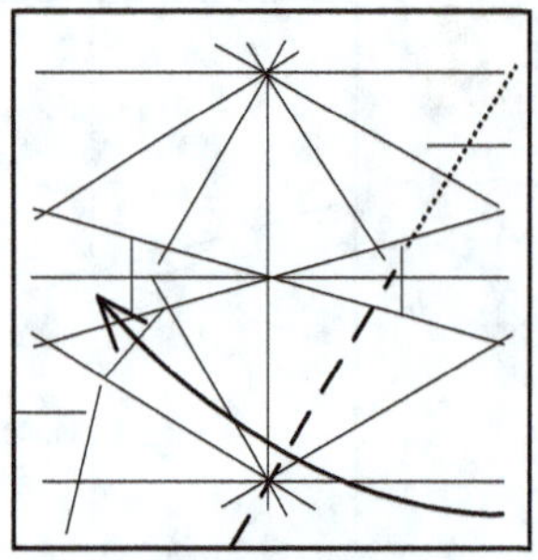

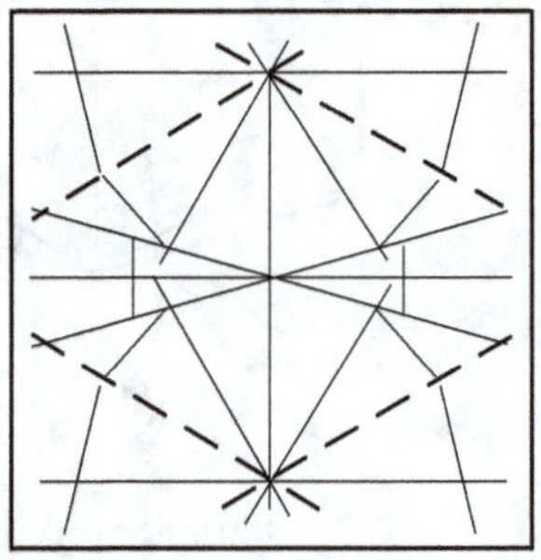

94 *Origami Symphony No. 12*

19

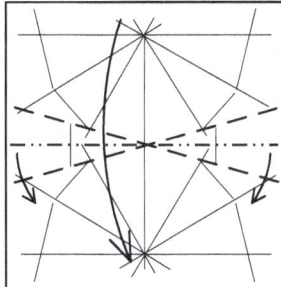

Fold along the creases.

 20

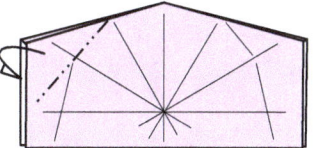

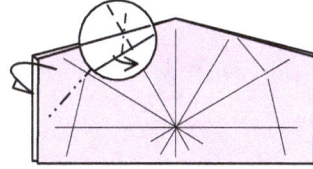

Inside view. Fold the inside layers together. Turn over and repeat.

21

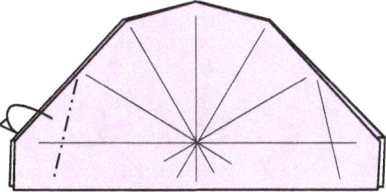

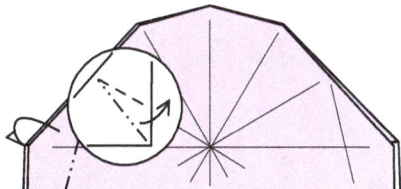

Inside view. Fold the inside layers together. Turn over and repeat.

22

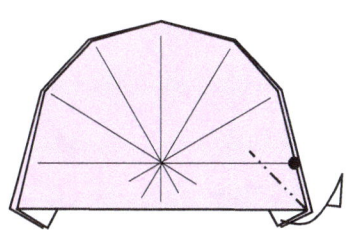

Fold the edge to the dot. Turn over and repeat.

23

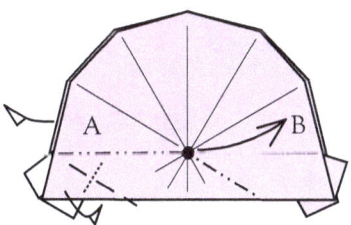

Lift up at the dot, reverse-fold on the left, and bring the dot to the right. Turn over and repeat.

24

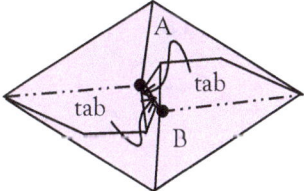

Tuck and interlock the tabs. The dots will meet.

25

Hexagonal Dipyramid

Hexagonal Dipyramid **95**

Fourth Movement

Allegro: Whimsical Gnomes are Everywhere

 Kindhearted and mischievous, there are several kinds of gnomes. Mountain gnomes live in caves deep in the mountains and hunt for treasures. Forest gnomes live in the woods, hiding under trees or beneath roots. Garden gnomes protect gardens. Tinker gnomes make all kinds of quirky machines that often don't work as intended. Everywhere there is a gnome, there is magic and adventures beyond imagination.

Quartz Pebblepocket

Quartz Pebblepocket carves safe stairways and tiny bridges for other gnomes. In his own cave, he shapes clear crystals into prisms and hangs them in the cave windows. When the sunlight filters in, the walls explode in rainbows.

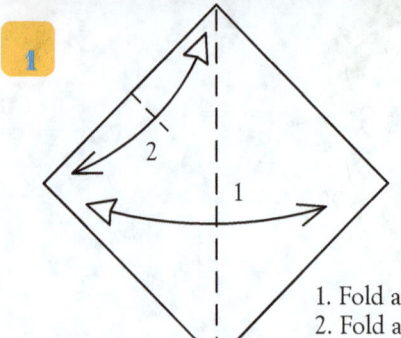

1. Fold and unfold.
2. Fold and unfold on the edge.

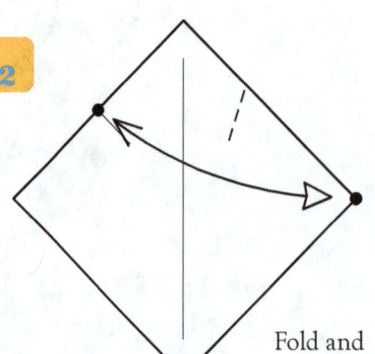

Fold and unfold.

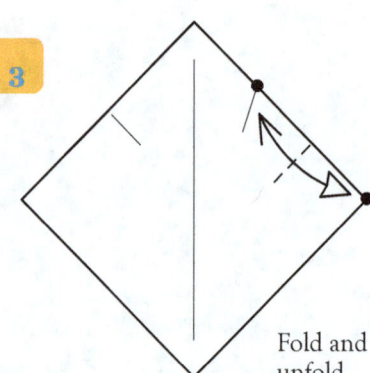

Fold and unfold.

96 Origami Symphony No. 12

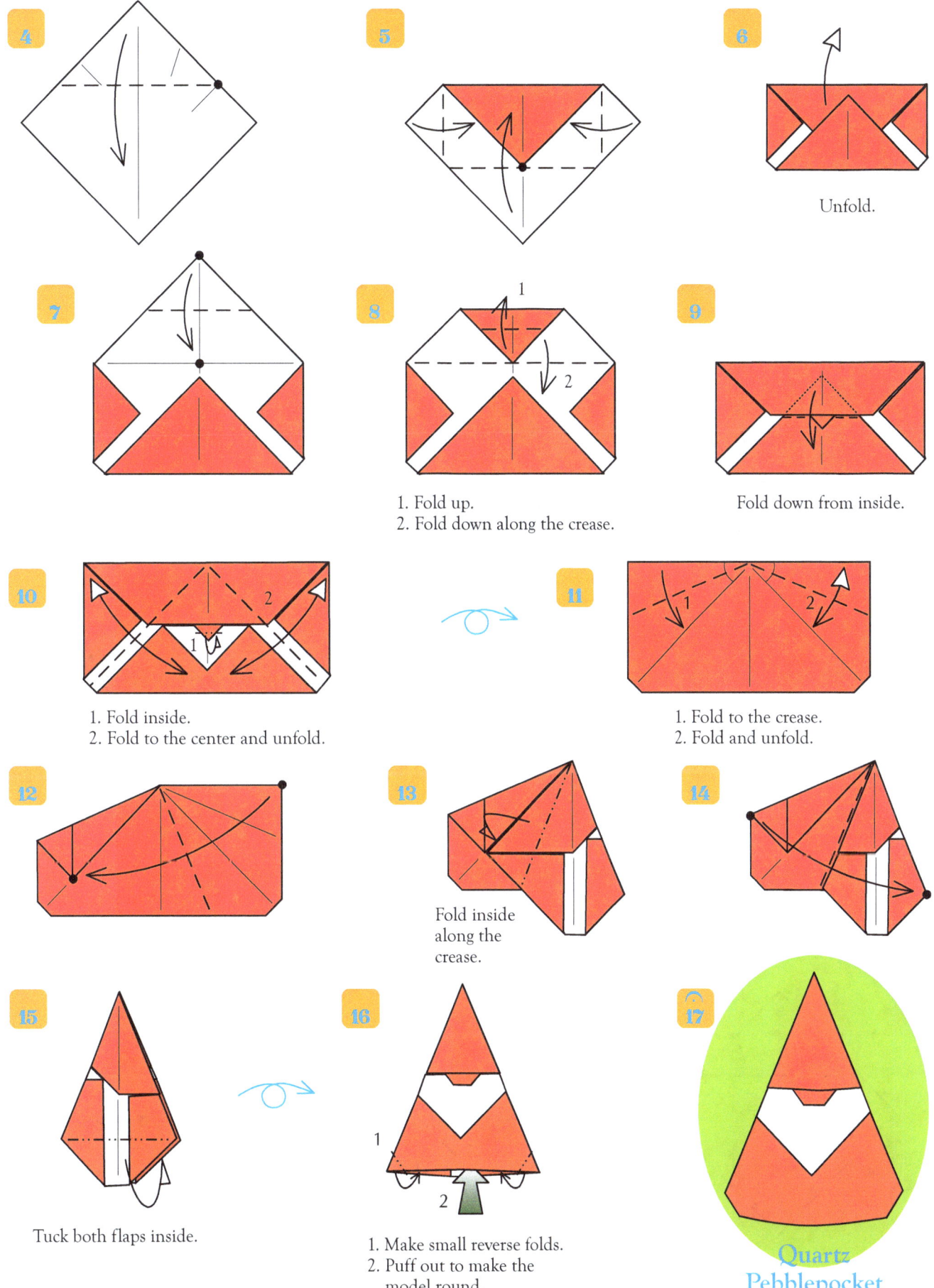

Unfold.

1. Fold up.
2. Fold down along the crease.

Fold down from inside.

1. Fold inside.
2. Fold to the center and unfold.

1. Fold to the crease.
2. Fold and unfold.

Fold inside along the crease.

Tuck both flaps inside.

1. Make small reverse folds.
2. Puff out to make the model round.

Quartz Pebblepocket

Quartz Pebblepocket **97**

Flint Coppercap

Flint Coppercap creates faceted stones that sparkle like starlight. He places these in tunnels to ensure safe travels for the other gnomes. From leftover crystal, he carves tiny stone owls to watch over his treasure box.

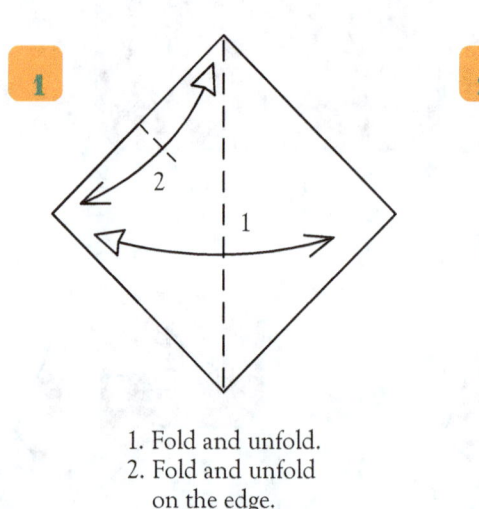

1. Fold and unfold.
2. Fold and unfold on the edge.

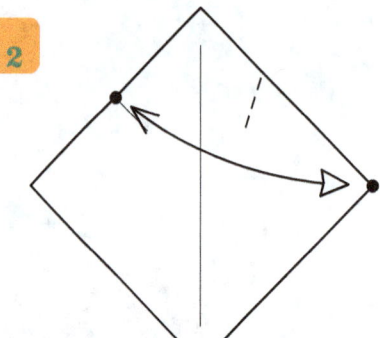

Fold and unfold.

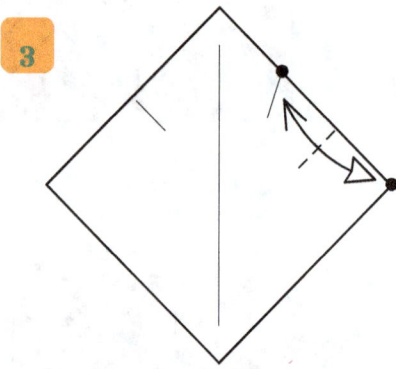

Fold and unfold.

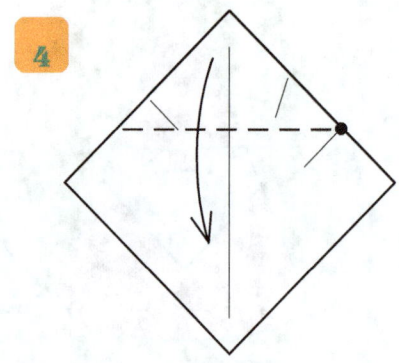

Fold and unfold.

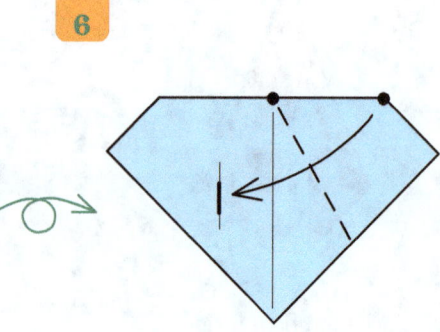

Bring the dot on the right to the crease.

98 Origami Symphony No. 12

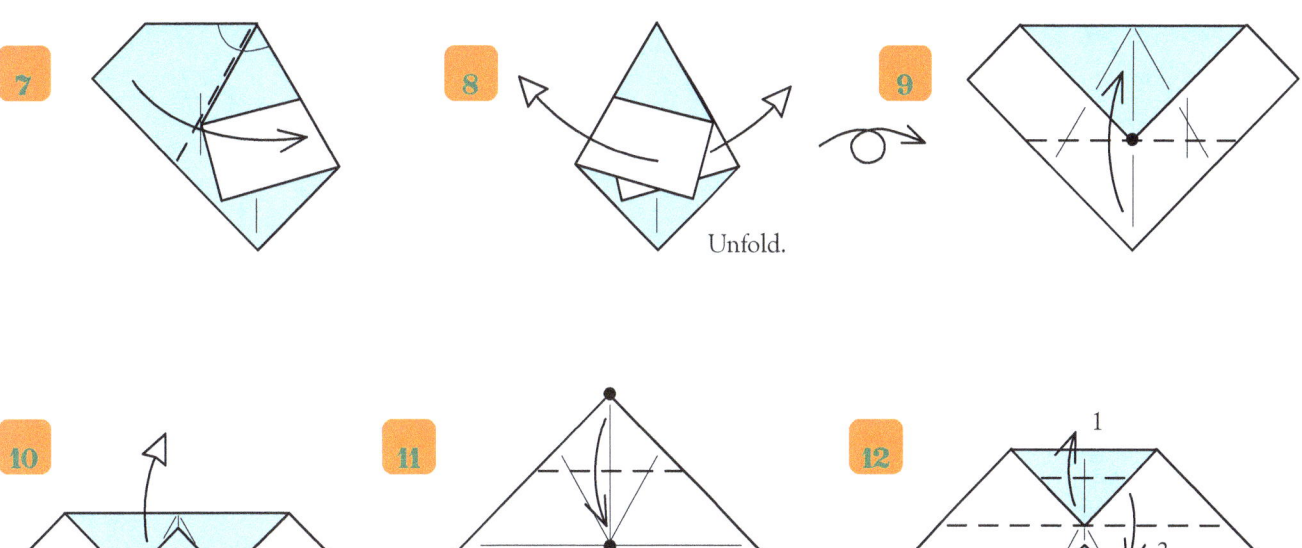

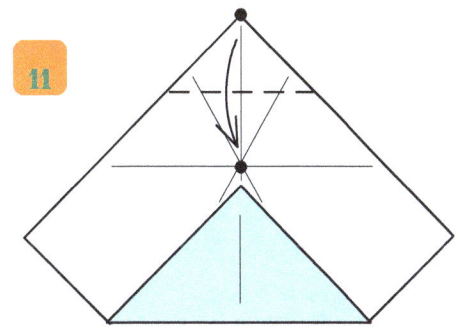

Unfold.

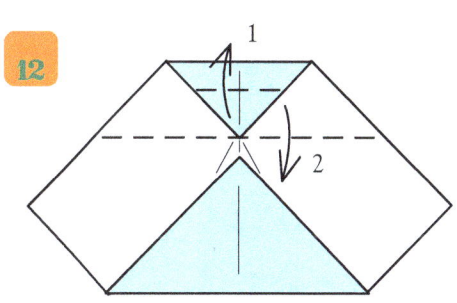

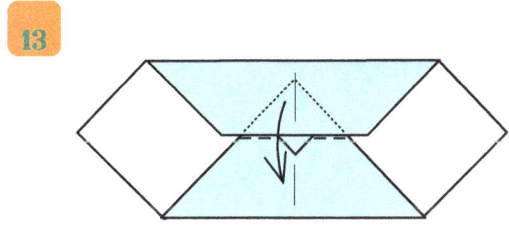

Unfold.

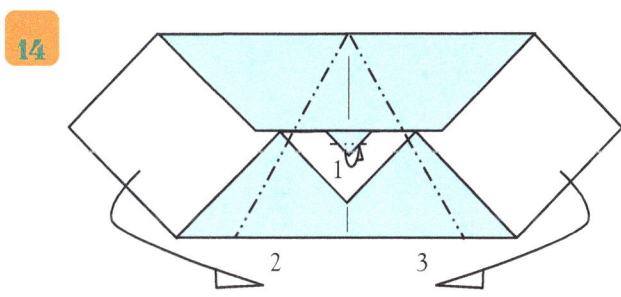

1. Fold up.
2. Fold down along the crease.

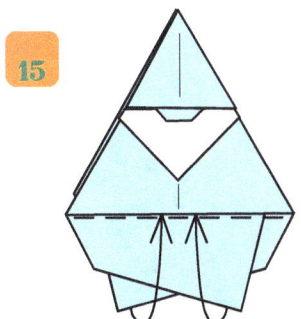

Fold down from inside.

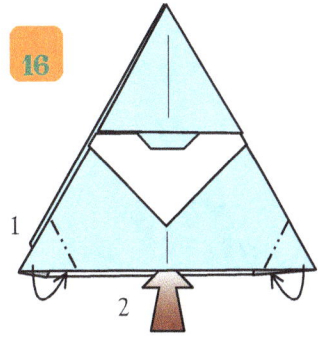

1. Fold inside.
2 and 3. Fold along the creases.

Tuck both flaps inside.

1. Make small reverse folds.
2. Puff out to make the model round.

Flint Coppercap

Snapdragon Honeywhisk

Snapdragon Honeywhisk is a garden gnome who chats with ladybugs, teaches beetles to line up in neat rows, and makes sure the snails don't nibble too much lettuce. He paints bright colors onto dull blooms to cheer them up.

1. Fold and unfold.

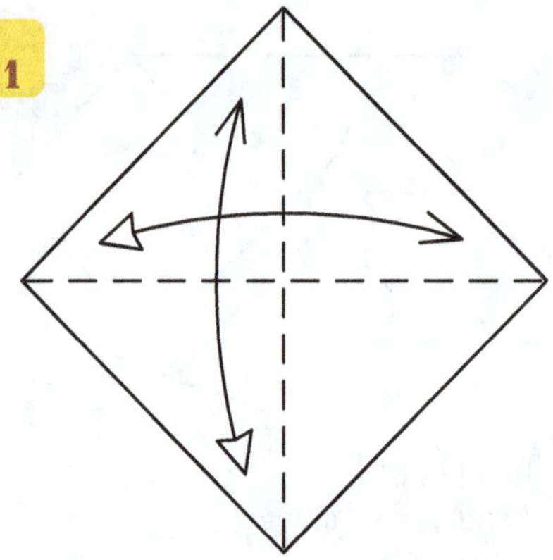

2. Fold to the center.

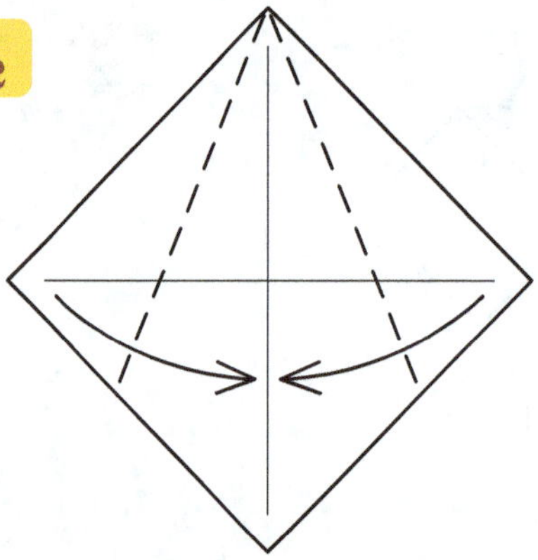

3. 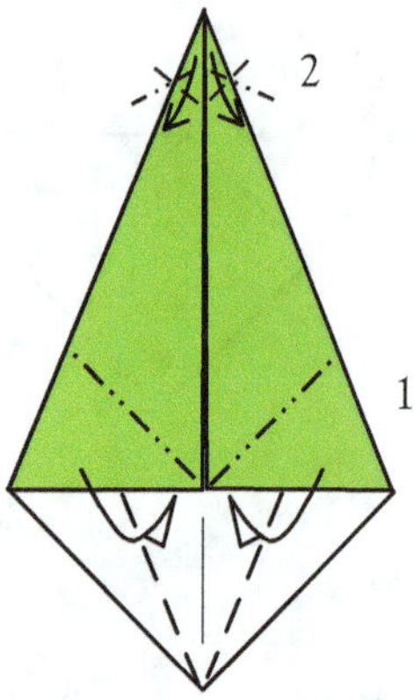
   1. Fold inside.
   2. Spread.

4. Fold behind.

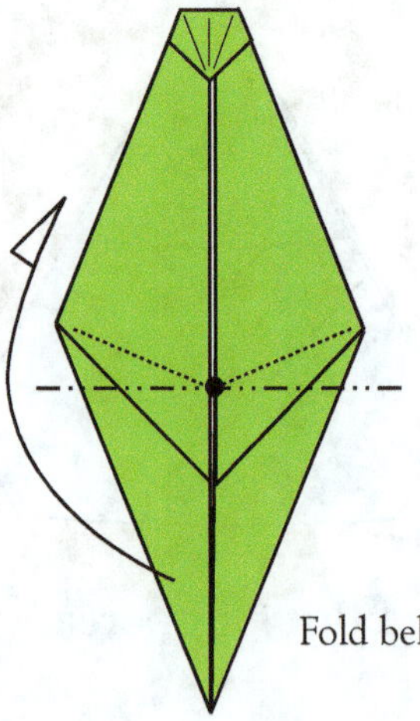

5.

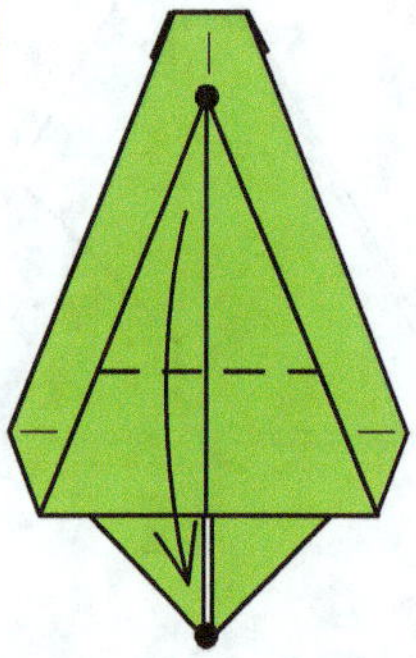

6. 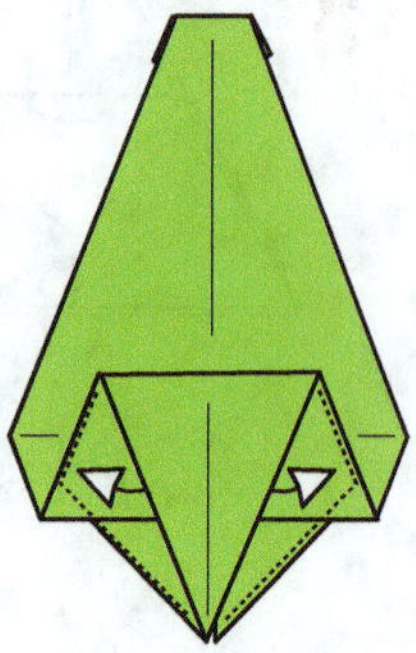 Pull out to the dotted lines.

100 Origami Symphony No. 12

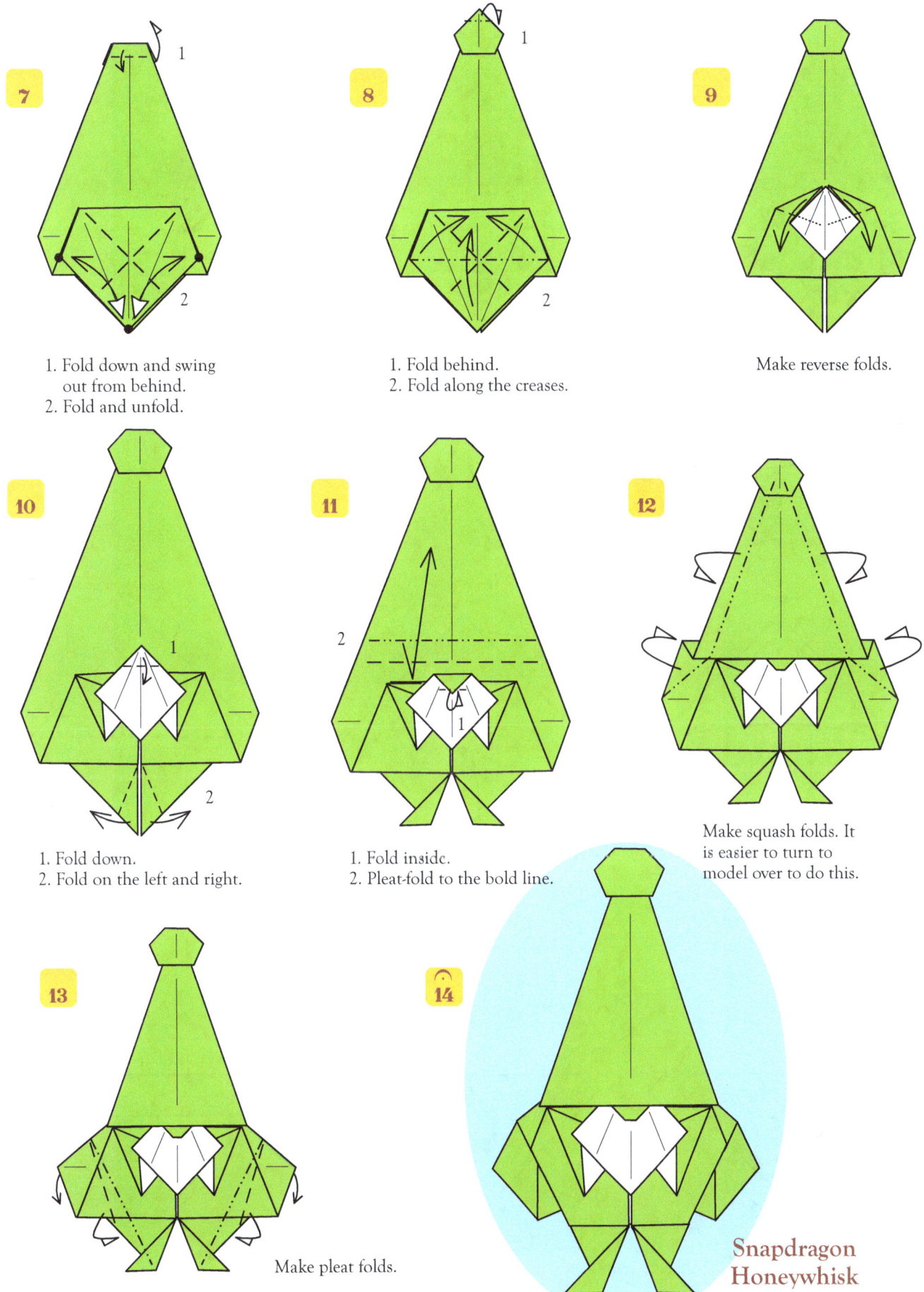

7.
1. Fold down and swing out from behind.
2. Fold and unfold.

8.
1. Fold behind.
2. Fold along the creases.

9. Make reverse folds.

10.
1. Fold down.
2. Fold on the left and right.

11.
1. Fold inside.
2. Pleat-fold to the bold line.

12. Make squash folds. It is easier to turn to model over to do this.

13. Make pleat folds.

14.

Snapdragon Honeywhisk

Snapdragon Honeywhisk **101**

Glimmer TinkerBlinker

Glimmer TinkerBlinker created a self opening umbrella that fits snuggly on his hat. When it rains it pops open and starts singing out of key. His motto is: always have a second plan, and hide it in your hat.

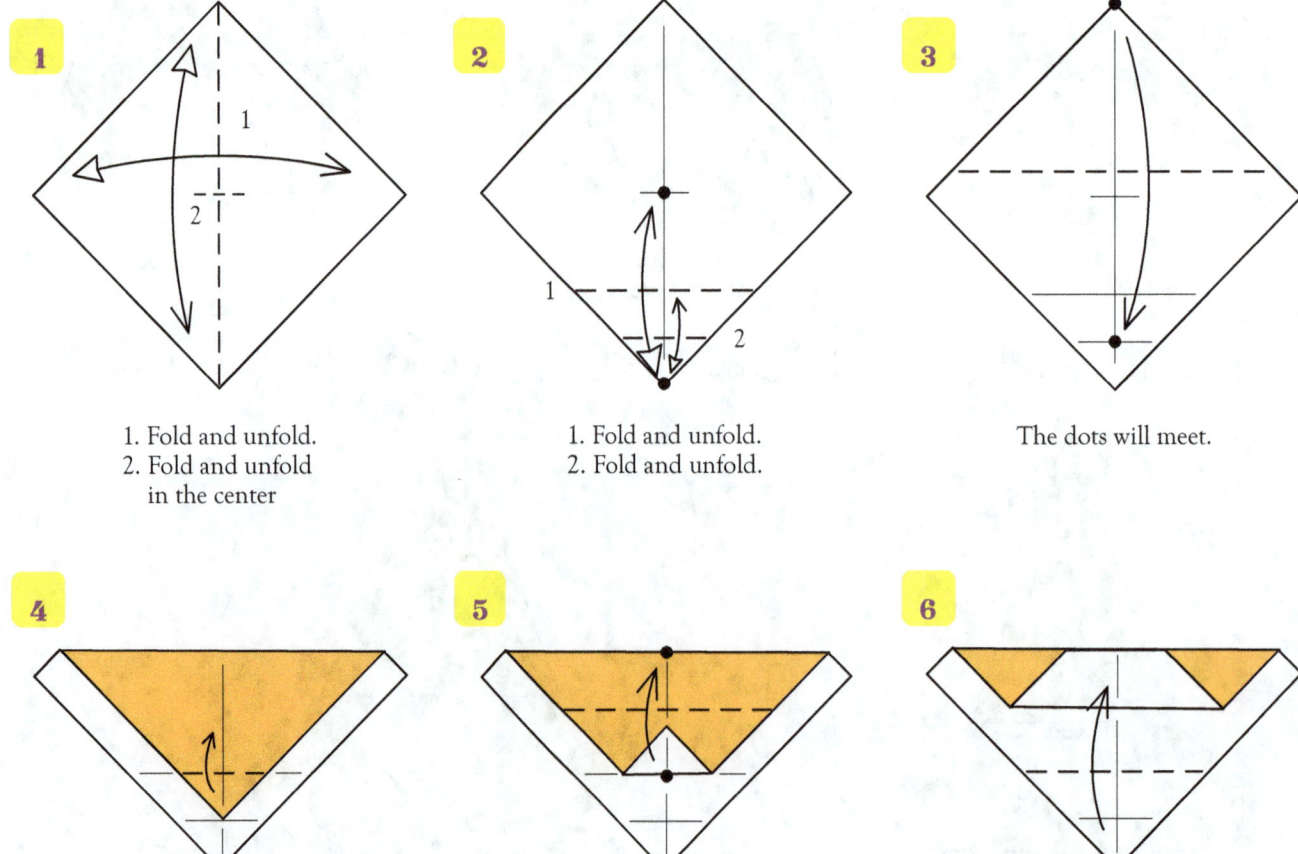

1.
1. Fold and unfold.
2. Fold and unfold in the center

2.
1. Fold and unfold.
2. Fold and unfold.

3. The dots will meet.

4. Fold up along the hidden crease.

6. Fold along the crease.

102 *Origami Symphony No. 12*

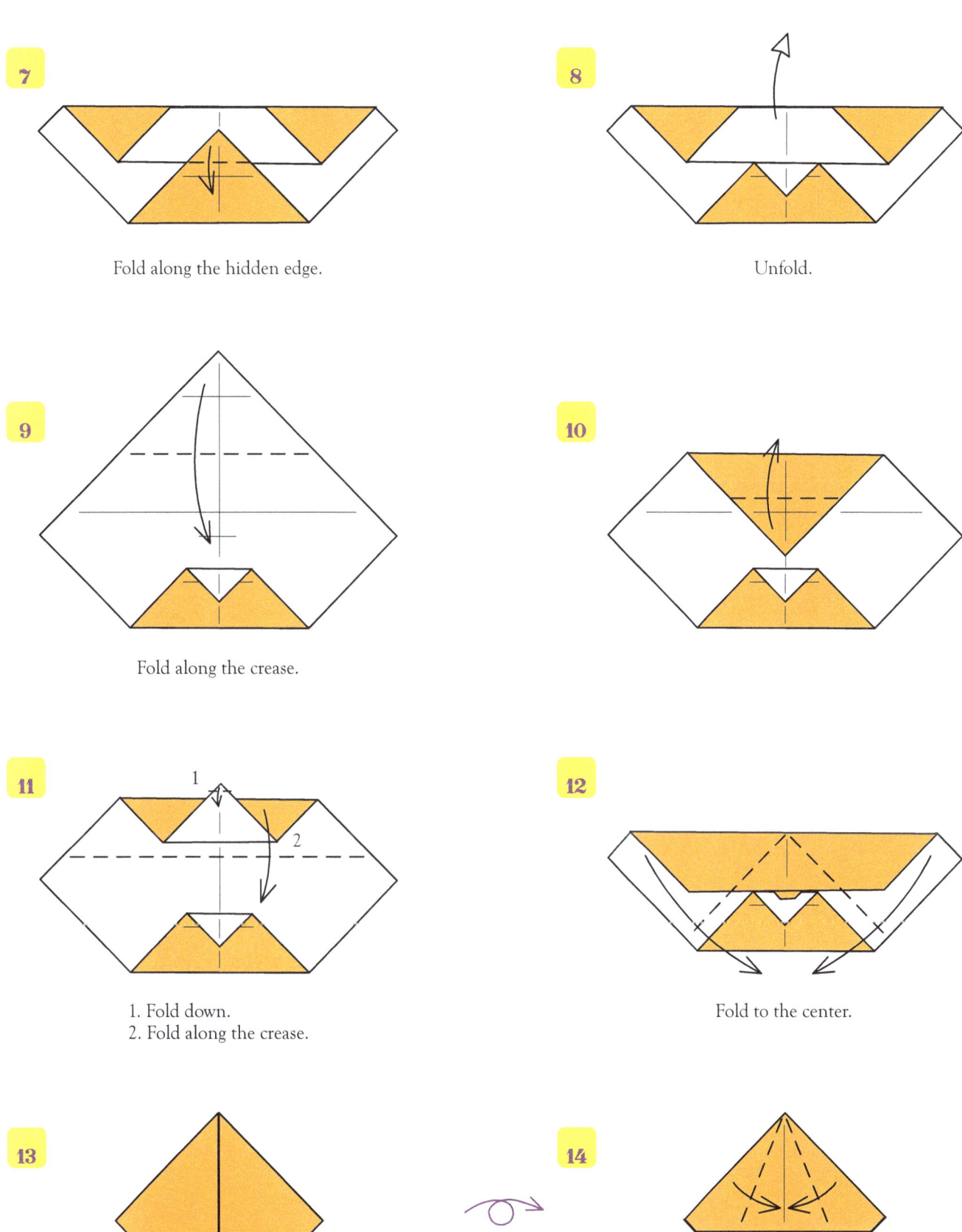

15 Unfold.

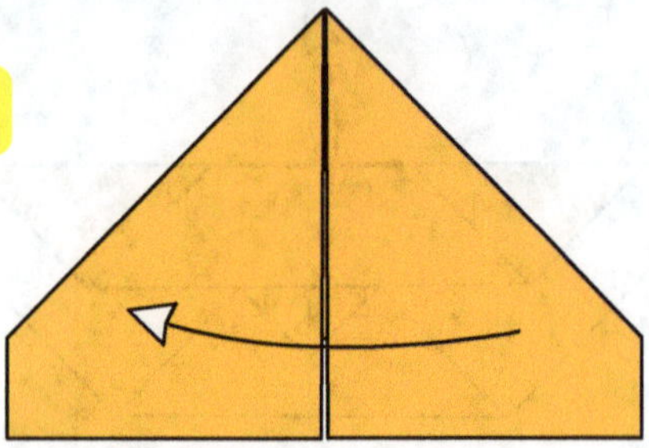

16 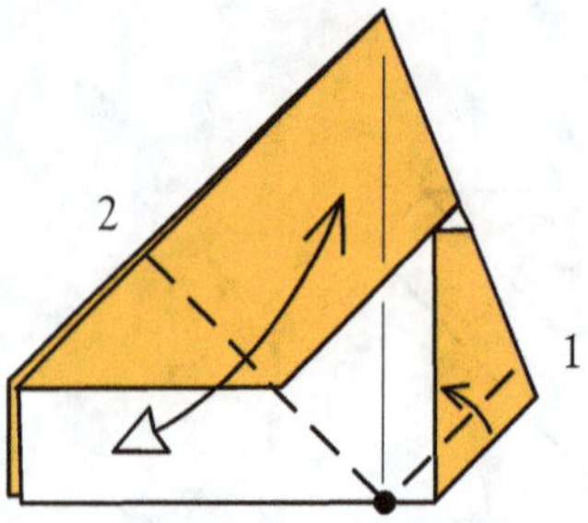
1. Fold a thin strip.
2. Fold and unfold.

17

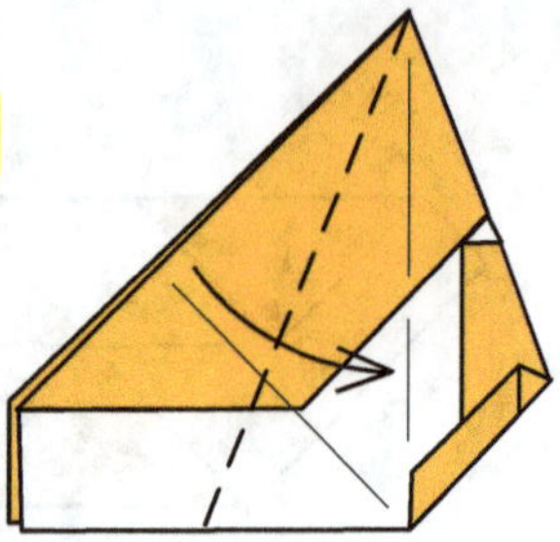

18  Squash-fold.

19

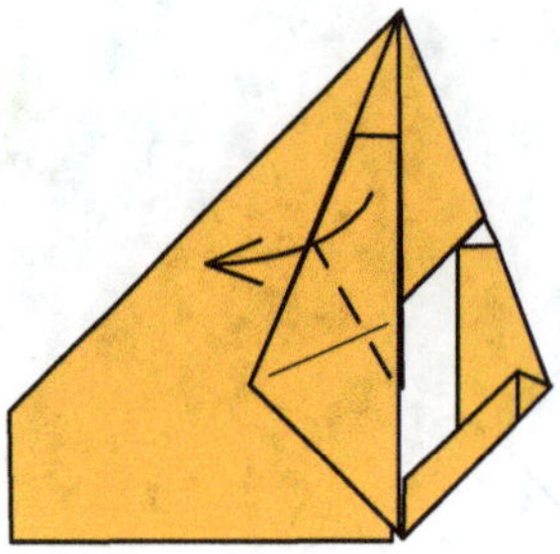

20

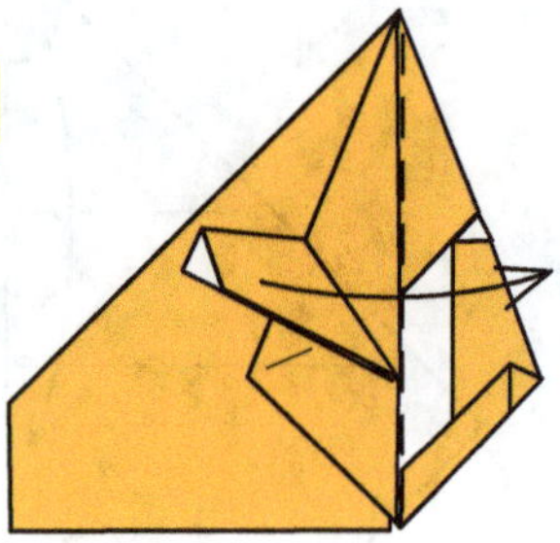

21 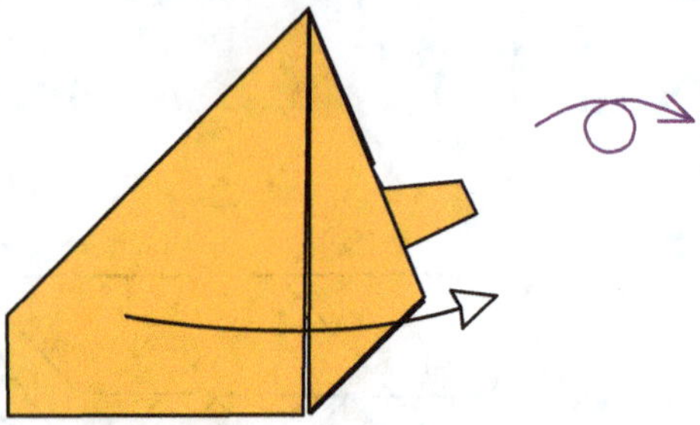 Repeat steps 15–20 in the opposite direction.

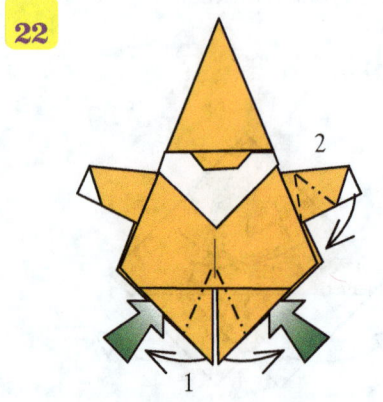

22
1. Make reverse folds.
2. Pleat-fold.

23

Glimmer TinkerBlinker

104 *Origami Symphony No. 12*

CoggleJam TinkerBlinker

CoggleJam TinkerBlinker built a breakfast machine complete with gears, fire explosions, and whirling buckets. When the machine splattered milk everywhere, he cried over spilt milk. Luckily, the machine broke after that, or he would have been scrambled, fried, and slightly roasted. Gnomes are all about making mistakes. They just hope to be around to make another one.

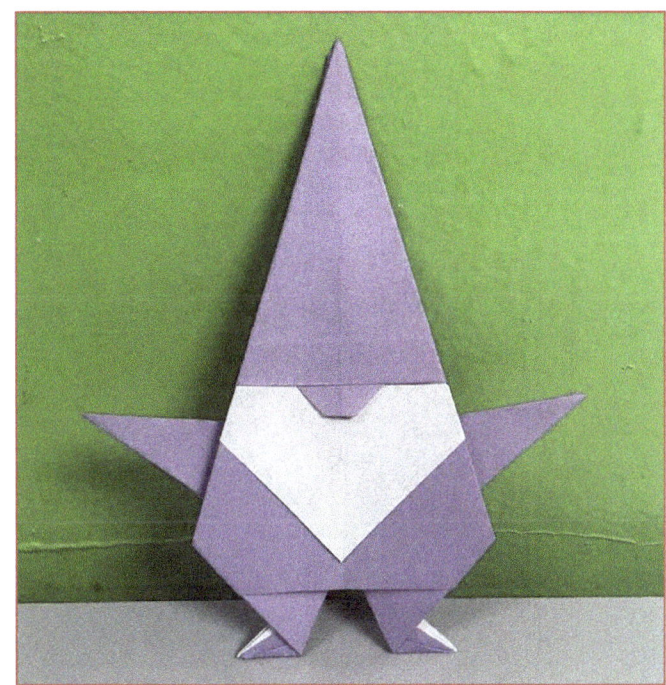

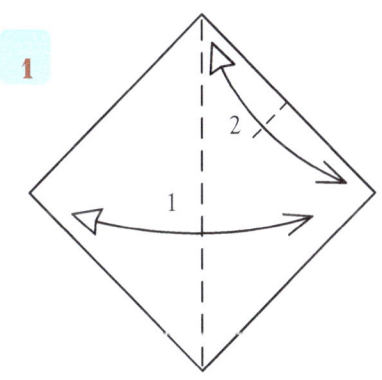

1. Fold and unfold.
2. Fold and unfold on the edge.

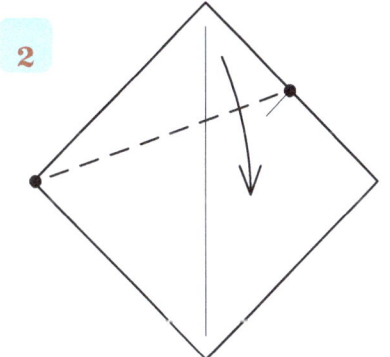

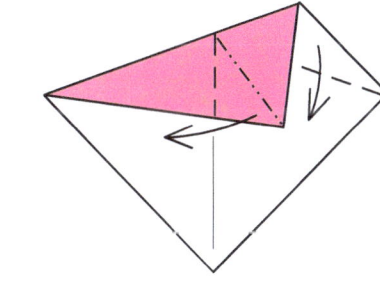

Squash-fold.

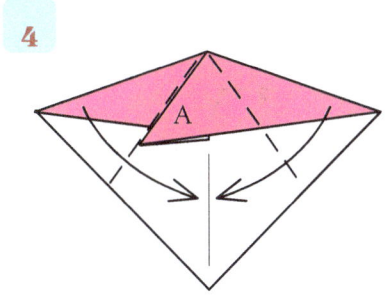

Keep flap A on top while folding to the center.

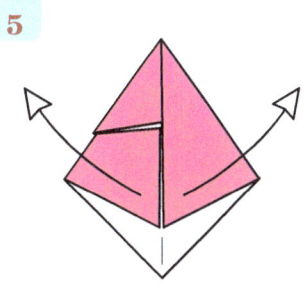

Unfold.

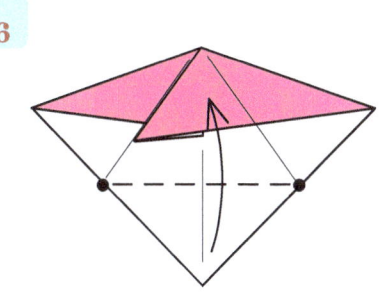

CoggleJam TinkerBlinker **105**

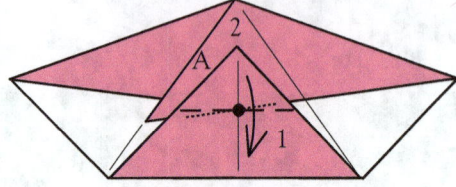

1. Fold down along a hidden line.
2. Bring flap A to the front.

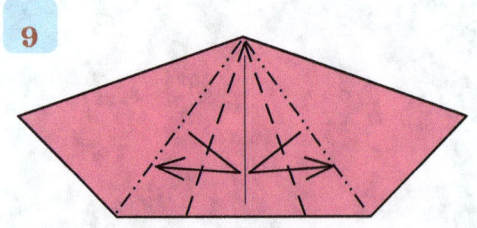

Pleat-fold to the center. Do not fold the hidden flap, shown as A in step 7.

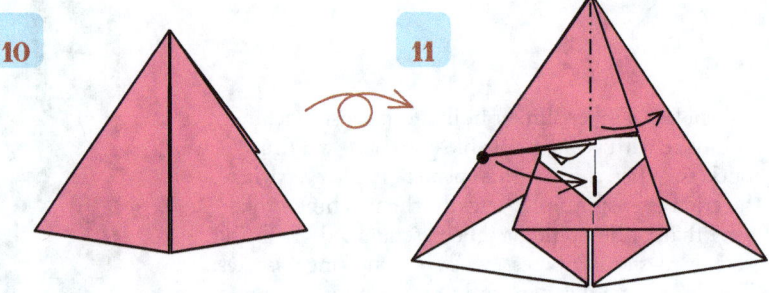

Spread and squash fold.

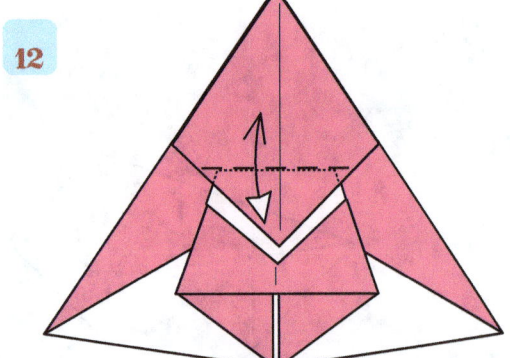

Fold and unfold along the hidden edge.

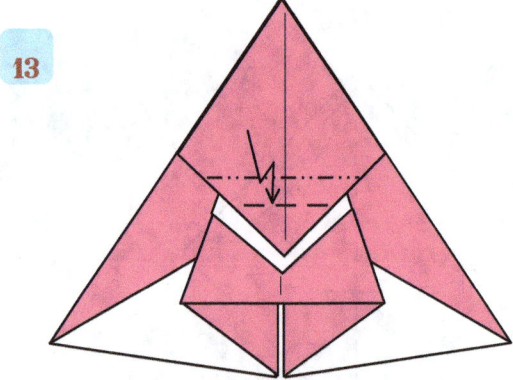

Mountain-fold along the crease for this pleat fold.

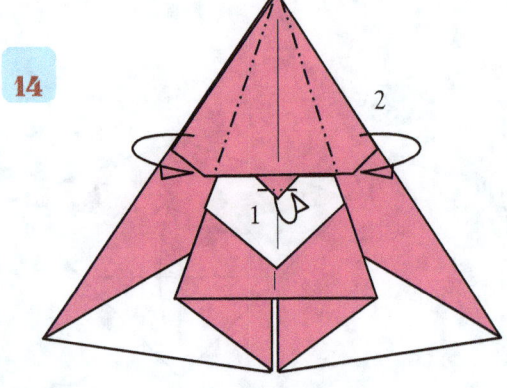

1. Fold inside.
2. Fold inside.

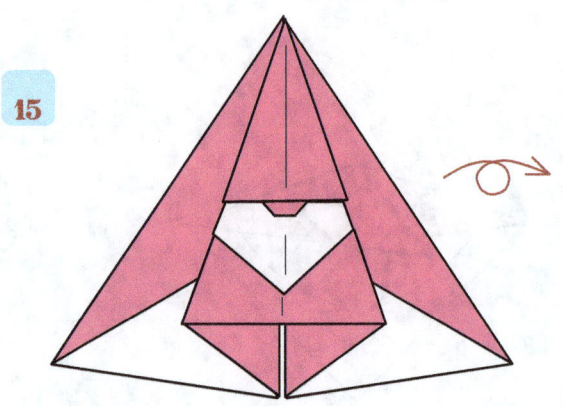

106 Origami Symphony No. 12

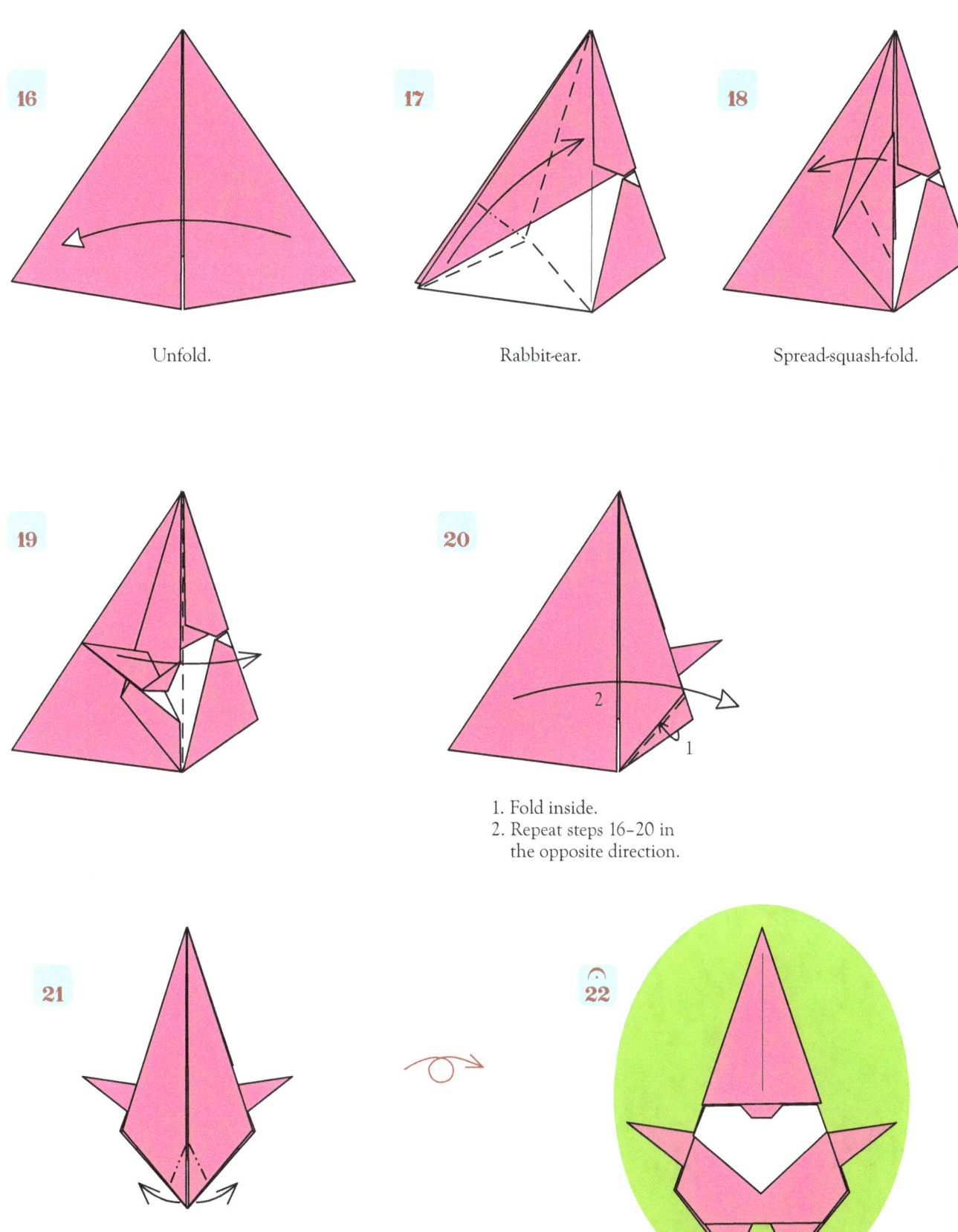

CoggleJam TinkerBlinker

Bramblethorn Whistlewind

Bramblethorn Whistlewind teaches the frogs how to hop across his mushroom patch, creating different musical notes on each mushroom. He has composed symphonic music if the frogs hop on the right mushrooms at the right time. For the past 400 years, Bramblethorn Whistlewind has been trying, perhaps next year the frogs will create his beautiful forest music.

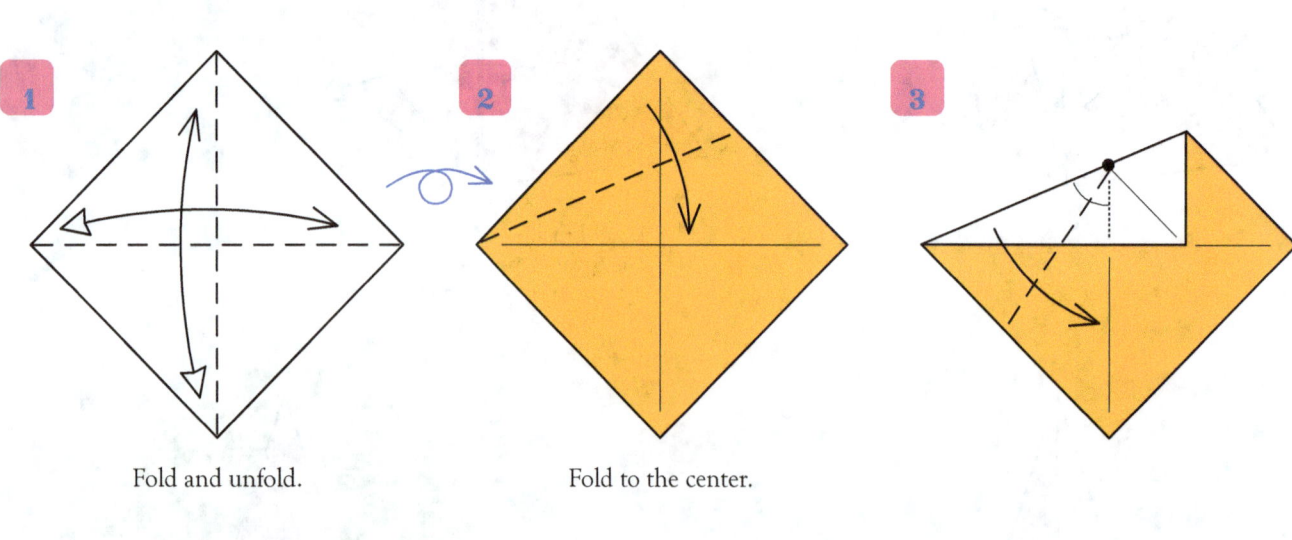

1. Fold and unfold.
2. Fold to the center.
3.

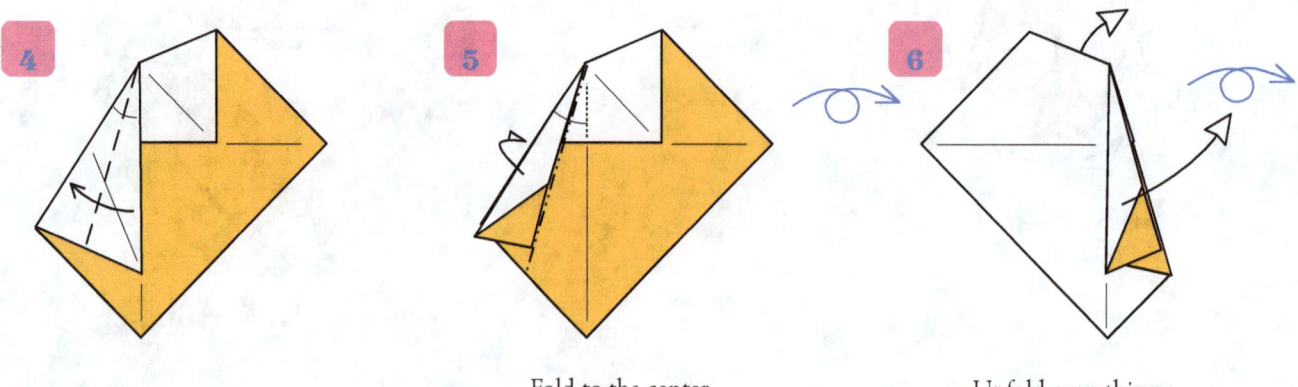

4.
5. Fold to the center.
6. Unfold everything.

108 *Origami Symphony No. 12*

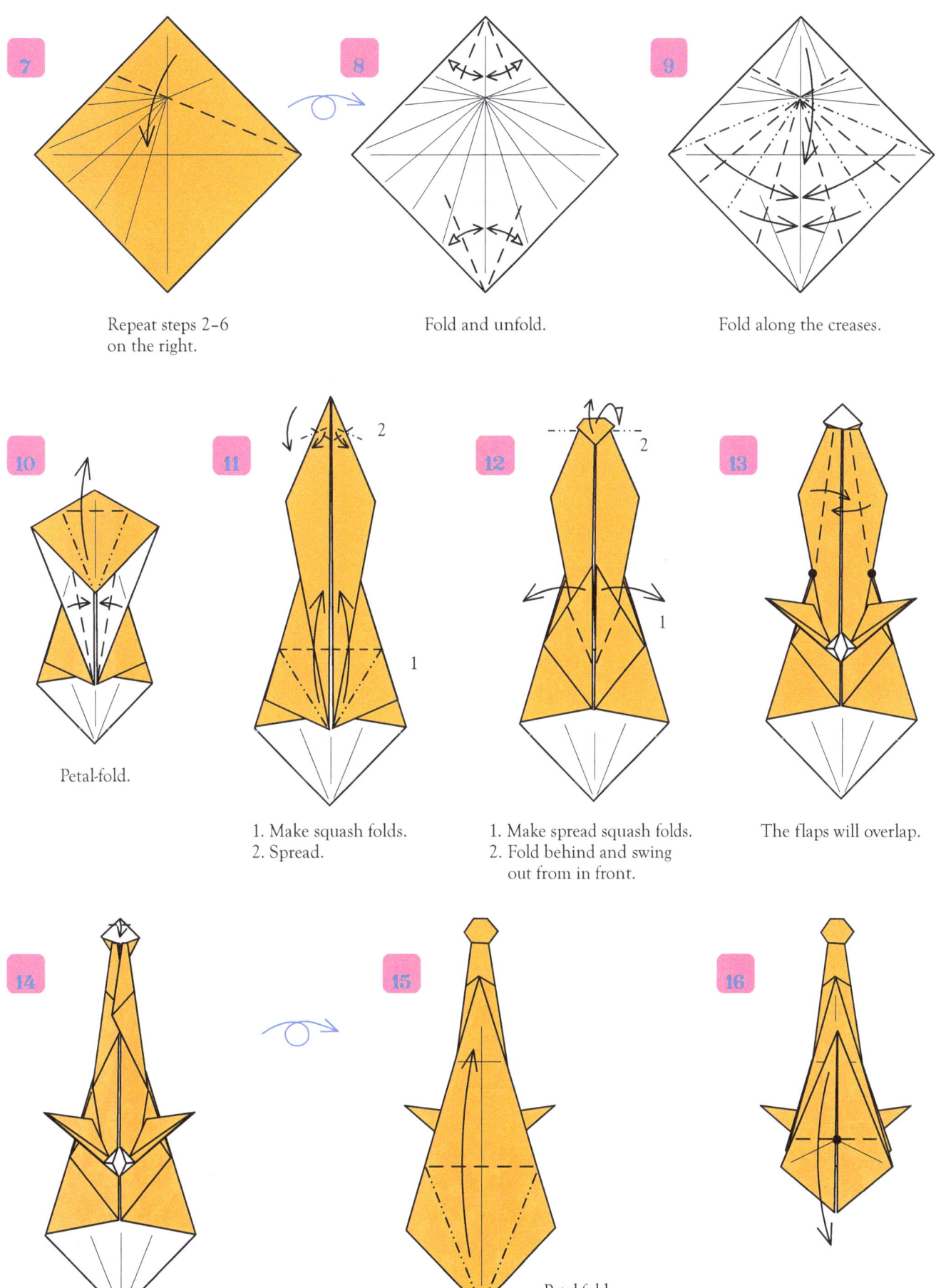

Bramblethorn Whistlewind

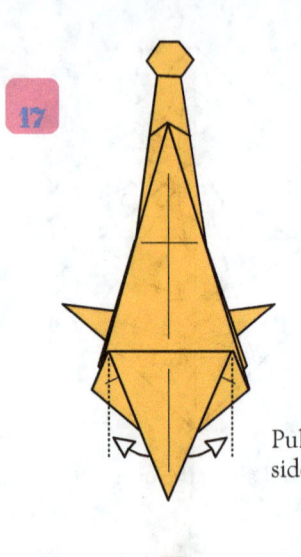

Pull out so the sides are vertical.

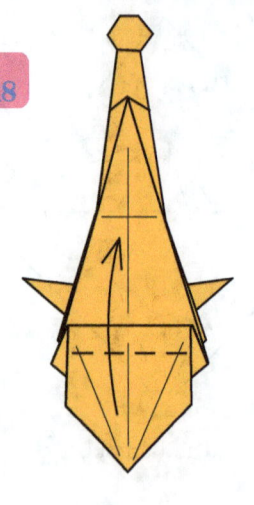

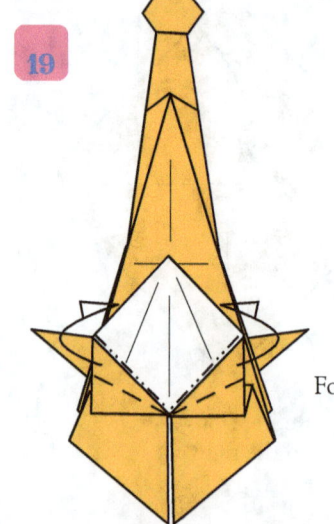

Fold inside.

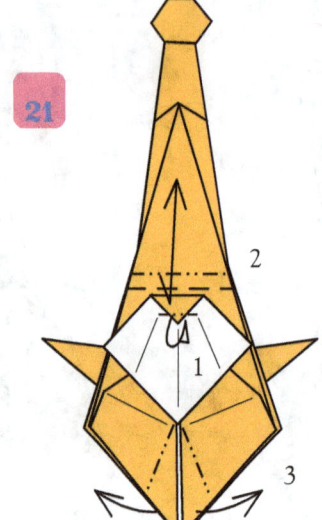

1. Fold down.
2. Fold inside along the hidden edges.

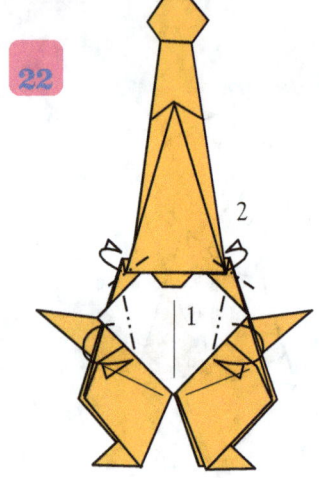

1. Fold inside.
2. Pleat-fold to cover the top of the nose. Mountain-fold along the crease.
3. Make reverse folds.

1. Fold inside.
2. Fold behind.

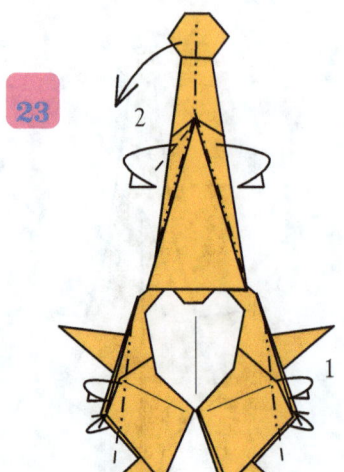

1. Fold inside on the front and back.
2. Rabbit-ear.

Squash-fold.

Bramblethorn Whistlewind

110 *Origami Symphony No. 12*

Crimble Bumbleknack

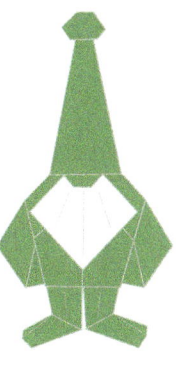

Crimble Bumbleknack tends to the forest bees that make golden honey. When the bees gift him some honey, he spreads in on his favorite oak leaves, for an afternoon snack. He likes telling mindless stories to the daisies because they listen with open petals. In return, he enjoys animal stories since they all have a tail to spin.

1. Fold and unfold.

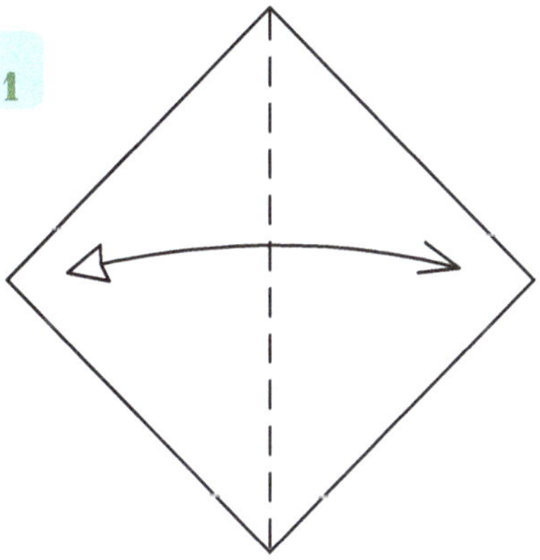

2. Fold to the center and unfold.

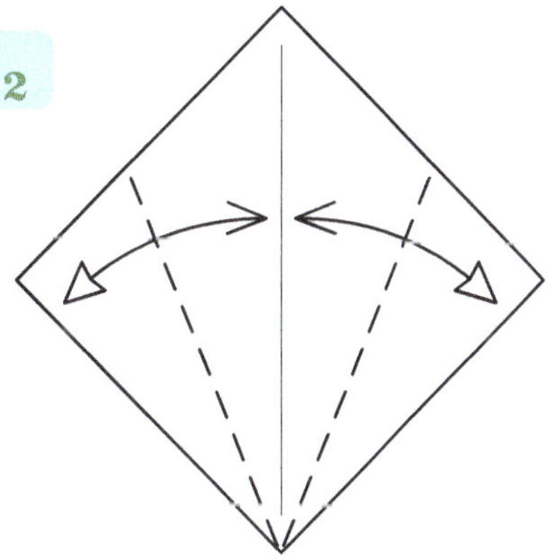

3. Fold and unfold.

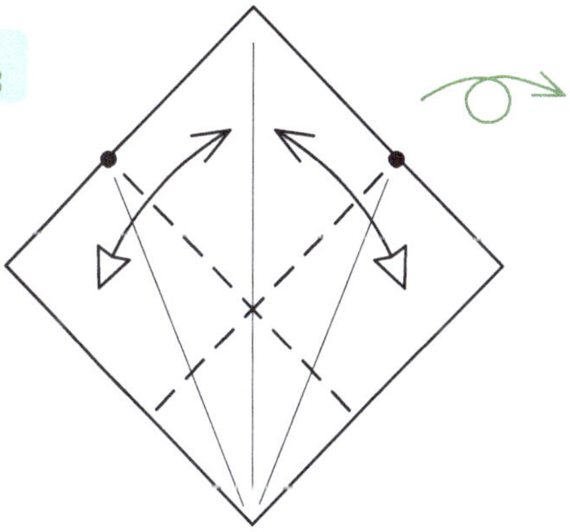

4. Fold and unfold at 1 and 2. Rotate 180°.

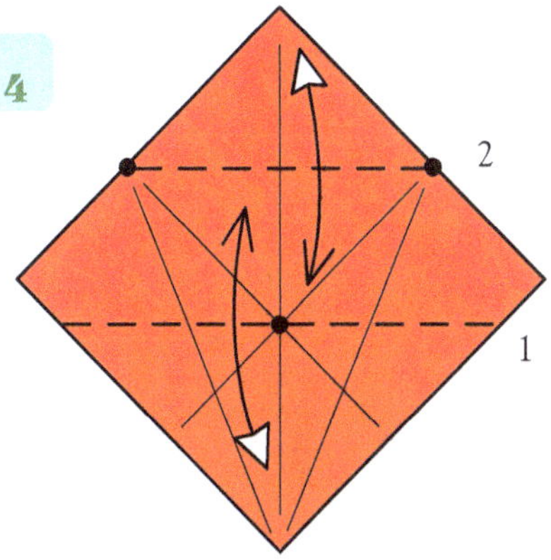

5. Fold along the creases.

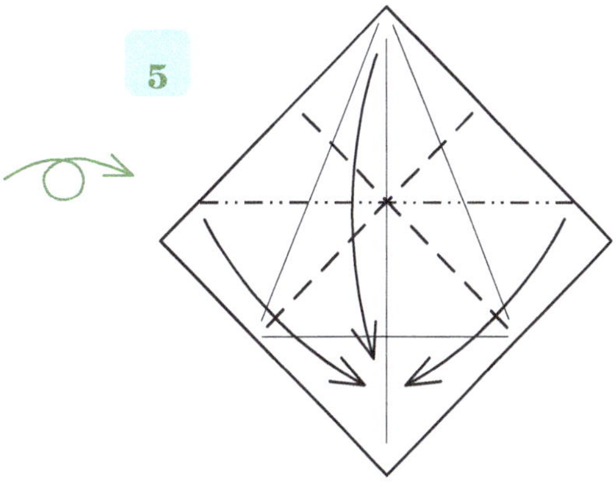

6. Petal-fold.

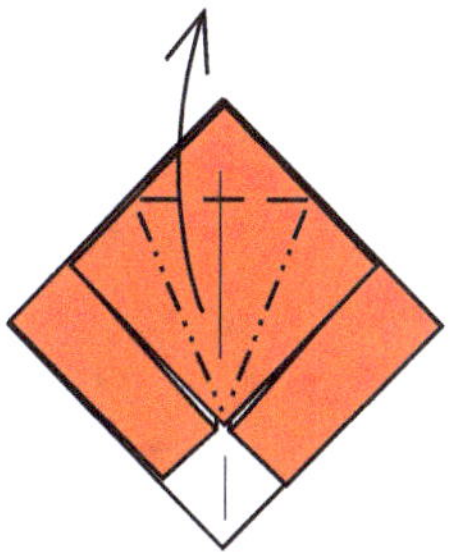

Crimble Bumbleknack 111

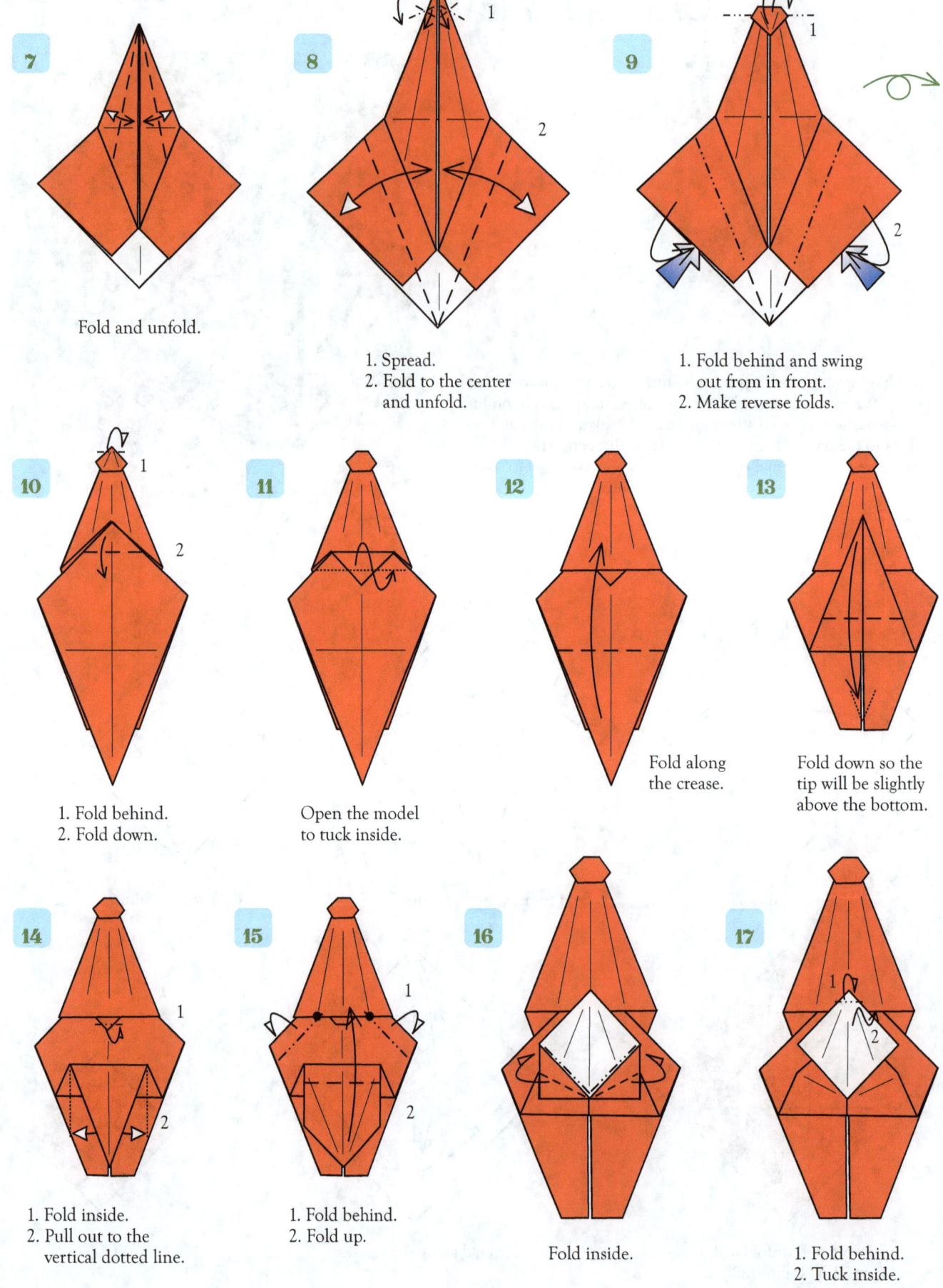

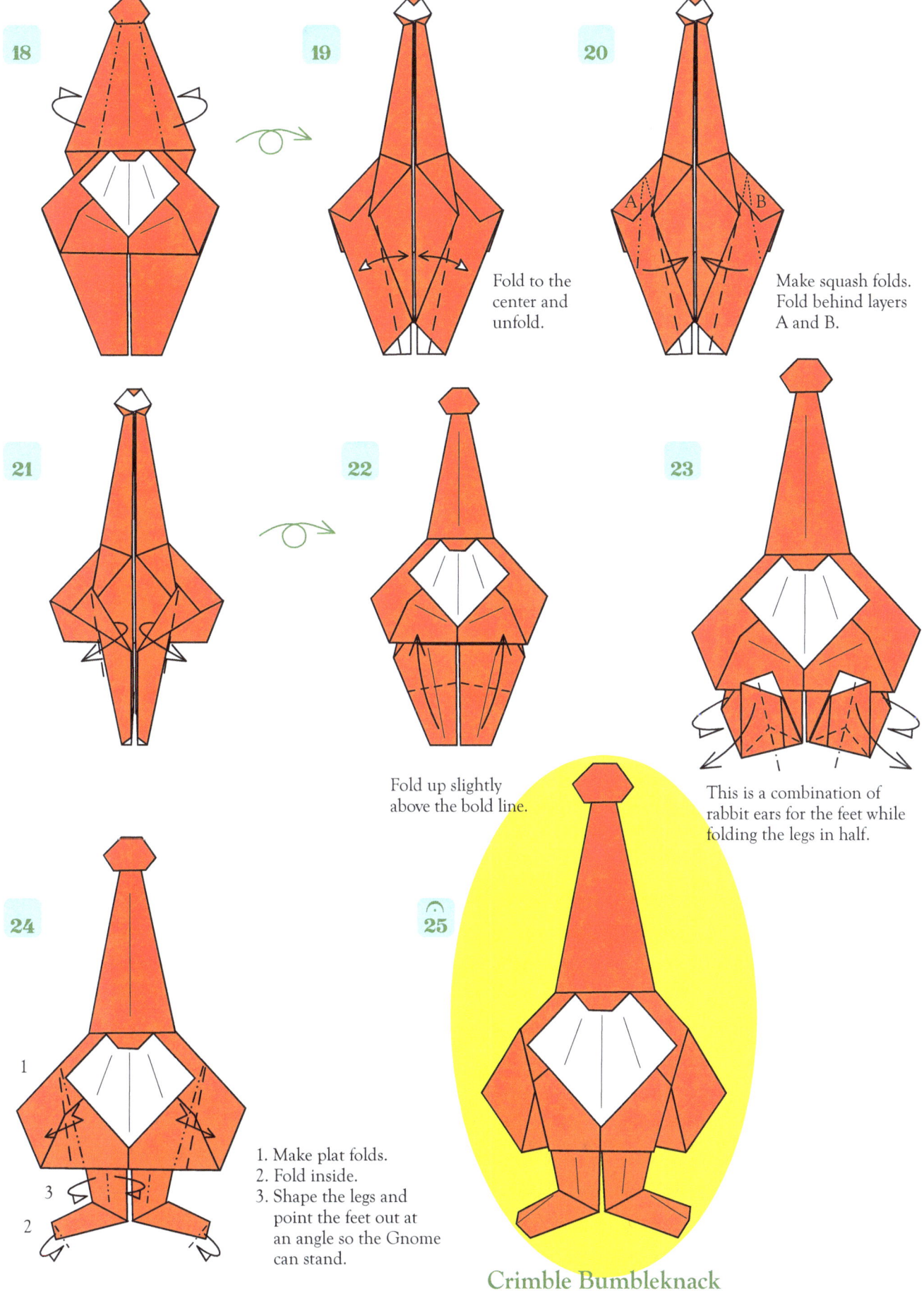

Cloverleaf Sparklebranch

Cloverleaf Sparklebranch makes snacks of dried berries and moss-covered nuts and hides them under roots so hungry animals find treats on cold nights. Every morning he scares the darkness away and wakes up the roosters, inviting them to sing their cheerful good-morning song.

1. Fold and unfold.

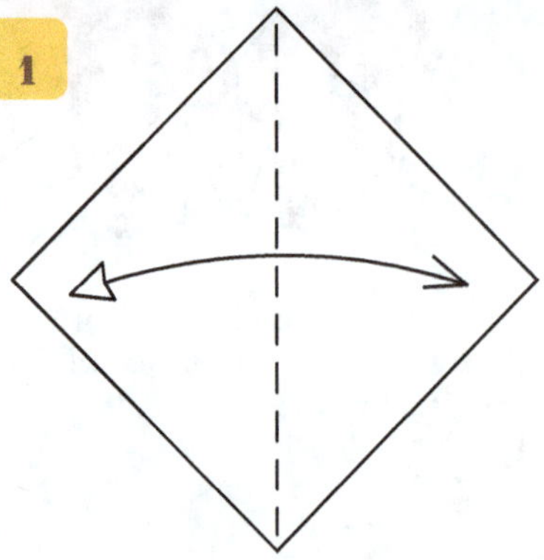

2. Fold and unfold on the edge.

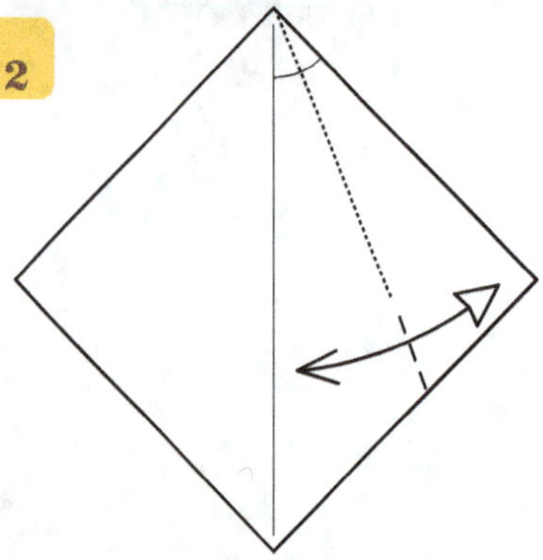

3. Fold and unfold on the edge.

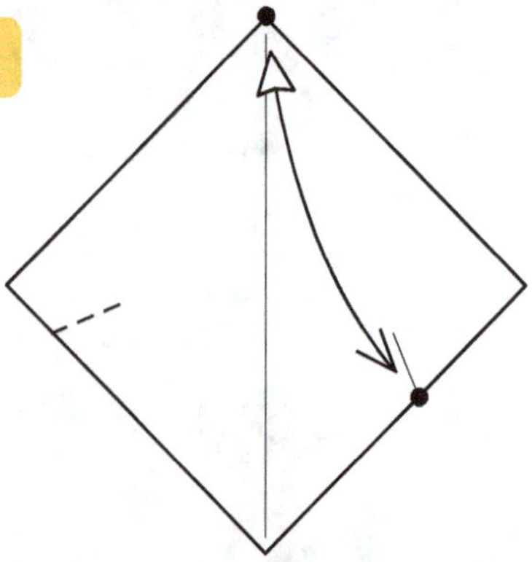

4. Fold and unfold on the diagonal. Rotate 180°.

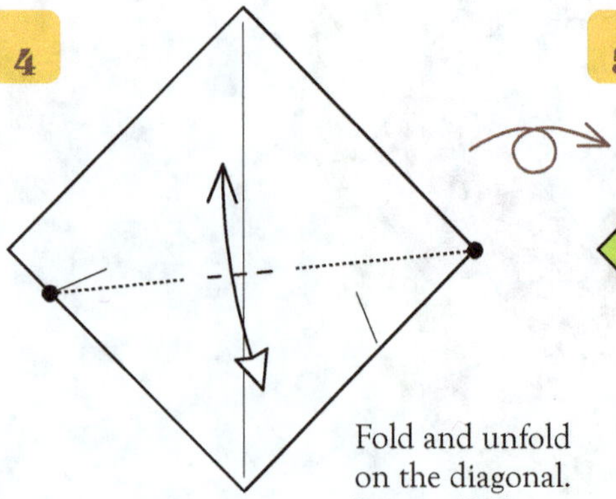

5.

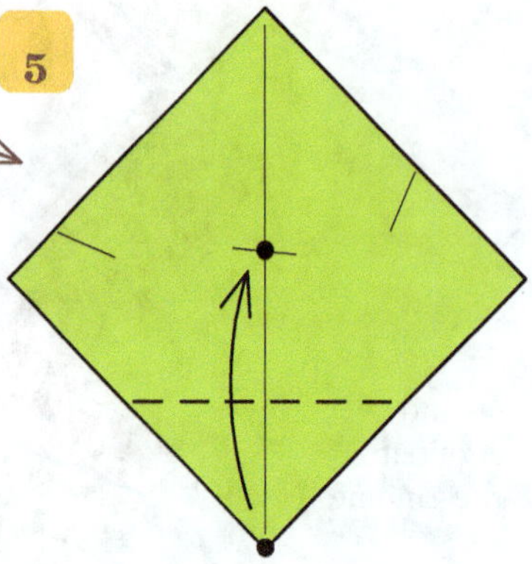

6. 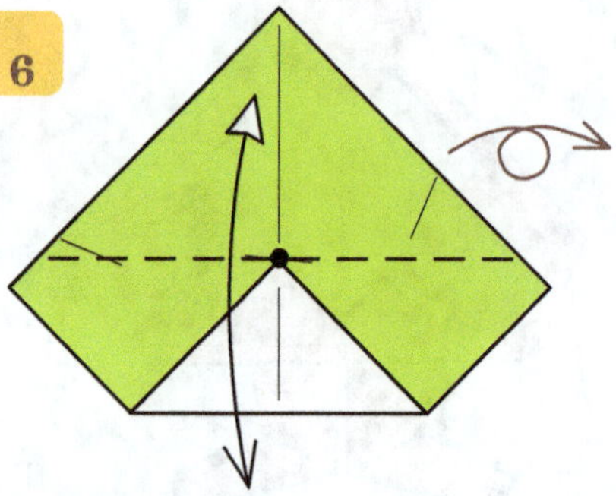 Fold and unfold.

114   Origami Symphony No. 12

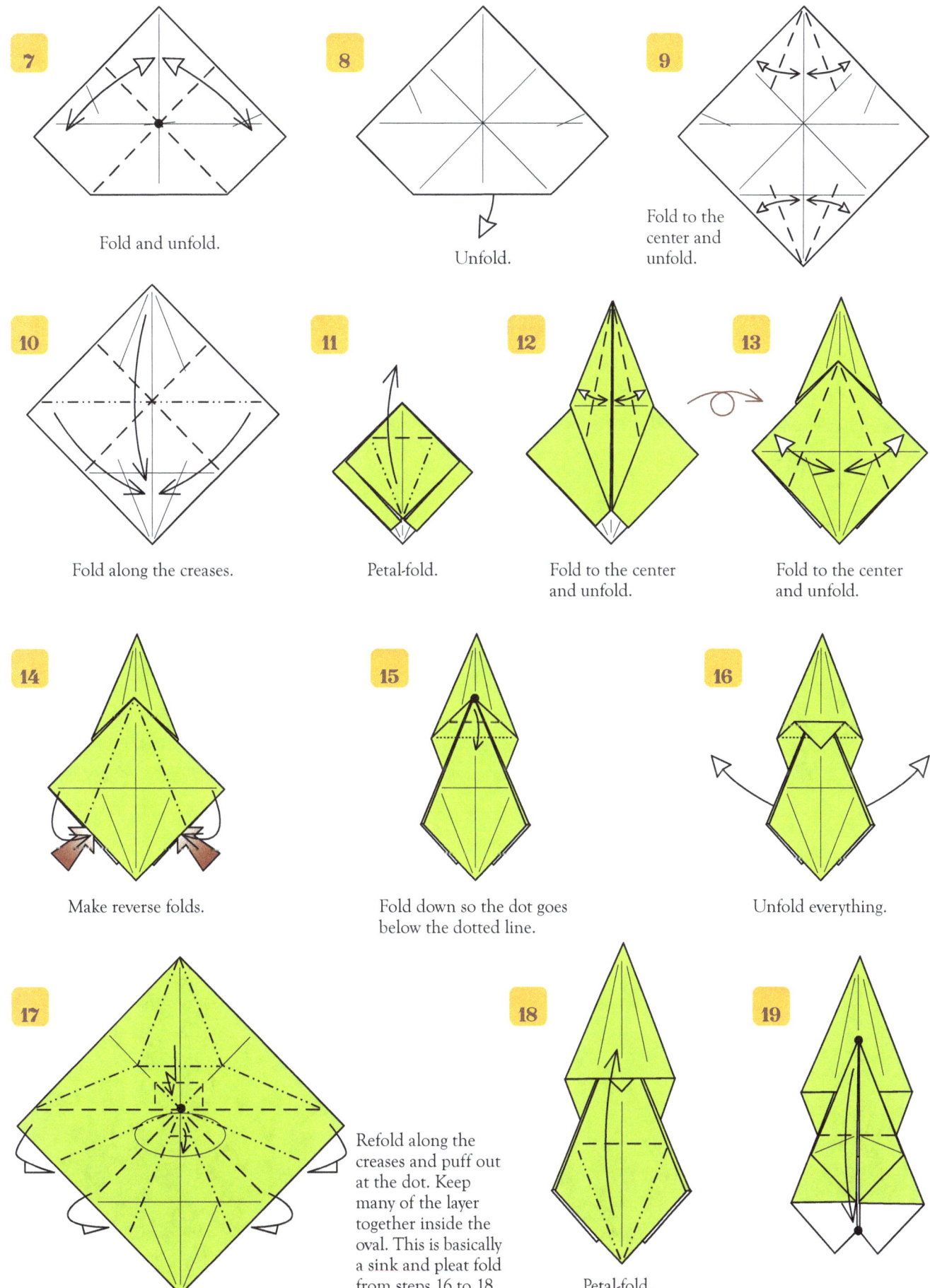

Cloverleaf Sparklebranch 115

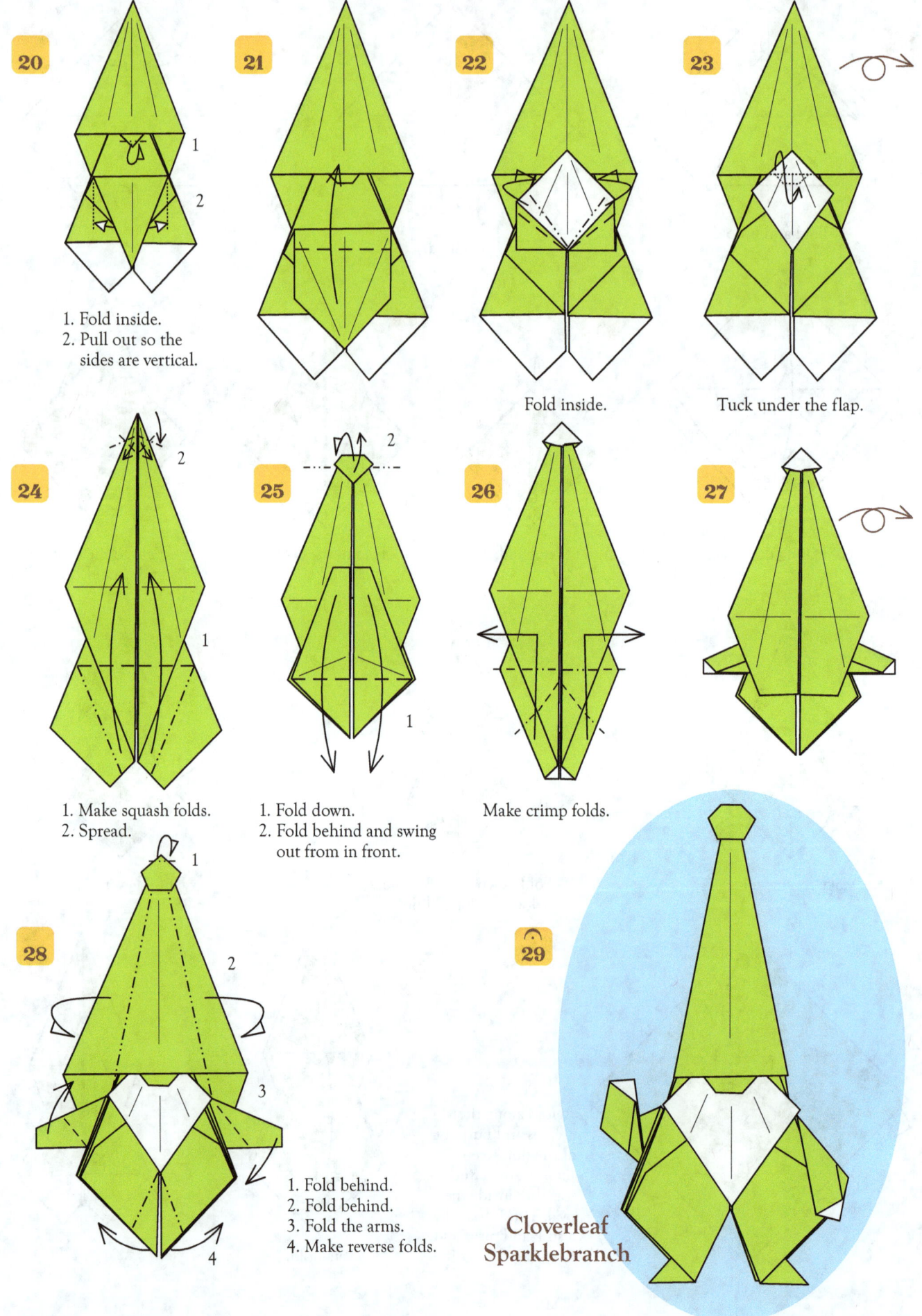

Zindle Snickerdash

Zindle Snickerdash is a mischievous gnome that makes their victims see everyone with giant, twirling mustaches until they take off their hats and break the spell.

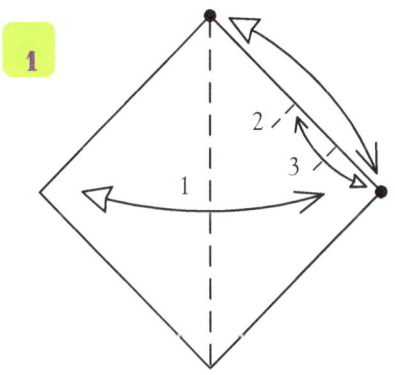

1. Fold and unfold at 1, 2, and 3.

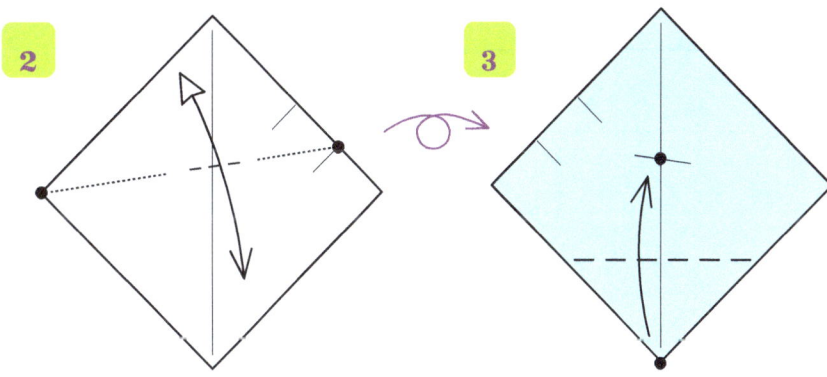

2. Fold and unfold along the diagonal.

3.

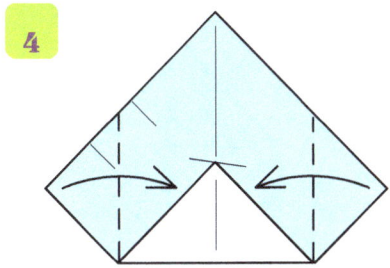

4.

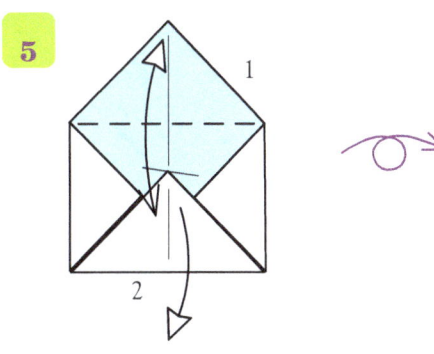

5.
1. Fold and unfold.
2. Unfold.

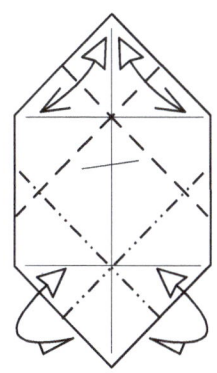

6. Fold and unfold.

Zindle Snickerdash 117

7

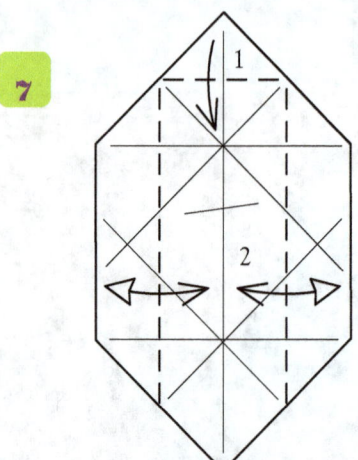

1. Fold down.
2. Fold and unfold the top layer.

8

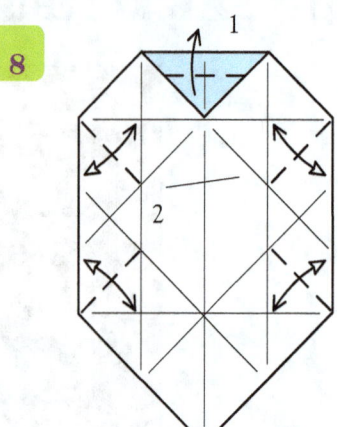

1. Fold up.
2. Fold and unfold.

9

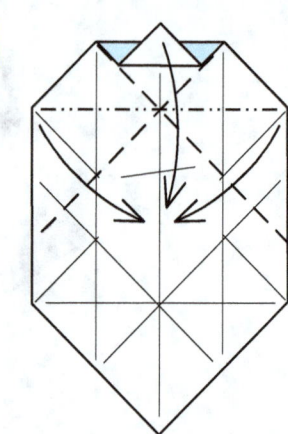

Fold along the creases.

10

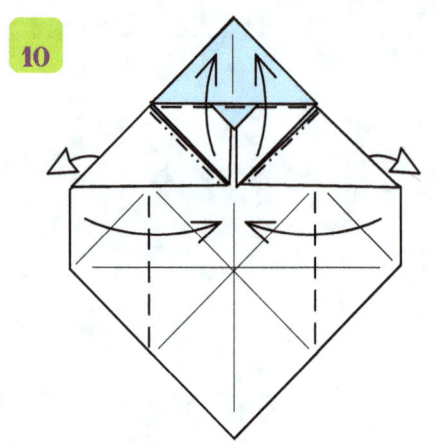

Make squash folds and swing out from behind.

11

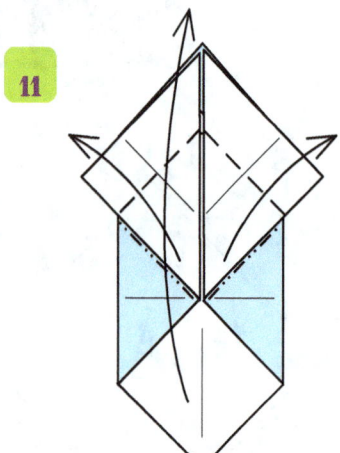

Petal-fold.

12

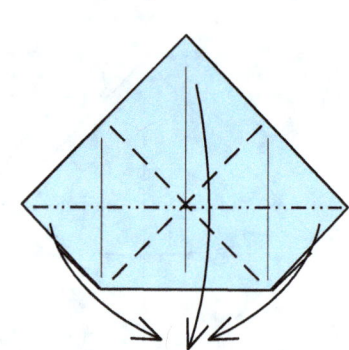

Fold along the creases.

13

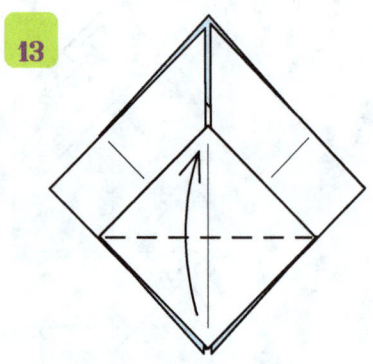

14

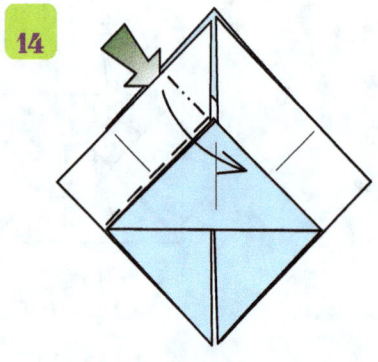

Squash-fold.

15

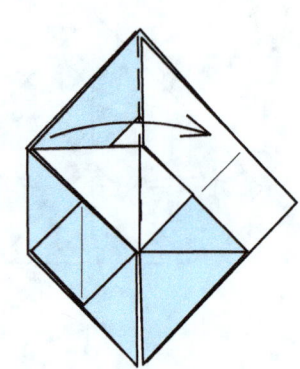

118   Origami Symphony No. 12

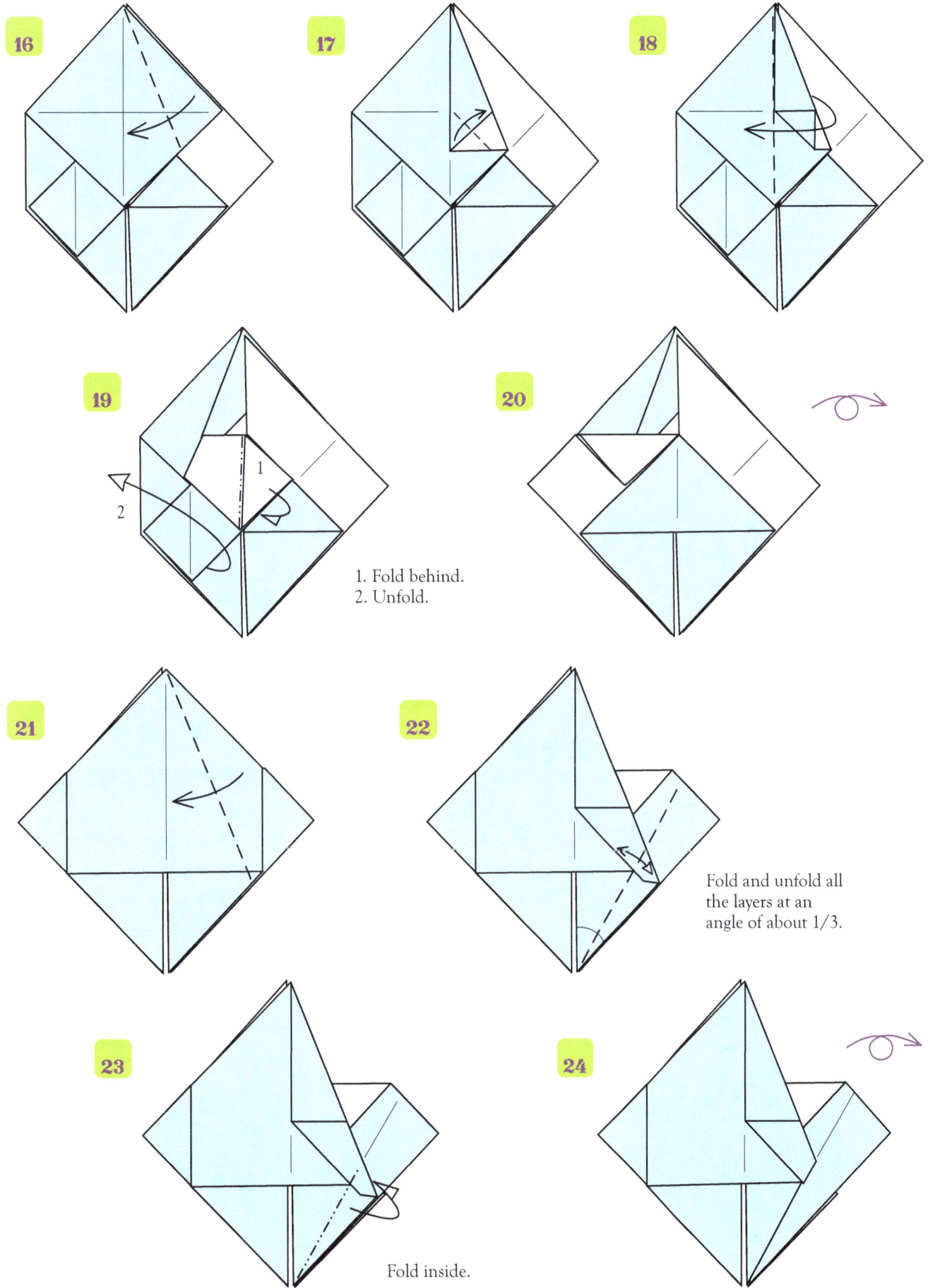

1. Fold behind.
2. Unfold.

Fold and unfold all the layers at an angle of about 1/3.

Fold inside.

Zindle Snickerdash **119**

25

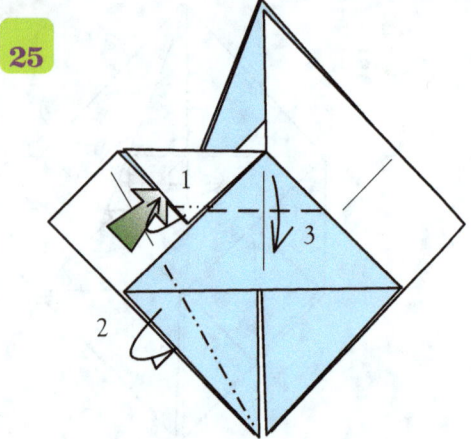

1. Reverse-fold.
2. Fold inside along the crease.
3. Fold down.

26

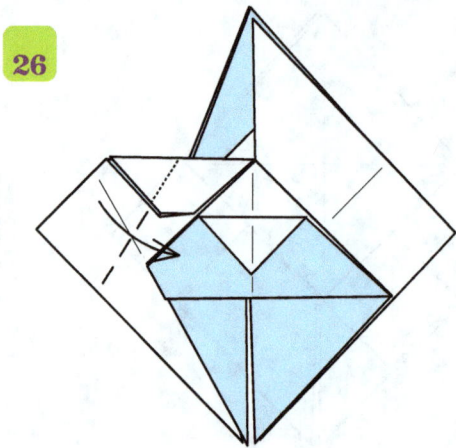

27

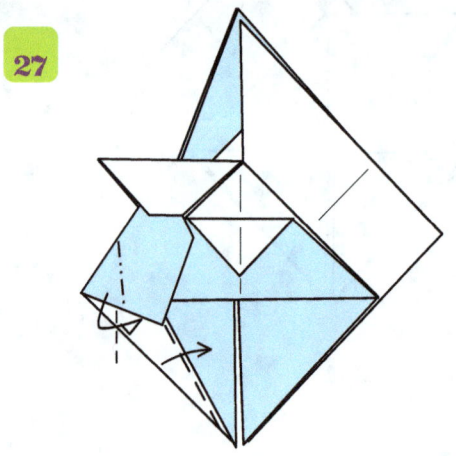

Reverse-fold.

28

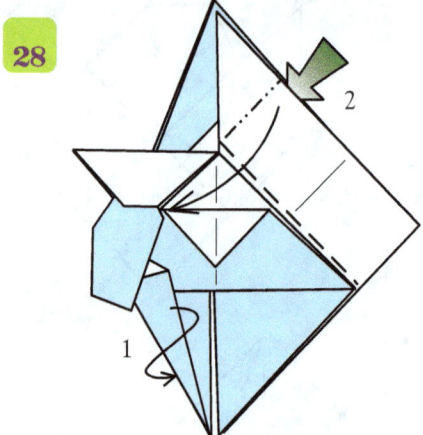

1. Tuck inside.
2. Repeat steps 14–28 on the right.

29

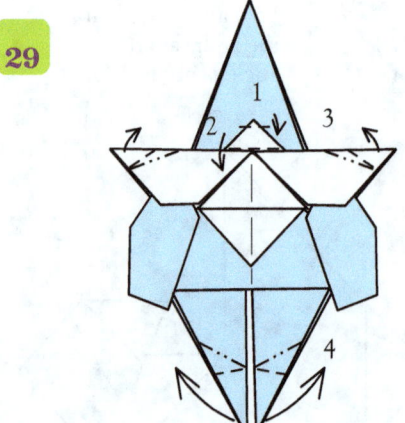

1. Fold down.
2. Fold down.
3. Make pleat folds.
4. Make crimp folds.

30

Zindle Snickerdash

120 *Origami Symphony No. 12*

Wizzlewick Wizzle

With a tap of his wand, Wizzlewick Wizzle can make a babbling brook sing notes as clear as crystal. When the frogs and dragonflies join the chorus, Wizzlewick summons the mushrooms to hop and bounce around. Hold tight to your hat because the wizard can make your hat lift up, spinning and twirling until you jump into a pile of leaves. When Wizzlewick Wizzle tried to do his invisibility spell, it didn't work because he couldn't see what he was doing.

1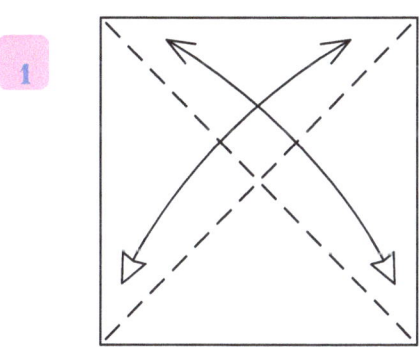

Fold and unfold.

2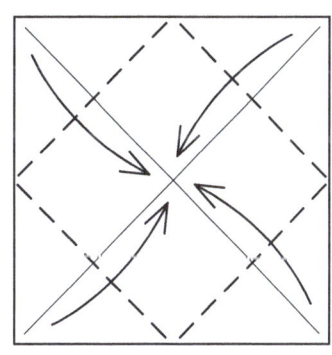

Fold to the center.

3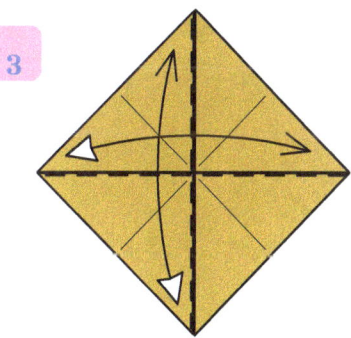

Fold and unfold.

4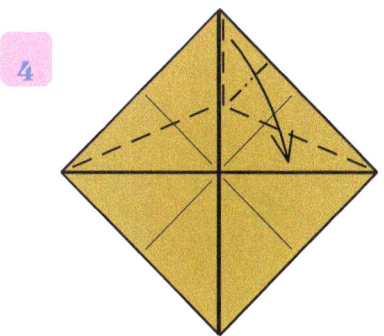

Rabbit-ear.

5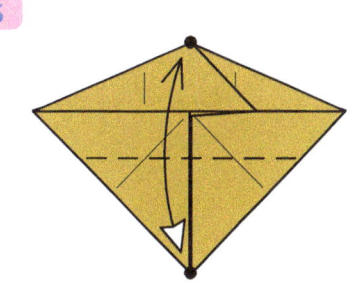

Fold and unfold.

6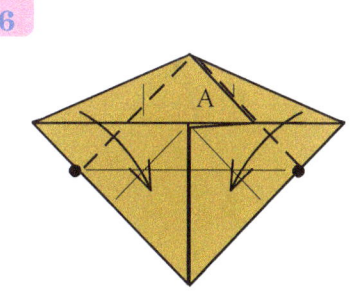

Fold behind A.

Wizzlewick Wizzle **121**

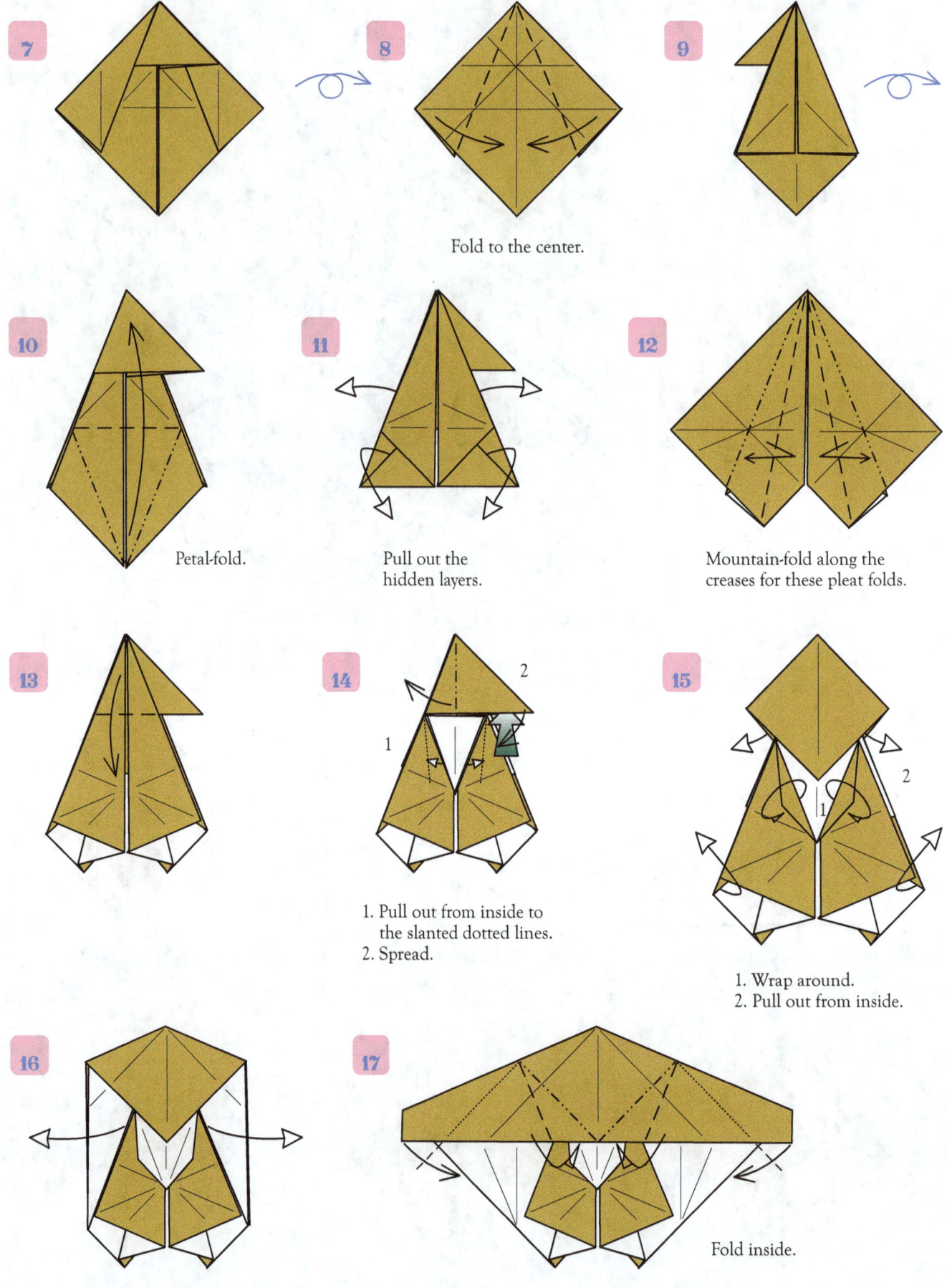

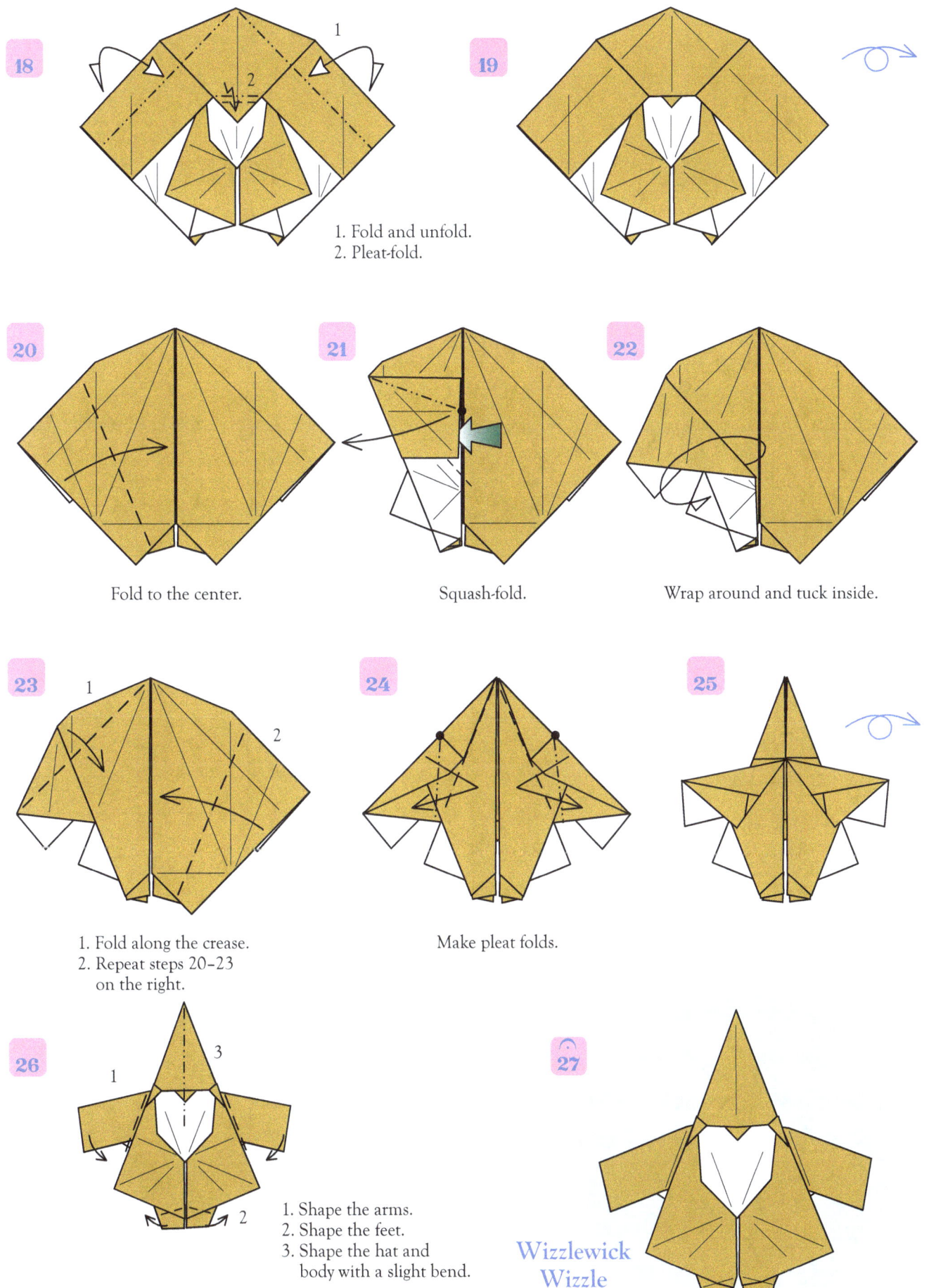

1. Fold and unfold.
2. Pleat-fold.

Fold to the center.

Squash-fold.

Wrap around and tuck inside.

1. Fold along the crease.
2. Repeat steps 20–23 on the right.

Make pleat folds.

1. Shape the arms.
2. Shape the feet.
3. Shape the hat and body with a slight bend.

Wizzlewick Wizzle

Wizzlewick Wizzle 123

Jibber Kelpwhistle

Jibber Kelpwhistle always sports fancy shoes and wears a super-tall hat. He makes everything taste better, makes hats seem so comfortable that you will want to sleep in them, and makes piles of gifts appear at the front door every day. A porcupine will guard your cottage at night. Butterflies and bluejays glisten in the distance. There's no place like Gnome.

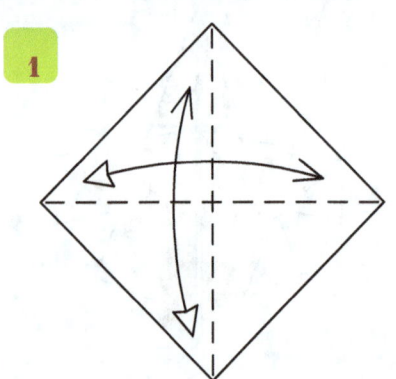

1. Fold and unfold.

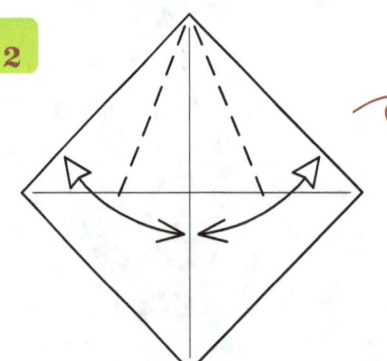

2. Fold to the center and unfold.

3.

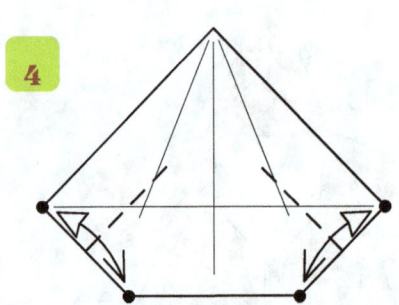

4. Fold and unfold.

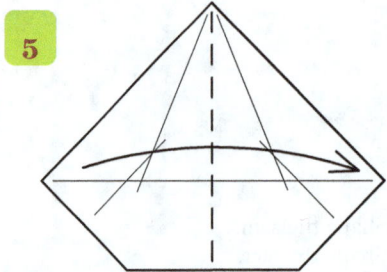

5.

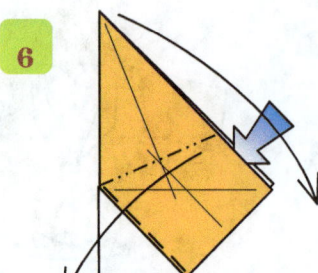

6. Squash-fold and rotate.

124 *Origami Symphony No. 12*

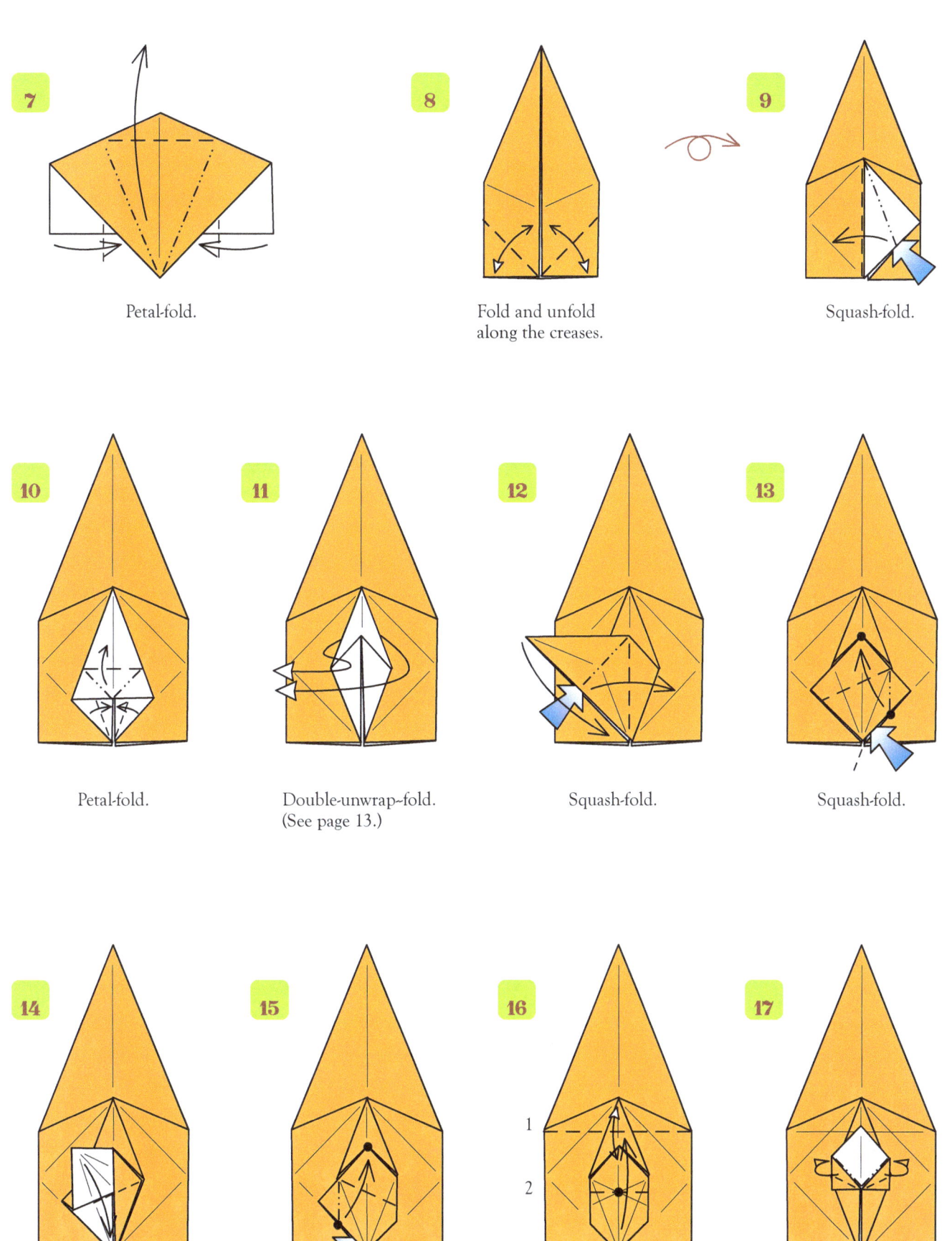

18

19

1. Fold to the crease.
2. Fold along the crease.

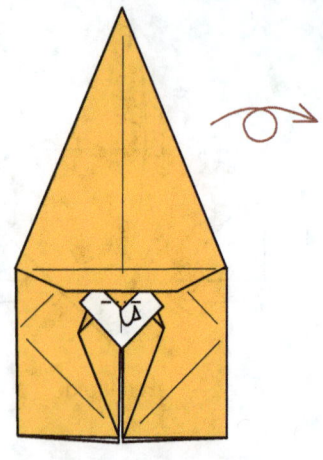

20

Fold inside.

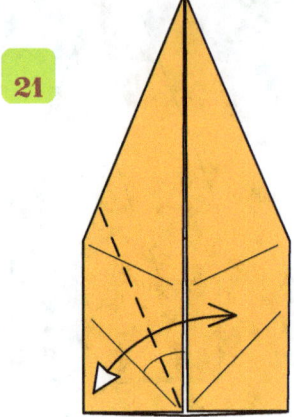

21

Fold and unfold.

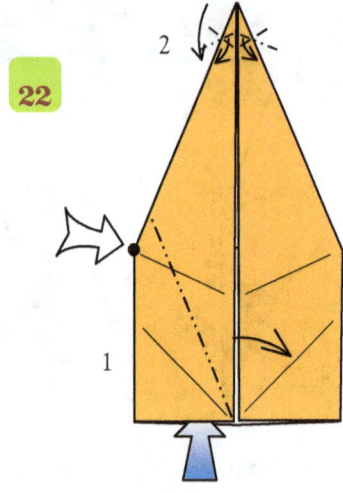

22

1. Push in at the dot for this reverse fold.
2. Spread.

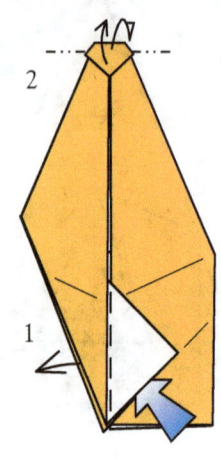

23

1. Reverse-fold.
2. Fold up and swing out from behind.

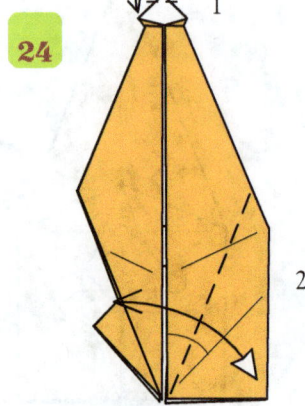

24

1. Fold down.
2. Repeat steps 21–23 at the bottom on the right.

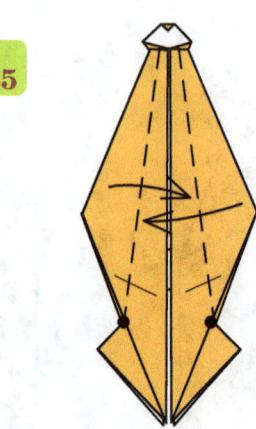

25

Divide the angle in thirds.

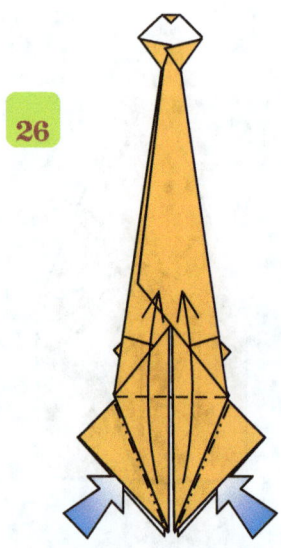

26

Make squash folds.

126 *Origami Symphony No. 12*

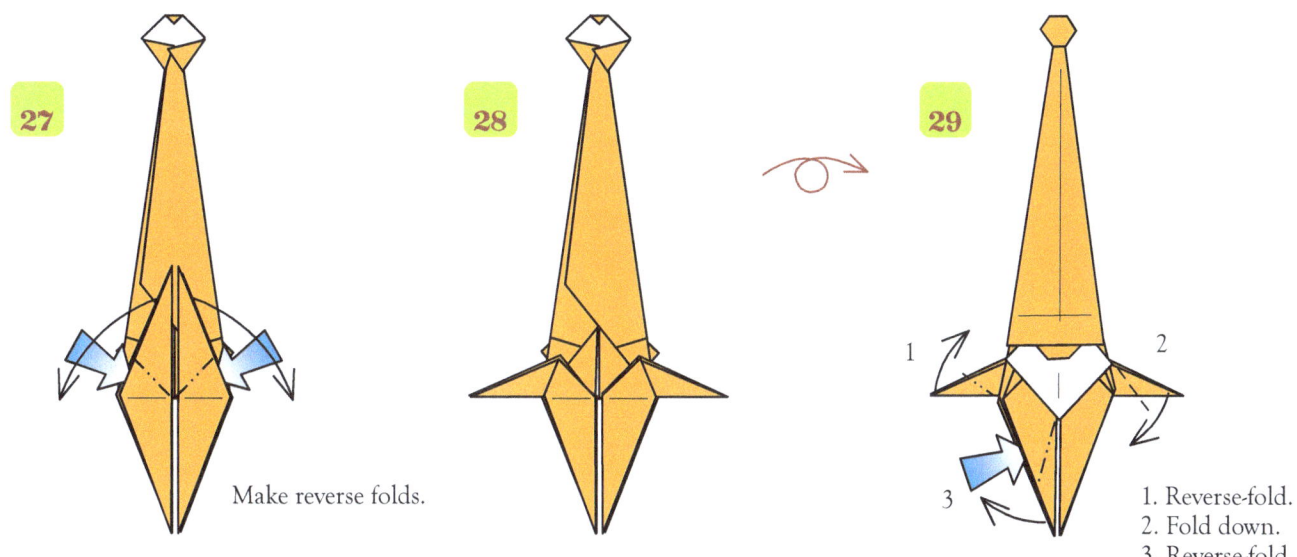

27 Make reverse folds.

28

29
1. Reverse-fold.
2. Fold down.
3. Reverse-fold.

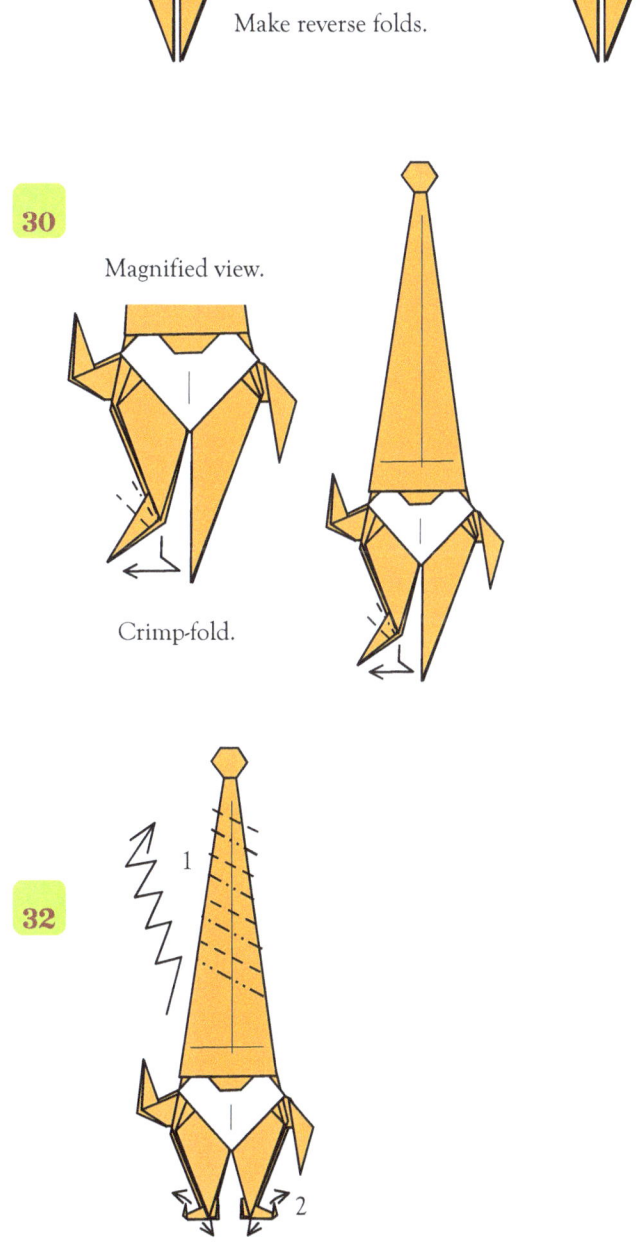

30 Magnified view.

Crimp-fold.

32
1. Pleat-fold.
2. Spread the feet at the bottom so the Gnome can stand.

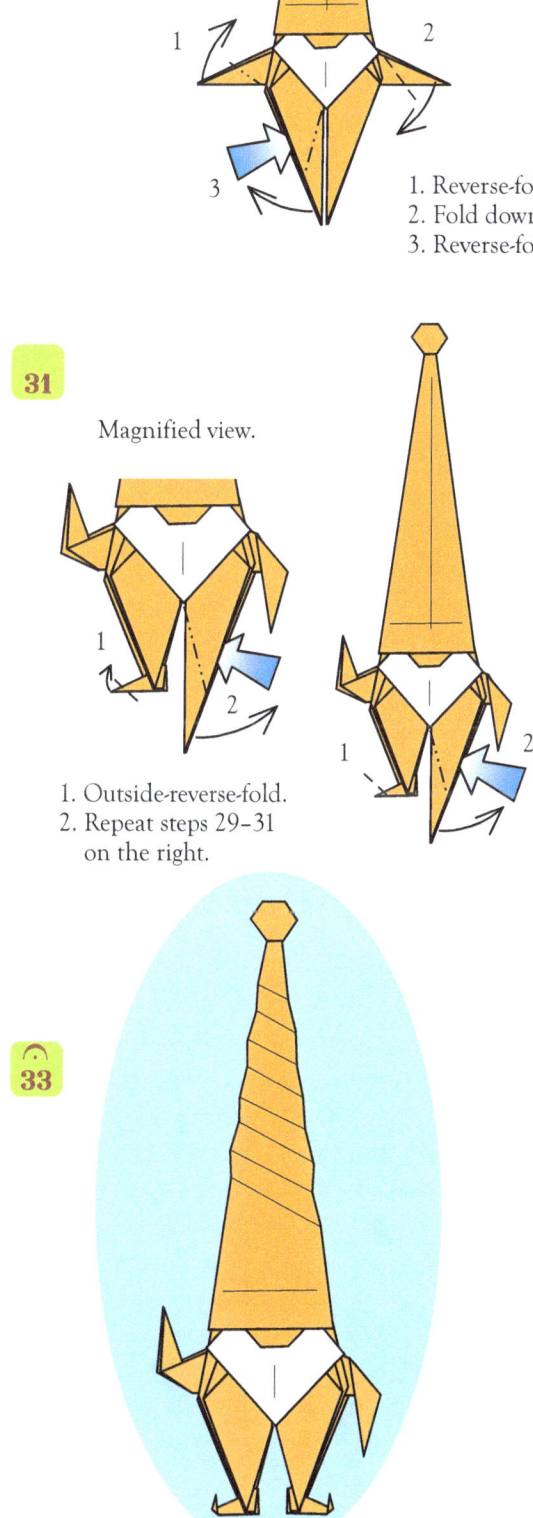

31 Magnified view.
1. Outside-reverse-fold.
2. Repeat steps 29–31 on the right.

33

Jibber Kelpwhistle

www.ingramcontent.com/pod-product-compliance
Lightning Source LLC
Chambersburg PA
CBHW051417070526
44584CB00023B/3470